Modern Women, Modern Work

RETHINKING THE AMERICAS

Series Editors
Houston A. Baker, Jr.
Eric Cheyfitz
Joan Dayan
Farah Griffin

A complete list of books in the series is available from the publisher.

Modern Women, Modern Work

Domesticity, Professionalism, and American Writing, 1890–1950

FRANCESCA SAWAYA

PENN

University of Pennsylvania Press

Philadelphia

Copyright © 2004 University of Pennsylvania Press
All rights reserved
Printed in the United States of America on acid-free paper

10 9 8 7 6 5 4 3 2 1

Published by
University of Pennsylvania Press
Philadelphia, Pennsylvania 19104-4011

Library of Congress Cataloging-in-Publication Data
Sawaya, Francesca.
  Modern women, modern work : domesticity, professionalism, and American writing, 1890–1950 / Francesca Sawaya.
    p. cm. — (Rethinking the Americas)
  Includes bibliographical references and index.
  ISBN 0-8122-3743-9 (alk. paper)
  1. American literature—Women authors—History and criticism. 2. Women and literature—United States—History—20th century. 3. Women—Employment—United States—History—20th century. 4. American literature—20th century—History and criticism. 5. Authorship—Sex differences—History—20th century. 6. Women authors, American—Biography. 7. Women in literature. I. Title. II. Series.

PS151.S38 2003
810.9'9287'0904—dc 22

2003060766

Contents

Introduction   We Other Victorians: Domesticity and Modern Professionalism   1

1. Domesticity, Cultivation, and Vocation in Jane Addams and Sarah Orne Jewett   19

2. Situated Expertise: Josephine St. Pierre Ruffin, Pauline Hopkins, and the NACW   36

3. Naturalist Sentimentalism and Cultural Authority in Frank Norris and George Santayana   56

4. "Going over to the Standard": The Paradoxes of Objectivity in Ida Tarbell and Willa Cather   80

5. Objective Domestic Critique: Anthropology and Social Reform in Ruth Benedict and Zora Neale Hurston   111

Afterword   139

Notes   147

Bibliography   181

Index   193

Acknowledgments   197

Introduction
We Other Victorians
Domesticity and Modern Professionalism

By the end of the nineteenth century, a variety of social commentators agreed that what characterized modern "civilization" was specialization.[1] This agreement depended on assumptions about sexual and racial difference. Members of the professional-managerial class[2] in particular historicized the rise of occupational specialization by citing the evidence of the "natural" evolution of the sexual division of labor from primitive homogeneity to modern differentiation.[3] They defined modernity not only through the divided labor of distinct classes but also through the divided labor of women and men, of domesticity and modern professionalism. At the same time, these professionals posed the undifferentiated work of "primitives" against the highly differentiated work of "moderns." The untrained, unspecialized homogeneous work of racial others, they argued, was quite distinct from the trained, specialized, heterogeneous work of modern professionals.

Such gendered and racialized progressive narratives about civilization conflate, but also separate, the sexual and occupational divisions of labor.[4] As a result, women are included in modernity because they engage in differentiated labor—in other words, domesticity. At the same time, women are excluded from modernity along with other "primitives" because domesticity is part of the untrained, undifferentiated labor of the past. The conflation and separation of the sexual and occupational divisions of labor, and the racializing of both, raise a number of questions about the discursive construction of professionalism: What effect did ideas about modern civilization, about sex and race, have on the development of professionalism? How are we to understand the relation between the putatively modern "culture of professionalism" and the putatively primitive "cult of domesticity"? Furthermore, how did the first generations of black and white women professionals negotiate ideas about modern occupational specialization, ideas that depended on women and other "primitives" to prove the high status of specialized, trained labor and yet that placed these "primitives" (in different ways) outside such labor?

Modern Women, Modern Work addresses these questions about the relations between gender, race, and professionalism in the United States in the late nineteenth and early twentieth centuries. It demonstrates the crucial ways in which Victorian domestic discourse structures modern professional culture and more specifically, how black and white women intellectuals helped shape the professions. The book reads fiction, memoirs, newspapers, speeches, popular histories, and academic monographs, showing the ways in which women relied on ideas from "the cult of domesticity" and "the culture of professionalism" to authorize interchangeably their writing and their work.[5] By exploring women's use of different kinds of narrative forms to engage in a range of professions, *Modern Women, Modern Work* challenges the histories we tell of modern U.S. literature and professionalism and the assumptions about gender and race that inform them.[6]

Until very recently, our accounts of the culture of professionalism in the United States have tended to ignore both how women helped form the professions and how racialized ideas about the division of labor shaped the ideology of professionalism. One of the central reasons for this neglect is that scholars have adopted a history of modernity from the moderns. They have narrated stories of progressive evolution similar to those that the moderns told. Scholars have argued that domestic discourse emerged in the United States in the 1830s out of the economic and social dislocations of the time and reached its standard and most powerful formulation during the 1850s and 1860s. Its ideology of the separate spheres of the sexes—of the private, moral, transcendent realm of woman and the family posed against the public, immoral, rationalized sphere of man and the market—is seen as expressing the tensions within a rising industrial capitalism and as particularly authorizing women.[7] By contrast, professional discourse is seen as emerging in the 1870s and reaching its standard formulation at the turn of the century. Professionalism's ideology of academic training, autonomy, community, and public service is described as developing out of corporate capitalism and as authorizing men.[8] As a result of this history, we continue to describe Victorian domestic culture, women, and racial "others" as outsiders to modernity. Modernity is thereby implicitly linked to masculinity and whiteness and premodernity to femininity and racial or ethnic otherness.

More recently, however, scholars have begun to revise these periodizations and definitions by scrutinizing the formation of what Raymond Williams calls the "modern absolute," or modernism's tendency to erase the historical specificity of its claims.[9] At the same time, scholars are also questioning what we could call the Victorian absolute or the static and generalized assumptions about the separate spheres of the sexes.[10] Across the disciplines, the particularities of gender, race, and class that constitute modernist and Victorian absolutes are being investigated. Such scholarship has resulted not only in new institutional and disciplinary histories but also in a reevaluation of the central tenets of Victorian and modern discourse and their relation to each other.[11] *Modern Women, Modern Work* contributes to the process of analyzing the modern and Victorian absolutes in the history of U.S. culture. It does so by showing how late nineteenth- and early twentieth-century professionalism was shaped by nineteenth-century domestic discourse of the separate spheres of the sexes. Specifically, the book demonstrates how black and white women negotiated the discourses of domesticity and professionalism in their narratives about work to contribute to modern professional culture.

Professional ambivalence provides an entry point for my exploration of modern and Victorian absolutes in U.S. culture. Professional discourse in the modern period was generally celebratory, but alongside its optimism runs a profound anxiety. Two sets of contradictory relations inform professional ambivalence in the period this book studies: first, professionalism's relation to democracy and second, its relation to the market. Professionals argued that their work was democratic and rational rather than aristocratic and irrational. They linked their authority to training rather than inherited status. Their claims to egalitarianism, however, enforced social exclusivity. The ideology of meritocracy—the notion that everyone has an equal chance to succeed through education and training—ostensibly promoted equal opportunity, but through its prohibitive forms of accreditation and refusal to acknowledge the power of institutions, it functioned to rationalize white, male, middle-class authority. Similarly, through disciplinary differentiation, the professions created the organizations and the accrediting methods that enabled them to construct community, but this community was based on the monopolistic policing of knowledge and access to knowledge.[12]

Equally important, professionals wanted to define their work as operating outside the determination of the capitalist market. Professional discourse emerged out of the nineteenth-century "cult of science"[13] and asserted that through objective analysis the economic and social problems created by laissez-faire capitalism could be solved and society progressively transformed in a rational, equitable, and ordered manner. Professionals depended on the notion that, unlike wage laborers, they were beyond the market, and hence disinterested experts, seeking knowledge for the betterment of society rather than themselves; they insisted that they must therefore be independent of the market, with complete control over their field of expertise. The professions, however, were (and are) dependent on the market; the difference between them and other forms of wage labor is that a large part of what they sell is precisely their claim to be outside the market.[14]

Modern Women, Modern Work shows that to resolve these two sets of contradictions—in which claims to democratic accessibility and market transcendence clash with institutionalized realities of elitism and market interestedness—U.S. professionals in the modern period used what they denominated as outmoded domestic ideology. Scholars have argued that professionalism relies heavily on appeals to tradition or the past to authorize its modern authority.[15] I focus specifically on how professionals relied on Victorian domestic ideology of the past. Such a reliance makes a great deal of sense, for domestic ideology was riven by similar contradictions as those that bedeviled professionalism. In Nancy Cott's classic formulation, domestic discourse was "Janus-faced," at once conventional and radical, both accepting and critical of capitalism and democracy.[16] In contrasting the private sphere of women and the home with the public sphere of men and the market, domesticity recognized "the capacity of modern work to desecrate the human spirit" (67). But in posing the home as the redemptive counterpart to an unstable and fractious democracy and a brutal market capitalism, domesticity functioned within the systems that it decried. It enjoined women to "absorb, palliate, and even to redeem the strain of social and economic transformation" (70), enforcing "secure, primary social classification for a population who refused to admit ascribed statuses" as well as fitting men "to pursue their worldly aims in a regulated way" (98). Domesticity came to be imagined as a full-time occupation for women, comparable in its aim and in its specialized description to the divided work of men, which it implicitly supported. Domestic discourse is, in other words, protoprofessional discourse, not only in its critique of labor specialization and social hierarchies but also in its insistence on them (72–74).[17]

Domesticity's contradictions and their structural similarity to those of professionalism enabled modernists, on the one hand, to displace the contradictions within and anxieties about professionalism onto a "premodern" domesticity. Domesticity's bad faith became a way professionals could either evade or reflect critically upon the bad faith that inhered in their own work. On the other hand, domesticity's logic of separate spheres, and its belief in the home's transcendence of the compromised political and economic spheres, could also provide professionals with an idealized model from the past of work that (supposedly) transcended the economic and political situation of the time. This book traces the narrative possibilities and kinds of work that the modernists' opposition of domesticity and professionalism enabled. It demonstrates the various and complex ways in which, because of professionals' ambivalence, domestic ideology ironically came to structure their work. I am particularly interested in the ways women used and criticized the discourse of domesticity in order to shape professional work for themselves. This work reveals women's ambivalence about professionalism that is shared with, yet has different contours than that of, their male counterparts.

As must be evident by now, while *Modern Women, Modern Work* challenges the story of rupture between Victorian and modern culture, it nonetheless relies on the terms and ideas that arise out of that story.[18] Because I focus on the ways the "modern" has been constructed, debated, and struggled over across the disciplines, I do not seek to create new periodizations. June Howard has pointed out that periodization "realizes its power as a practice of interpretation and explanation, not classification."[19] In other words, hard and fast definitions about different eras are easily shown to be inaccurate, but periodization nonetheless remains effective because it functions in the past and present to provide explanatory models of historical change. This book analyzes the gendered and raced struggles over the powerful tool of modernist periodization and our continuing and unexamined reliance on a dominant account of historical change that emerged from those struggles. We need to think critically about the naturalized tropes of modernism (particularly that of rupture), even as we remain attentive to the important social and cultural shifts articulated and created by modernists through their tropes. I therefore challenge our traditional accounts of modernity through an analysis of the struggles over periodization without creating new classifications or terms.

To illustrate more concretely the powerful uses of modernist periodization that this book specifically explores, I turn briefly to Emile Durkheim's influential *The Division of Labor in Society* (1893, 1902). Described as the first major analysis of professionalization and social order, Durkheim's sociological treatise spells out the complex and ambivalent gender and race politics of the relation between domesticity and professionalism.[20] His book demonstrates the optimism as well as the anxieties inhering in modern professionalism and how an "outmoded" domesticity serves as antithesis and model to resolve the contradictions of professionalism. The first chapter of the book most clearly reveals the influence that domestic ideology has on the conceptualization of modern professionalism. Significantly, this chapter serves to explicate not only Durkheim's thesis but also his methodology. In this chapter, he dramatizes the book's argument—that occupational specialization in modern society creates social solidarity rather than conflict—by constructing an analogy between the sexual and occupational divisions of labor.[21] The sexual division of labor in the modern bourgeois family, Durkheim asserts, provides the most "striking example" of a case comparable to the one he is making for disciplinary differentiation.[22] While Herbert Spencer had argued that sexual specialization was the hallmark of modern civilization, Durkheim sees sexual specialization not only as a hallmark of modernity but also as analogous to modern disciplinary differentiation.[23] This analogy, we will see, reveals both Durkheim's ambivalence about professionalism and his reliance on domesticity to resolve that ambivalence.

To Durkheim, the evolution of the sexual division of labor parallels but is not reducible to the occupational division of labor. He begins by citing the then-standard history of the sexual division of labor: "The further we look into the past," he asserts, "the smaller becomes the difference between man and woman" (*DL*, 57). At "the beginning of human evolution" (57), men and women are not very different either physically or in terms of their social and political roles (57–58). As a result, he asserts, "conjugal solidarity . . . [was] itself very weak" (59). By contrast, Durkheim argues, in modern times, not only are women physically weaker than men (57), but also their role is highly differentiated from that of men: "Long ago, woman retired from warfare and public affairs, and consecrated her entire life to her family ... Today, among cultivated people, the woman leads a completely different existence from that of the man. One might say that the two great functions of the psychic life are thus dissociated, that one of the sexes takes care of the affective functions and the other of the intellectual functions" (60). In Durkheim's account, the sexual division of labor results in "Conjugal solidarity ... [,which] makes its action felt at each moment and in all the details of life" (61). Durkheim concedes that while "economic utility" may be a factor in creating this solidarity between men and women, such solidarity "passes far beyond purely economic interests, for it consists in the establishment of a social and moral order *sui generis*. Through it, individuals are linked to one another" (61). The family, Durkheim writes, represents the realm of extraeconomic morality and affect—particularly the "moral" emotion of disinterestedness: "[T]he sexual division of labor is the source of conjugal solidarity, and that is why psychologists have very justly seen in the separation of the sexes an event of tremendous importance in the evolution of the emotions. It has made possible perhaps the strongest of all unselfish inclinations" (56). What is of interest here is not only that Durkheim sees the separate spheres of the sexes as representing evolution from a primitive, homogeneous past to a civilized, specialized present but also, and more crucially, that he relies uncritically on nineteenth-century domestic ideology in order to theorize the progressive effects on society of occupational specialization. Durkheim uses the notion that the sphere of domestic relations passes "far beyond" market determination and interestedness to describe professionalism's comparable transcendence of the market.

Durkheim's reliance on domestic ideology to describe modern occupational specialization is particularly striking for the way it helps him articulate the terrain of study unique to professional sociology, its autonomous status, and what authorizes it as a discipline. *The Division of Labor* is not simply an analysis of professionalization but is, like much of Durkheim's work, a manifesto for the new field of sociology and its importance in effecting social change.[24] Durkheim's text analyzes the significance of the way modern "[o]ccupations are infinitely separated and specialized" (*DL*, 39) so that each discipline has its own "object, method, and thought" (40). The text enacts this idea by theorizing how sociology differentiates itself from other modern disciplines. He argues that the domain of "unselfish inclinations," of morality and disinterestedness (which, as we have seen, are also the domain of domestic relations), is not only what sociology studies but also what inheres in sociology's methodology and what it subsequently fosters. Taking on economists who naturalize the division of labor as well as philosophers who moralize over it (44–46),[25] Durkheim argues that the sociologist, by contrast, studies as "an objective fact" the "moral value of the division of labor" and comes to "scientific conclusions" (*DL*, 46) that will help society. For Durkheim, the extraeconomic morality of the family exemplifies, and thereby authorizes, the disciplinary autonomy and disinterestedness of sociology.

While Durkheim uses domestic ideology to illustrate his argument about occupational specialization generally and the independence of sociology specifically, his reliance on domesticity raises two problems of chronology that highlight his ambivalence about modernity, a modernity which his text generally insists upon and embraces. The first seems like a minor issue. Since intellectual work or science is the modern to Durkheim, women's specialization in "affective functions" (60) suggests that their domestic work is anachronistic or premodern. This is, of course, not an unusual way to describe women and domesticity at the turn of the century, and as *Modern Women, Modern Work* demonstrates, such a description can be used to very different intellectual and political ends by men and women alike. The effect of Durkheim's particular version, however, is implicitly to exclude women and other premodern or primitive individuals from modern professionalism. The second chronological problem is linked to the first but presents an active challenge to Durkheim's central thesis that increasing occupational division promotes growing social solidarity. Durkheim concedes that the highest form of sexually differentiated labor occurs only among the "most cultivated people" (61, also 60) and that the uncultivated have not yet reached this advanced stage of evolution. Only a small percentage of the population, in other words, are modern. These two problems of chronology—of women's and the home's primitive status and of uneven evolutionary development in which only cultivated men and women have achieved solidarity—throw into relief the text's larger hesitation over the actually quite detrimental effect that modern occupational specialization is having on society. While two-thirds of *The Division of Labor* works to prove that "organic solidarity" results from occupational specialization, one-third is devoted to abnormal forms of and responses to the occupational division of labor that result not in social solidarity but in conflict and anomie.

In Durkheim's famous preface to the second edition, "Some Notes on Occupational Groups" (1902), he tries to address directly the ambivalence and hesitation evident in his earlier argument about modern work. He does so by rethinking the two problems of chronology that the 1893 text left unresolved and by imagining an institutional force that could bridge the gap between the social solidarity that the division of labor theoretically should produce and the conflict and anomie it has in fact produced. In this characteristically modernist text, the "home" is simply eliminated as a major factor in contemporary society.[26] At the same time, however, Durkheim embeds the home's extraeconomic significance even more firmly into his conception of the modern in order to imagine a solution to the social problems that occupational specialization has created. In this preface, Durkheim focuses on the chaos and alienation of modern life, "the state of juridical and moral anomie in which economic life actually is found" (*DL,* 1–2). The "anarchy" of contemporary society, he argues, "is an unhealthy phenomenon, since it runs counter to the aim of society, which is to suppress, or at least to moderate, war among men" (3). It is evident, Durkheim says, that "a multitude of individuals" spend their lives "almost entirely in the industrial and commercial world . . . [and] that world is only feebly ruled by morality" (4). The sociologist's new question therefore must be, "If in the task that occupies almost all our time we follow no other rule than that of our well-understood interest, how can we learn to depend upon disinterestedness, on self-forgetfulness, on sacrifice?" (4). Durkheim's answer to this question of market and personal interestedness is that the "ancient" (7) "corporation or occupational group" (5) (in other words guilds or trade unions) can be adapted to become an effective tool in modern society (7–8, 18). It will be "indispensable . . . not because of the economic services it can render, but because of the moral influence it can have" (10). In other words, the "occupational group" will create the extraeconomic morality that is crucial to social solidarity and that in the 1893 edition he described as being fostered by the "home," or family.

While Durkheim remains interested in his 1902 preface in what he describes as the family's historic role in creating morality (12–18), the point here is that the home, imagined by domestic ideology as a social formation working outside market determination, is dead. Instead, Durkheim argues, the market permeates every level of society. Hence the occupational group or corporation must take on the family's role in creating "moral influence" and "moral power" (10). Despite this account of the market's ubiquity, Durkheim returns anxiously and nostalgically to the family as imagined in domestic ideology to theorize how this occupational group might work: [T]he family, in losing the unity and indivisibility of former times, has lost with one stroke a great part of its efficacy. As it is today broken up with each generation, man passes a notable part of his existence far from all domestic influence. The corporation has none of these disturbances; it is as continuous as life. The inferiority it presents, in comparison with the family, has its compensation (16–17). Because "domestic influence" plays a very small role in modern social life, extraeconomic factors have been marginalized. There is "compensation" possible in a re-creation of the occupational group of the past, but even in the resuscitation of this institution, a superseded domesticity remains the ideal form in which morality can be created. Domesticity is a model, in other words, for modern professionalism, a professionalism Durkheim has posed in both the 1893 and the 1902 texts (albeit in a different manner) as domesticity's analytic and temporal opposite.

Modern Women, Modern Work shows that the paradoxes evident in Durkheim's argument recur throughout professional discourse in a variety of ways. The belief that professionalism represents civilization, combined with the worry that it is breaking down social order; the contrasting of the domestic with the professional, but also the reliance on the "primitive" domestic as a model to delineate professional transcendence of the market—these are the paradoxes at the heart of this book. Why does Durkheim's notion of professionalism oppose itself to, rely on, and embed within itself premodern domestic ideology? How are we to understand the manner in which domesticity serves to help Durkheim imagine and illustrate the functions and status of the discipline of sociology, even as it also works to exclude women and "primitive" others from that discipline? How are we to read the relation of Victorian domesticity, imagined as feminine and premodern, to the construction of professionalism, imagined as masculine and modern? What is the significance, in other words, of the engendered and racialized histories of modern progressive professionalism? And, equally important, how might these paradoxes have been used or even reshaped by those positioned as primitives in modernity, as outsiders to professionalism? How did women and racial others engage the paradoxes of professional discourse?

Durkheim's text demonstrates clearly that we need to think about the break as well as the continuity between Victorian domestic and modern professional culture. The ways in which modern texts compulsively oppose the domestic to the professional, the feminine to the masculine, the primitive past to the civilized present have been crucial in shaping modern ideas about work, as evident in the split between fields and disciplines designated as women's (teaching, nursing, social work) and those customarily viewed as the province of men (science, medicine, law), as evident more broadly in the struggles by women and racial and ethnic minorities to gain entrance into the professions and their relative exclusion from them. At the same time, when we focus only on these oppositions, we ignore the important historical and ideological overlap between the domestic and "primitive" and the professional. In particular, we ignore the relays between engendered and raced forms of work, relays that elaborate precisely the anxieties that the oppositions seek to elide, allay, or contain.[27]

If the paradoxes we see in Durkheim's *The Division of Labor* suggest that we need to read the relation between modern professional and Victorian domestic culture against the grain of the "modern absolute," that book's ambivalence and hesitation also suggest that we need to read against the grain of what we could call the Victorian absolute, the static and universalistic assumptions about the separate spheres of the sexes. To reevaluate the Victorian absolute, *Modern Women, Modern Work* focuses on how women fiction writers—as well as activists, academics, and professionals—combined the discourses of domesticity and professionalism in their vocations to shape and reform their work and society. Such a focus on women's texts is not meant to imply that women alone combined these discourses. Nonetheless, the scholarly neglect of both women's participation in the formation of the professions and the importance of "feminized" discourse to that formation demonstrates how the opposition between

Victorian and modern culture structures modern thinking; neglect registers how the (often effective) attempts by the moderns to exclude or limit women's participation in the professions make us read women as "out of it," as outside the culture of professionalism.[28]

There is, however, another more complicated and equally significant reason for our failure to read women's involvement in professionalism, namely the continuing ambivalence that feminist scholars themselves feel about professionalism.[29] Professionalism, as I have already argued, has elicited mixed feelings from professionals and nonprofessionals alike. While entry into the professions was one goal of the women's movement, it was a contested goal with contested effects. Many feminist scholars have shown not only that professionalism ended up containing much of the radicalism of the women's movement (as is evident in the term *women's professions*) but also that it was often achieved at the expense of working-class and minority men and women.[30] Professionalism uncomfortably highlights not only fractures within women's fight for equality but also how women's history is imbricated in the dominant ideologies and institutions of U.S. capitalism. Calling the Victorian absolute into question, therefore, entails exploring the inequities that women professionals enforced, even as they criticized and battled other inequities. An important example will suffice to demonstrate this point.

In her feminist manifesto, *Women and Economics* (1898), Charlotte Perkins (Stetson) Gilman argues that society can progress only if woman's economic dependence on man ends and woman is trained to engage in specialized or professional labor. One of Gilman's most popular books,[31] *Women and Economics*, follows the basic outlines of the Durkheimian narrative, defining modernity as specialized labor that promotes collective and progressive, rather than individualist and hence destructive, aims. Gilman writes, "To specialize any form of labor is a step up: to organize it is another step. Specialization and organization are the basis of human progress, the organic methods of social life."[32] Gilman, however, uses this standard progressive narrative about labor specialization to different ends than Durkheim. In keeping with this argument, Gilman associates modernity with professional work and social solidarity but argues that for full modernization to be achieved, women cannot be relegated to domesticity. Highlighting rather than evading the way modern professionalism imagines women and their domestic labor as anachronistic, Gilman writes that society's progress has been stymied by the fact that specialization and organization "have been forbidden to women almost absolutely" (*WAE*, 67). Because woman's economic activity is "of the earliest and most primitive kind" (8), she "hinders and perverts the economic development of the world" (121). Once woman is trained to do specialized labor for the common good, Gilman asserts, social evolution will proceed apace. Women's recent demand for economic independence and the rise of women's organizations therefore reveal, says Gilman, "one of the most important sociological phenomena of the century,—indeed, of all centuries," namely "the first timid steps toward social organization of these so long unsocialized members of our race" (164).

This triumphal evolutionary narrative insists on the link made by the professional-managerial class between specialized labor and progress, but Gilman claims that narrative for women as well as men. Even as she naturalizes occupational specialization, she nonetheless denaturalizes the usual association, one that Durkheim exemplifies for us, between the specialized division of labor and the sexual division of labor. This denaturalization involves two moves. First, Gilman criticizes the natural as representing the uncivilized and unevolved. Nature represents not just primitive homogeneity but also individualistic competition and conflict. It is coterminous, therefore, with the inefficient, immoral workings of laissez-faire capitalism. For example, sex selection (the choosing of mates) is indeed natural, but that means it is guided by the same uncivilized logic as that of the market. "Natural" sex selection is therefore the same as prostitution: women must sell themselves to men, while men must sell their labor to the highest bidder to acquire goods to buy women (105–14). Writes Gilman, "The sexuo-economic relation in its effect on the constitution of the individual keeps alive in us the instincts of savage individualism which we should otherwise have well outgrown" (121). As a result, neither men nor women can work "disinterestedly for the social good" but instead must act "in their own immediate interests" (114). This critique of the "natural" market is indebted not only to a progressive belief in modern civilization but also to a domestic belief in the possibility and superiority of domains outside the market.[33] Gilman repeatedly compares the inefficiency and immorality of nature to the work of the trained professional who transcends the natural (*WAE*, 169–99, 225–47). For Gilman, natural sex selection must be eliminated in order for men and women to pursue the highest ideals, ideals she describes—through a domestic critique of the market and a domestic belief in transcendence of that market—as professional and scientific ones that function outside market determination (113–14, 230–47).

If Gilman's first move in denaturalizing the sexual division of labor is to appeal to domestic ideology's notion of realms of labor outside the market, her second and related move is to do so by enforcing a virulent naturalized racism. Gilman's feminist thought, as Gail Bederman has shown, is "at its very base racist." Thoroughly imbued in the discourse of civilization of the late nineteenth century, Gilman as early as 1890 was arguing that "race function does not interfere with sex function."[34] In other words, natural or essential, differences are racial, not sexual. At the end of her book, she drives home this point in a dramatic fashion by comparing the contemporary marriages of savage domestic women and educated professional men to scandalous cross-evolutionary, cross-racial pairings. Writes Gilman: "Marry a civilized man to a primitive savage, and their child will naturally have a dual nature. Marry an Anglo-Saxon to an African or Oriental, and their child has a dual nature.

Marry any man of a highly developed nation, full of the specialized activities of his race and their accompanying moral qualities, to the carefully preserved, rudimentary female creature . . . and you have as result what we all know so well,—the human soul in its pitiful, well-meaning efforts, its cross-eyed, purblind errors, its baby fits of passion" (*WAE*, 332). Gilman threatens her audience with evolutionary stasis, even devolution, if they do not allow white women to enter the professions. Modernity, she argues, is white racial progress. It is racial others, not white women, who are and must be excluded from modernity and the modern professions.

Women and Economics suggests that we need to be attentive to the nuances of what Alice Gambrell calls women's "insider-outsider" status in modern professionalism, an insider-outsider status that functions differently according to class, ethnic, and racial variables.[35] We cannot simply assume that any group of women was "out of it," separated in their professionalism from the ideas that were formative to professionalism more generally. In Gilman's case, for example, the benefits that accrue to her feminist argument for denaturalizing the sexual division of labor cannot be extricated from the historically specific, naturalized racism on which they depend. But while women's professionalism highlights feminism's participation in the culture it criticizes, it is, after all, through that culture, through the struggles over power within that culture, that change takes place. While Gilman's racist, feminist revision of the basic progressive narrative of professionalism was influential, it was not by any means the only narrative of women's professionalism. Middle-class, African American women also laid claim to professionalism and contested both the engendered and racialized periodizations of mainstream professionalism in their constructions of their expertise.[36] We see such contestations in (among other important examples) Ida B. Wells's careful depiction of herself in her 1890s antilynching journalism as a lady accepted into the highest and most cultivated echelons of British society, a depiction intended to counter representations of black women as primitive, sexually promiscuous savages; in the brief, pointed histories by Fannie Barrier Williams, Anna Julia Cooper, Sarah J. Early, and Hallie Q. Brown of black women's educated and organized professional activism, histories that directly protest black women's exclusion from the Ladies Board of Managers at the Chicago World's Fair in 1893; in Mrs. N. F. Mossell's comprehensive list in *The Work of the Afro-American Woman* (1894, 1908) of every black woman professional in the U.S. whom her research has discovered, a list that directly contests Annie Nathan Meyer's all-white account of women's professionalism in *Woman's Work in America* (1891).[37] Middle-class, African American women, like their white counterparts, negotiated the complex relation between ideas about the sexual and occupational divisions of labor, about the past and the present, in a broad range of ways that have not been fully charted.

I argue throughout *Modern Women, Modern Work* that as feminist scholars we must historicize our own claims to expertise, making distinctions between better and worse forms of professionalism and better and worse ways of authorizing analysis, critique, and reform.[38] Our professional work and our critiques depend historically on how professionalism was negotiated and criticized by our predecessors. We cannot simply escape the past or the present of women's vexed relation to the professions. Bruce Robbins has made this point about professionalism more generally. Analyzing the contemporary attack on academic professionals' interestedness, an attack launched ironically enough by both the right and the left, Robbins writes, "[W]e have to stop positing spaces of freedom which, like domesticity . . . inevitably mask someone's servitude. . . . Not disembodied freedom, but diverse embodiedness and incomplete servitude have to become the common sense view of intellectual work" (*SV*, 10). Robbins's use of an analogy to domesticity underlines how domesticity continues to function as both antithesis to and model for professionalism. As antithesis, domesticity designates women's role as the primitive in the modern sexual division of labor. As model, domesticity describes an imagined realm of unalienated and transcendent labor. Robbins insists, however, that a normative and idealized account of domesticity is analogous to a normative and idealized version of professionalism. Such a reading of domesticity—which erases both the working-class domestic's poorly paid productive labor outside the home, and the bourgeois and working-class woman's unpaid, productive labor in the home—is comparable, Robbins argues, to the version of professionalism that erases its relation to the market. As feminists, we could add that to insist that women's professionalism must be transcendent is to disable us from seeing the differences between how women relied on and criticized normative and idealized accounts of domesticity to authorize their professionalism *and* to what very different ends they did so. Discourses create reverse discourses—across as well as within different social groups—but we need to refuse the temptation of imagining that these reverse discourses are transcendent.[39] *Modern Women, Modern Work*, therefore, highlights the diverse embodiedness and incomplete servitude of women's professionalism by exploring discourses and reverse discourses within women's ideas about professionalism, particularly across and between black and white women, who have historically been situated in very different ways in U.S. society and culture.

Modern Women, Modern Work focuses on the years between the turn of the century and the 1940s in the U.S. These are crucial years for U.S. professionals, years in which they are struggling to solidify their self-definition as democratic and disinterested experts. These definitions are being challenged, on the one hand, by the pressures of what has been called the corporate and consumer capitalism of the U.S. that disproves the ideology of meritocracy and autonomy,[40] and on the other hand, by women and minorities, who are using such definitions to enter the professions. To tell the story of these complicated struggles within and over professionalism, the book relies on a methodology at once historicist, comparativist, and feminist. Each chapter of the book pairs selected fictional texts with contemporaneous, nonfictional writings in other professional fields. Such an approach allows for an examination of moments within the history of disciplines when the opposition between the domestic and the professional was deployed in a productive and characteristic way to shift debates about society and women's role in it. The book insists that, as Joan Scott puts it, "Changes in the organization of social relationships always correspond to changes in representations of power, but the direction of change is not necessarily one way."[41] Each chapter therefore begins with a localized problem about representation (in, for example, the narrative forms of regionalism, sentimentalism, naturalism, and modernist experimentation). I show how this local problem opens up a nexus of social and political debates surrounding the engendering and racializing of modern expertise in corporate and consumer capitalism and how women intellectuals negotiated those debates. My focus is on professions in which black and white women gained noteworthy (if not always permanent) access: literature, social work, political activism, journalism, anthropology. These professions would not all be included in classic studies of the history of the professions, and that is part of the impetus for studying them.[42]

In recent years, new historicism has been associated with the kind of work that, like mine, redefines "the boundaries" of the archive by focusing on discourse across the disciplines.[43] By rethinking what is background and foreground material in different disciplines, Catherine Gallagher and Stephen Greenblatt explain, new historicist work seeks to interrupt the "Big Stories" and the "epochal truths."[44] The use of the "anecdote," Gallagher and Greenblatt further argue, has been particularly helpful in challenging traditional narratives of change and continuity.[45] While similar counterhistorical impulses to the ones Gallagher and Greenblatt describe shape this book, I am not convinced that the anecdote is a satisfying formal analogue to those impulses. The anecdote, it seems to me, does not sufficiently trouble the relation between background and foreground. Instead, I would argue that epochal truths can be more thoroughly reexamined through an extensive investigation and comparison of archives seen as anecdotal to different disciplines. Juxtaposing texts across disciplinary lines, and engaging in equivalent explorations of them and the institutional frameworks in which they operate, can better demonstrate the pervasiveness and varied effectiveness of certain discourses than the anecdote. While problems and paradoxes of representation in literary texts are the site on which my analyses begin, that site opens up comparable issues in other disciplines. *Modern Women, Modern Work* therefore analyzes common tensions—between transcendence and situatedness, abstraction and specificity, objectivity and subjectivity, and exclusiveness and inclusiveness—across the disciplines in this time period and the ways in which women used domestic and professional discourses to address those tensions.

It is also true, however, that crossing disciplinary boundaries need not necessarily interrupt the "Big Stories" we have told about modernity, a point I discuss in Chapter 3 in relation to certain versions of new historicism. For that reason, this book is more deeply indebted to the ethics and polemics of contemporary feminist thought than to the counterhistorical impulses of new historicism. Specifically, it depends on what Carla Kaplan describes as feminism's historic "privileg[ing]" of "conversational themes and dialogic methods" and feminism's self-critique of the profound misunderstandings, appropriations, and conflicts that have ensued from essentialist assumptions about that dialogue.[46] Adapting Kaplan's notion of a feminist "erotics of talk"[47] (which Kaplan adapts from Audre Lorde), I examine, on the one hand, moments of dialogic identification between women, where certain kinds of intellectual and political struggles about professional work were conceptualized across women's texts in common ways. On the other hand, I also explore the power dynamics that preclude identification between women and how disidentification enables important forms of social critique.[48] I focus thus on the ways white women have attempted to shut African American women out of the conversation about, and practices of, professionalism and the ways, in turn, that African American women have contested those attempts and reshaped the dialogue. I also explore (though less fully than the first conversation between women) the complex dialogue between progressive men and women about women's professionalism.[49] A feminist polemic about both the possibilities of, and problems with, the dialogue between women, and between men and women—between social groups situated historically in different ways—guides the principle of selection of thinkers and texts in *Modern Women, Modern Work*.

I need to make one final and important point about methodology. While I do not shy away in this book from the power differentials that have led to conflict as well as cohesion in the dialogue between women and between men and women, I do not explore all those differentials. Most obviously, my focus on professionalism tends to subordinate analyses of class conflict to those of race and gender. Nonetheless, my hope is that a historicist and comparative analysis—sharpened by a feminist focus on the power dynamics in the dialogue between black and white women, and between men and women—outlines a different history of modernity, one that will continue to be filled in by scholars in the years ahead. More crucially, and a point that bears repeating, I hope that my analysis will help us to think through and shape better models of feminist professionalism in the present.

The first two chapters of the book explore how black and white women in the U.S. used domesticity and professionalism to create new kinds of socially activist work for themselves. In Chapter 1, I compare the critical use of nos-

16   Introduction

talgia for a rural, domestic past in *The Country of the Pointed Firs* (1896) by Sarah Orne Jewett with that in *Twenty Years at Hull-House* (1910) by Jane Addams. I argue that educated women at the turn of the century combined Victorian ideas about middle-class domesticity with newer ideas about women's leisured cultivation to depict women as better than men at mediating social conflict. This creation of a feminized transcendent expertise, while crucial to the foundation of professional social work, provided white women with a powerful version of authority but denied it to women from putatively primitive or hybrid cultures.

Chapter 2 continues to explore how women used domesticity and professionalism to authorize and shape their work. Here, however, I focus on women who were excluded from the kind of expertise created by Addams and Jewett. Both the novelist Pauline Hopkins in *Contending Forces* (1900) and the club organizer Josephine St. Pierre Ruffin in her newspaper, *Woman's Era* (1894–95) contest the claims to transcendence of domesticity and cultivation. Adapting the narrative form of regionalism, they rethink the region-nation and private-public divides and argue for a new kind of professional expertise that is situated rather than abstracted. The chapter demonstrates the close connection between black women's narrative forms and their organized, political activism, an activism which complicates the transcendent expertise that Jewett and Addams created and that the culture of professionalism more generally promoted.

While the first two chapters show how women were able to deploy domestic and professional discourse productively, the third and fourth explore the ways some important thinkers attempted to stabilize the opposition between domesticity and professionalism through a contrast made between (domestic) subjectivity and (scientific) objectivity. Chapter 3 demonstrates that this contrast was used to curtail the supposed feminization of cultural authority. The novelist Frank Norris in *The Octopus* (1901) and the philosopher George Santayana in "The Genteel Tradition in American Philosophy" (1911) criticize Victorian, sentimental aesthetics and women's central role in producing them, arguing that such aesthetics disguise and support the functioning of capitalism. Their analysis—posed as masculine, professional, and objective—paradoxically returns them to a notion of transcendent aesthetics inherited from feminized sentimentalism, an aesthetics that became central to the creation of modern literary expertise. Norris and Santayana's depiction of women and their cultural power illustrates perfectly the influence that domestic discourse had on standard forms of modern professional discourse, how modernists tried to erase that influence, and how that influence has been ignored by subsequent readers. Norris and Santayana's thinking represents the powerful and resilient narrative of modernity and its complicated progressive antifeminism that I call into question throughout this book.

It was not simply men, however, who sought to stabilize the opposition between domesticity and professionalism. Chapter 4 explores how Willa Cather and Ida Tarbell also attempted to do so in order to insist on their professional authority. Relying on notions of the journalist's independence from the market, Cather and Tarbell contrasted their work to the "interested," best-selling women's writing of the past. Their journalistic belief in the modern writer's autonomy, however, functioned to highlight not so much the truth of their work as the truthfulness of their individual character. Cather and Tarbell's professionalism was, in short, a contradictory notion, pointing both to and away from the author's involvement in the text, both to and away from a critique of the market, as Cather's *The Professor's House* (1925) and Tarbell's *The History of Standard Oil* (1904) show. These women's claims to professional authority are undermined by their own construction of their expertise, demonstrating how professionalism for women could as much reinforce the status quo as undermine it.

Chapter 5 provides a coda to the book as a whole. It does so by comparing the manner in which two women anthropologists combined domestic and professional discourse to shape new kinds of authority for themselves, as well as the different ways that authority was understood, and the conflicts between them over their authority. Specifically, it focuses on how Zora Neale Hurston in *Seraph on the Suwanee* (1948) and Ruth Benedict in *Patterns of Culture* (1934) linked and criticized both Victorian domesticity and modern professionalism through their analysis of the problematic nature of any claim to transcendent authority, whether subjective or objective. The chapter investigates how Hurston and Benedict productively combined and interrogated domestic and professional discourse in order to engage in broad forms of social and disciplinary critique. At the same time, however, the chapter shows that while these women's writings enabled them to become public intellectuals, it was difficult to maintain a balance between using the binary of domesticity and professionalism and simply enforcing that divide. This is evident in the quite different reception of their work, their complex personal and professional relationship, and the changes their work registers over time.

Modern Women, Modern Work revises our literary histories as well as our theories of professionalism. It calls into question the assumptions about gender and race that animate the opposition between Victorian domestic and modern professional culture on which modernists relied. It argues not only for the importance of what we could call the Victorian others of modern culture but also, following Michel Foucault, for the historical indebtedness of our modern ideas about the professions and disciplines to Victorian culture more broadly.[50] In focusing on the relation between ideas and institutional change, the book demonstrates how women's narratives helped to shape modern professionalism in the U.S. These narratives, however, did not always work to make professionalism either more inclusive or democratic. In mapping out the constraints that women in particular faced as they shaped their writings and their work, in tracing the slippery compromises they embraced and the brilliant adaptations they made, *Modern Women, Modern Work* problematizes the naturalized histories we have told about modern professionalism and helps us to rethink our own work within the culture of professionalism.

Chapter 1

Domesticity, Cultivation, and Vocation in Jane Addams and Sarah Orne Jewett

In her preface to the 1893 edition of *Deephaven,* Sarah Orne Jewett describes her call to vocation some twenty years earlier as having arisen out of her "dark fear that townspeople and country people would never understand one another."[1] She felt as a "young writer" (*DH,* 3) that "the individuality and quaint personal characteristics of rural New England" were being "swept away" (5) by the rise of "fast-growing ... cities" (1), which had not only "drawn to themselves ... much of the best life of the remotest villages" but also in summer had sent countryward "the summer boarder" (2) or tourist. "[G]rave wrong and misunderstanding" between rich "timid ladies" and laboring "country people" ensued. Jewett attempted to remedy this misunderstanding in her writing: "There is a noble saying of Plato that the best thing that can be done for the people of a state is to make them acquainted with one another." She tried to offer an "explanation" (3) of the country to the city in order to defuse the tension between the two—a tension so extreme, she suggested, that it threatened to divide the nation.

Three questions arise here about Jewett's formulation of her call to vocation.[2] Why does she rewrite the classic pastoral division of city and country as that between tourist and laborer? Further, why does she see the tension between this tourist and laborer as a "misunderstanding" (3), a kind of failed communication rather than a class conflict? And last, why does she imagine herself as a mediator between the two, defusing this grave danger by "introducing" one part of the nation to the other, along the lines Plato suggested?[3] In other words, what qualifies her to negotiate this conflict?

Jewett was not alone in envisioning a division in post–Civil War America between city and country. Nor was she alone in seeing this division as a fearful one. Historians and literary scholars have traced how the growth of cities, rise in immigration, and expansion of the country westward made the New England countryside seem increasingly marginal to the nation's development and identity. Because New England had long functioned as the mythic "seed-bed" of American democracy, anxiety about this region's displacement manifested itself in a variety of ways.[4] Rural decline, or rather fears about it, must be (and usually are) recognized as crucial to Jewett's work and to the literary movement called regionalism more generally, a movement in which she is seen as an exemplary figure. But while regionalism has been a useful way to categorize Jewett's work within the context of late nineteenth-century rural decline, it has been a difficult term to pin down with any precision. Its malleability is evident in the history of criticism of Jewett.

In the early years of the institutionalization of American literary study, regionalism was used not only to analyze but also to dismiss Jewett and other authors who wrote about rural decline. Her writing, literary critics argued in the 1920s and 1930s, represented the death throes of the feminized genteel tradition in New England letters, a tradition characterized by colonial dependence on English cultural forms. Regionalism described an elitist and backward form of literature against which importantly critical and nonelitist American literature was struggling to free itself.[5] When Jewett was recuperated in the work of feminist critics in the 1980s and 1990s, *regionalism* was again adopted as a term to discuss her work. This time, however, the term was used in order to highlight and deconstruct the gendered assumptions about literary value that inflected the earlier criticism. Feminists argued that Jewett was a regionalist in the sense that women's culture was more generally—marginalized by mainstream American culture because it was produced by women and because it promoted a very different vision of the world. Jewett figured prominently in evaluations of how the critical establishment had homogenized American literature and ignored dissenting or minority views.[6] More recently, the term *regionalism* has been used yet again to describe writings by women (and minorities) as marginal to the major American literary traditions. In response to feminist criticism, this historicist work has sought to show that in order to succeed, regionalist writers did not dissent from but rather relied on mainstream views about gender and race that constricted them and their work. *Regionalism*, in these historicist accounts, is a useful term for analyzing how women and minority writers are tragically compelled by the literary market to become complicit in making their work minor, in contrast to that of the "major" American writers who avoid such complicity with the market.[7]

These very different accounts of Jewett's regionalism show, first of all, that while definitions of form are historically mutable, they are nonetheless real in the sense that they do certain kinds of ideological work for those who use them.[8] At the same time, these different accounts of regionalism also demonstrate that while definitions of form change over time, what has remained the same are the values that inform those definitions.[9] Despite the malleability of the term *regionalism*, and despite the very different accounts of Jewett produced by the use of that term, what *is* agreed on is that the worth of her writings depends on her being an "idealized agent," on her "authorial transcendence" of hegemony, as Lora Romero describes this traditional measuring of worth.[10] While there are important differences between old and new historicists, feminists and nonfeminists,[11] all have tended to assume that if Jewett's regionalist fiction has value, it must stand apart from and above mainstream discourses of its period.

As this chapter explores, it is precisely this powerful notion of idealized agency that Jewett herself calls upon, in two different but linked ways, in order to authorize her regionalist writings. On the one hand, she relies on Victorian domestic ideology about woman and the home's transcendence of market relations, a transcendence that unites the competitive and fragmented nation in an oasis from itself. As Romero has shown, since the nineteenth century, this domestic woman has been crucial to debates over idealized agency because she can be described as embodying either hegemony or resistance.[12] On the other hand, even as Jewett calls upon the idealized agency of domestic woman, she subordinates domestic ideology temporally to, and combines it with, what she figures as newer ideas about woman's role. In these newer ideas, woman is described as an individual who has "leisure, culture, grace, social instincts, artistic ambitions," as Henry James described this new woman, or who experiences "vicarious leisure," as Thorstein Veblen said more sarcastically.[13] In Jewett's description of her vocation, woman's historical ability to unite a divided nation through the home is enhanced by her new-found leisure and educated understanding of the (supposedly) unifying power of culture, of art. Stephanie Foote has recently shown that a double-pronged temporality characterizes regionalist texts of this period. Foote argues that these texts both look away from and look toward the present of U.S. industrialization, urbanization, immigration, and imperialism as they construct their fictions of the nation's past.[14] Jewett uses a double-pronged progressive temporality, I likewise argue, to construct her mediating authority. Designating touristic cultivation as woman's civilized modern present, she turns domesticity into the past of nature, instinct, and the body. The modern, cultivated woman tourist subsumes into herself the universality of the body but moves beyond that to the more transcendent universality of high culture.

This careful work of combining the "past" of domesticity with the "present" of leisured cultivation, and subordinating the former to the latter, is not unique to Jewett but rather involves her in a larger progressive and professional discourse about woman's labor at the turn of the century.[15] By reading Jewett's *The Country of the Pointed Firs* (1896) with Jane Addams's *Twenty Years at Hull-House* (1910), we can see how the first generation of aspiring white women professionals used ideas about what they designated as women's past and present to authorize their intervention in social conflicts within the nation.[16] By embedding outmoded domestic ideas within newer cultivated and leisured ones to shape new kinds of female expertise, they created a powerful version of authority for themselves. At the same time, they implicitly denied that authority to women and men imagined as uncultivated, unleisured, uncivilized. In short, they sought to gain professional work for themselves by turning the educated, middle-class white woman (as opposed to the domestic woman) into an idealized agent of culture.[17]

In this chapter, I focus on the ways Addams and Jewett rely on what they themselves describe as an older discourse of woman's domesticity while very carefully and subtly subordinating it to and combining it with a newer discourse about woman's leisured cultivation. The classed racialism of their progressive temporality provides the glue that binds together their accession to mainstream ideologies of the time as well as their challenge to those same ideologies.[18] Addams and Jewett, in other words, are particularly appropriate figures with which to begin a book about how women negotiated the relation between domesticity and professionalism in modernity because their work demonstrates powerfully how women used mainstream logic about progressive modernity to change dominant ideologies about woman's sphere. Their thinking reveals how women usefully created new kinds of authority for themselves as well as the problems that resulted from those new forms of authority.

What is it that led Jane Addams, a college-educated heiress from "the pastoral community"[19] of Cedarville, Illinois, to found Hull-House in the center of one of Chicago's slums? Further, what is it that Hull-House expressed to women of Addams's generation so that thousands of them flocked to settlement homes throughout the country?[20] While Addams links the founding of Hull-House to her childhood experience with rural democracy and to her education at one of the first women's colleges, she describes the formative moment as occurring during a visit to Europe. In a continuation of her college education and in "preparation" for a professional career for which she is filled with "enthusiasm" and "driving ambition" (*H-H*, 52), she travels to Europe "in search of culture" (64). One day, she is taken by a "city missionary" to London's East End with "a small party of tourists" so she can "witness the Saturday night sale of decaying vegetables and fruit" to the impoverished "masses" (61). Because of the "moral revulsion" (66) she experiences, she becomes afraid of wandering about London, "afraid to look down narrow streets and alleys lest they disclose again this hideous human need and suffering" (62). She realizes that her desire for education, her search for culture, is indicted by the poverty she sees: "For two years in the midst of my distress over the poverty which, thus suddenly driven into my consciousness, had become to me the 'Weltschmerz,' there was mingled a sense of futility, of misdirected energy, the belief that the pursuit of cultivation would not in the end bring either solace or relief" (64).

However, Addams does not simply reject her education and cultivation in this formative moment, as one might expect. As it is through her "search [for] culture" that she discovers poverty, so it is only *through* culture that she can understand poverty. Her "painful" view of the "masses" leads her to remember De Quincey's "The Vision of Sudden Death," which shows that "we were . . .

lumbering our minds with literature that only served to cloud the really vital situation spread before our eyes" (63). While her first response to the "unlovely" masses is to avoid seeing them, her second response is to look everywhere for them, to be "irresistably drawn to the poorer quarters of each city" (62) in Europe. She sees poverty through the lens of her education and cultivation and searches for it as "feverishly" (66) as she did for culture.

These two contradictory responses toward urban poverty in this crucial moment of vocation, both centered around "culture," need to be explained since they become integral to Addams's vocation and to what she describes as the philosophy behind Hull-House. In the first response, Addams finds the pursuit of cultivation futile. She rejects cultivation as a "snare" (60), especially for women. It is "American mothers and their daughters who cross the seas in search of culture," not American fathers and sons. While Addams had traveled to Europe because she believed that education would liberate women from their domestic lives, education now becomes that which prevents women's involvement in the world outside the home. And subsequently, Addams imagines a domestic role for women as the solution: "I gradually reached a conviction that the first generation of college women had taken their learning too quickly, had departed too suddenly from the active, emotional life led by their grandmothers and great-grandmothers[,] that the contemporary education of young women had developed too exclusively the power of acquiring knowledge and of merely receiving impressions; that somewhere in the process of 'being educated' they had lost that simple and almost automatic response to the human appeal, that old healthful reaction resulting in activity" (64). In this first response to poverty, Addams associates the domestic past with activity, with labor that is natural, nearly instinctual ("that simple and almost automatic response"). The present, by contrast, is associated with passivity, with an experience of reality so mediated that it has become ungrounded and unreal ("merely receiving impressions"). To remedy her alienation in the present, she must return to the past. From education and culture, she must return to domesticity and nature.

A central paradox of Hull-House, then, is that an intentionally reactionary rhetoric, inextricably tied to an imagined biological or natural truth, is used in the service of a progressive political agenda. The lady's useless and alienated leisure can be remedied only by a return to labor because labor is instinctual. Thus, Addams argues, "young people" (91), especially "young girls" (93), "bear the brunt of being cultivated into unnourished, oversensitive lives" and "have been shut off from the common labor by which they live which is a great source of moral and physical health" (91). "There is something primordial," Addams says, in the way that these young people "long" to work, a longing that is almost biological: "We all bear traces of the starvation struggle which for so long made up the life of the race. Our very organism holds memories and glimpses of that long life of our ancestors which still goes on among so many of our contemporaries . . . These . . . [memories and glimpses] are the physical complement of the 'Intimations of Immortality' . . . (92)

In order to share the "life of the race" (92), however, labor needs to be preindustrial. Addams's plan for Hull-House follows this understanding of the bodily, biological need for preindustrial labor: "I gradually became convinced that it would be a good thing to rent a house in a part of the city where many primitive and actual needs are found, in which young women who had been given over too exclusively to study might restore a balance of activity *along traditional lines* and learn of life *from life itself*" (72, emphasis added).

Addams suggests not only that the bodily struggle against "starvation" is "life itself," and that observing that struggle means a return to life, but also that preindustrial, "traditional" labor returns one to life. By laboring in the house, women will discover their own nature. It is thus that we can understand the significance of Hull-*House*. The house is a "settlement," an oasis of civilization in the middle of a territory not yet reached by civilization, but it is also a nostalgic escape from modern civilization, a return to the labor of one's mother, grandmother, and great-grandmother.[21] Food, child care, facilitation of social events, and recreation are the primary activities at Hull-House in the early years, while the residents of the area are described as neighbors and friends. And importantly, this early reliance on domestic discourse gave the inhabitants of Hull-House leeway to pursue, in later years, activities not traditionally associated with women.[22]

Appropriately, Hull-House's Labor Museum, which depicts preindustrial forms of labor, becomes a crucial means in *Twenty Years at Hull-House* by which Addams can create relationships with her "neighbors," particularly her female neighbors. The idea for the Labor Museum arises out of a walk she takes where, "perturbed in spirit, because it seemed so difficult to come into genuine relations with the Italian women "in her neighborhood," she decides to "devise an educational enterprise" that will provide "a dramatic representation of the inherited resources of . . . daily occupation" (*H-H*, 172). Addams specifically emphasizes her "yearning to recover for the household arts something of their early sanctity" (175), to show "the charm of woman's primitive activities" (176). Around this representation of older forms of labor, women will unite, just as they do around and in Hull-House. Because of the natural instinct to labor, because of the universality of domesticity, the similarities between Addams and her female neighbors will outweigh their differences.

But if labor generally, and preindustrial domestic labor specifically, are to Addams the bodily inheritance of humanity, and thus the great ameliorative force between classes and races, the Labor Museum also reveals Addams's second response to poverty—a belief in the even greater power of culture and representations to unify disparate groups. In the moment when Addams formulates her desire to recover the sanctity of woman's "primitive activities" as a solution to poverty, her mind fills with "shifting *pictures* of woman's labor *with which travel* makes one familiar" (175, emphasis added). That is, the very leisured and cultivated existence she has castigated and is resisting becomes her model for the active laboring life she praises and wants to live. By this I mean that not only do her leisured travel experiences create her view of the significance of labor, and not only does she see a museum as a form of communication between cultures, classes, races, and generations, but also that the traveler and museum goer are models for understanding differences. Thus, Addams recounts how the Hull-House Social Extension Committee attempts to bridge the "distinct social 'gulf' " between Irish-American and Italian neighbors by giving a party. Afterward one of the members of the committee tells Addams, "I am ashamed of the way I have always talked about 'dagoes.' They are quite like other people." Addams comments on this:

To my mind at that moment the speaker had passed from the region of the uncultivated person into the possibilities of the cultivated person. The former is bounded by a narrow outlook on life, unable to overcome differences of dress and habit, and his interests are slowly contracting within a circumscribed area; while the latter constantly tends to be more a citizen of the world because of his growing understanding of all kinds of people. We send our young people to Europe that they may lose their provincialism and be able to judge their fellows by a more universal test, as we send them to college that they may attain the cultural background and a larger outlook; all of these it is possible to acquire in other ways, as this member of the woman's club had discovered for herself. (249–50)

It is the cultivated person who is able to discern and understand differences disinterestedly, and while it is "possible" that such disinterest can be acquired elsewhere, the museum visitor and the tourist represent the exemplary forms in which understanding can be attained. Culture is what "lumber[s] our minds" (63) and is also "an understanding of the long-established occupations and thoughts of men, of the arts with which they have solaced their toil" (175), an understanding of the universal which results in the ability to "interpret opposing forces to each other" (167).

Inhering in Addams's two notions of culture are conflicting assumptions about civilization. On the one hand, educated cultivation reveals the divisions that modernity has created. The civilized have become alienated from their own labor and from their racial history and biological selves.[23] On the other hand, educated cultivation is precisely what enables the transcendence of the racial and the biological, of the primitive world in which the impoverished masses of the East End of London and the racial and ethnic others to whom Hull-House ministers are embedded. There are indeed moments in *Twenty Years at Hull-House* where cultivated Americans are unable to transcend what is figured as the racial and biological, and likewise there are moments when ethnic and racial others do transcend them. Addams notes, for example, how Greeks "are filled with amazed rage when their very name is flung at them as an opprobrious epithet," while Addams approvingly notes the respect with which these Greeks listen to an address by W.E.B. Du Bois "with apparently no consciousness of that race difference which color seems to accentuate so absurdly" (*H-H*, 183). The crucial issue, however, is that for Addams, transcendence is the criterion by which cultivation and civilization are judged. The contemporary Greeks that Addams describes are unconscious of racial difference because they know the history of their civilization and are cultivated; they are, as Addams says, "cosmopolitan" (183).[24]

Having traced Addams's description of her call to vocation to two models of woman's sphere—one that she links to the past (domesticity), the other to the present (education, tourism, cultivation)—we might usefully ask why she feels compelled to use both of them in her solution to vocational crisis, and how they might function for her. At a practical level the answer seems clear. College-educated women in particular flocked to settlement houses in America because few professional avenues were open to them and those that were, limited their advancement. The settlement house enabled middle- and upper-class women to work outside the home and to involve themselves in the social issues of the day. It also gave them an acceptable rhetoric with which to describe their activity.[25] They were "neighbors" and "friends," cultivated and humane ladies, not economists, sociologists, or politicians; they were, as Addams calls them, "public housekeepers."[26] They represented themselves as unprofessionalized, and therefore acceptable.[27]

In fact, Hull-House workers argued that this unprofessionalism was exactly what made them effective and what enabled, paradoxically, their uniquely female professional authority. In the early years of the settlement house movement,[28] these women argued that because they were "public housekeepers," they could not only have truer and more democratic relations with the poor but could also be more disinterested, better able to understand social problems and create solutions to them. Their account of their unique effectiveness reveals more clearly than practical explanations how the two models of woman's sphere could be brought together to create professional authority. The sphere of woman (upper-class, white woman, that is), as Addams experiences it in her European travels, is a kind of cultivated leisure. While this cultivation is at first castigated and replaced by its figured opposite—domesticity—cultivation remains, taking on the characteristics ascribed to domesticity. Cultivation becomes the glue that binds society together, just as in "the cult of domesticity" the home was the universal glue that would bind the competitive and fragmented American society together. Thus, in the final pages of *Twenty Years at Hull-House*, Addams argues that to unite and stabilize the nation, culture must be made accessible to all. It is the "profound conviction" of the settlement "that the common stock of intellectual enjoyment should not be difficult of access because of the economic position of him who would approach it, that those 'best results of civilization' upon which depend the finer and freer aspects of living must be incorporated into our common life and have free mobility through all elements of society if we would have our democracy endure" (310).

Along with being a neighbor and friend, the rich and educated settlement worker also dispenses culture to the poor and uneducated. Because of her education, she understands and can explain cultural as well as political differences and so becomes an "interpreter" (170) of truths. Addams even theorizes a neutral interpretive power and activism based on an idea of pure cultural value that will have the same "universal" acceptance as that of pure cultural value. The settlement worker, she says, should have "nonresistance or rather universal good will" and perform "disinterested action" that would be "like truth or beauty in its lucidity and power of appeal" (115). While the idea of pure cultural value is clearly not unique to women or to the time period, Addams's particular version of it (that such value can transcend history and social differences and be neutral), coincides with and contains the claims to authority of domesticity.

The settlement worker in particular is modeled on the figure of the tourist, the educated traveler who knows pure cultural value and who understands the "language" of the foreign country. Thus, one of the first major projects of Hull-House was the publication of a book called *Hull-House Maps and Papers* (1895). The maps, made for the United States Bureau of Labor's investigation into "the slums of great cities" (117), delineate the different ethnic neighborhoods and list the occupations and salaries of individuals in them. While the papers treat a variety of concerns, the map is a crucial metaphor for the project as a whole. It assumes that a guide through and an explanation of different areas will provide objective understanding of problems, which, in turn, will precipitate change. Making a problem visible is understanding and solving it. This reliance on a kind of touristic model of vision was common to the settlement house movement and Progressive politics generally.[29] But in Addams, domestic ideology is implicit in her high valuation of tourism. A man's "predatory instinct" makes him "carelessly indifferent" to what he sees, while women, "traditional housekeepers," grounded in a realm of natural and unalienated labor, see and know what to do.[30] Because of their experiences in housekeeping and cultivated leisure, Addams figures women as particularly qualified to engage in civic work. Their domestic unprofessionalism and cultivated disinterestedness create their very professional authority and expertise.

A novel without tension, a conflict, or denouement, and in which the main activity is visiting, Jewett's *The Country of the Pointed Firs* may seem to have little to do with the problem of vocation for women at the turn of the century. But it is through the activity of visiting that the book's thematic conflict, that between city and country, reveals itself; and it is through the vocation of the text's narrator—a writer and summer visitor from Boston—that this conflict is defused. Just as Addams attempts to claim, through her gender, a position for herself as a political arbiter, to represent herself as a neutral interpreter of conflicting interests, so Jewett in this text attempts to claim a neutral and transhistorical position for her writing. This claim inheres in Jewett's understanding and depiction of woman's relation to work. Like Addams, Jewett separates and combines the "older" discourse of the "cult of domesticity" with woman's new leisured cultivation to construct a special form of professional expertise for herself.[31] While imagining domesticity as a human instinct, Jewett sees culture as transcending even the universality of instinct, and hence depicts the cultivated woman as uniquely able to understand, interpret, and finally overcome differences. I want briefly to spell out the differences between city and country the novel depicts; then, I will describe the ways Jewett's text and narrator are figured as defusing these conflicts.

During one of the most ecstatic moments of community in *Pointed Firs*—the Bowden family reunion—the narrator suddenly makes explicit all the differences between city and country, between herself and the rural inhabitants, that until now she has left implicit. At the same time, and in a typical gesture, she works to contain and deny the differences she herself explicates:

> As the feast went on, the spirits of my companion [Mrs. Todd] steadily rose. The excitement of an unexpectedly great occasion was a subtle stimulant to her disposition, and I could see that sometimes when Mrs. Todd had seemed limited and heavily domestic, she had simply grown sluggish for lack of proper surroundings. She was not so much reminiscent now as expectant, and as alert and gay as a girl. We who were her neighbors were full of gayety, which was but the reflected light from her beaming countenance. It was not the first time that I was full of wonder at the waste of human ability in this world, as a botanist wonders at the wastefulness of nature, the thousand seeds that die, the unused provision of every sort. The reserve force of society grows more and more amazing to one's thought. More than one face among the Bowdens showed that only opportunity and stimulus were lacking—a narrow set of circumstances had caged a fine able character and held it captive. One sees exactly the same types in a country gathering as in the most brilliant city company. You are safe to be understood if the spirit of your speech is the same for one neighbor as for the other.[32]

The differences between city and country inhabitants are many. From the narrator's citified perspective, Mrs. Todd is "sometimes . . . limited and heavily domestic" because she lacks "proper surroundings"; that is, she is stuck in a "narrow set of circumstances"—the countryside. The narrator's belief that Mrs. Todd and many other Bowdens are "caged" by their rural surroundings is inextricably tied to a distinction between classes. The narrator's experience of the city is also an experience with "the most brilliant city company." While she claims that "One sees exactly the same types" in the country as in an upper-class city gathering, such a claim paradoxically suggests that this is not obvious to her reader, not obvious even to the narrator herself, who must state it. If the "spirit" of the words one uses is the same, the words themselves are not. Finally, that the narrator is able to generalize in such a fashion about the limitations of rural life means that she has choices Mrs. Todd and the others lack. She can see that the country is confining because she knows something that is not confining. In comparison to the sometimes "sluggish" Mrs. Todd (with her mental as well as physical immobility), the narrator has money and so mobility (mobility translated as the leisure to travel) to be cultivated and educated, and to understand differences.

The narrator also links city and country to different temporalities. Under even the "subtle" stimulation of the reunion, Mrs. Todd becomes "expectant" and "alert" rather than "reminiscent." The countryside is associated with memory and the past, the city with the rush and bustle of the present. While memory is usually highly valued in *Pointed Firs*, here the narrator suggests that living in the past is an act of necessity. She gives Mrs. Todd's usually reminiscent state a negative connotation and makes "limited," "sluggish," and "heavily domestic" synonymous, implying that the "domestic" labor that Mrs. Todd does and that is characteristic of the past is part of the problem of "narrow" circumstances. Meanwhile, the narrator metaphorically links herself to a profession not traditionally associated with women. She compares herself to "a botanist" in her wonder at the "waste of human ability in the world." She is beyond the "heavily domestic" worldview of past generations of women and can see the world from a broad and scientific perspective.[33] The movement from the limited and provincial to the objective and universal also resonates with another division in the book—that between the region, with all its individual peculiarities—and the nation. The narrator, representing the nation, depicts scientifically the activities and thoughts of the idiosyncratic region. The rural characters speak in dialect, which the narrator records precisely *as dialect* within the national language she uses to tell the story.

It is here, in the movement of narrative agency from an individual case study (Mrs. Todd), to a more universal perspective ("the waste of human ability"), and finally to a directive (how one should talk to people from the country) that we can see how the narrator attempts to deny or contain the differences between city and country that she herself has explicated. The reunion passage starts in the first person, compares the first person to a third person (the botanist), becomes the impersonal third person (one), and then uses a second-person plural to direct the actions of the reader as well as presumably to explain the actions of the narrator. First, the narrator presents herself as subjective agent of the story with her own opinions and interpretations, then as a kind of objective agent, then as an agent integrated into a community of agency (the community that reads her book). This movement from a specific to a more general narrative agency occurs continually in the book, and to understand its significance, we need to understand the narrator, who moves between these different agencies.

We learn almost all the facts that we ever learn about the narrator in the first chapters of the book. She is from Boston, is wealthy, leisured, and well traveled and thus discovered Dunnet Landing "two or three summers before in the course of a yachting cruise" (*CPF,* 2); she has so much leisure she cannot exactly remember when she first went to Dunnet Landing. She is condescending about the simplicity and ignorance of the landing, a simplicity and ignorance that she also romanticizes and aestheticizes so that at her return she discovers "the same quaintness of the village with its elaborate conventionalities; all that mixture of remoteness, and childish certainty of being the centre of civilization of which her affectionate dreams had told" (2). In addition, she is an independent career woman, a "single passenger" (2) traveling to Dunnet Landing on her own and looking for "seclusion and uninterrupted days" (6) in order to write. While the other characters' names and backgrounds are presented, hers are not. In other words, all that we learn about the narrator and her existence outside of Dunnet Landing underlines her distinction from the village and its people. The very privacy in which her history is enclosed separates her from the villagers, whose personal histories are described in detail.

Nevertheless, from the moment she arrives, the narrator attempts with more and more facility to bridge the divisions between herself and the community not only by taking part in the activities and interests of the community, but also by remaining exactly what she is—a wealthy, leisured, traveling lady. These attempts correspond with her two methods for defusing conflict in the book—involvement in the community's labor (particularly domesticity) and cultivated and leisured perception of that labor. Involvement in the community entails for the narrator, first of all, that she learn *how* to involve herself in it, how to empathize with the people in it. While the narrator's empathy does not evolve in clearly defined stages, she seems to become accretively more empathetic under Mrs. Todd's guidance. As the book progresses, the narrator no longer needs to ask Mrs. Todd about the meaning of actions but rather begins to understand and interpret actions on her own, even begins to visit people on her own.

What the narrator particularly learns to understand through her involvement in the community is the universal nature of domesticity. As the narrator visits from house to house, she shows us the way that the house and housekeeping of various individuals reveal their common, as well as their individual, histories. The house (and family) becomes the bond that unites everyone despite their differences. So it is at the Bowden reunion, where the narrator has given us the most explicit description of division (of city and country) that she also gives us the most explicit description of unity through domesticity. She describes the "old Bowden house" as standing "low-storied and broad-roofed, in its green fields as if it were a motherly brown hen waiting for the flock that came straying toward it from every direction" (*CPF,* 159). The old house stands in the midst of the natural world as a unifying point, the mother-creator around which all the "straying" individuals "from every direction" gather. More specifically, as in Addams, domesticity represents a part of the biological makeup of all individuals: "The sky, the sea, have watched poor humanity at its rites so long; we were no more a New England family celebrating its own existence and simple progress; we carried the tokens and inheritance of all such households from which this had descended, and were only the latest of our line. We possessed the instincts of a far-forgotten childhood" (163). The semicolons between sentences suggest that the ideas are equivalent and explain each other. Nature has watched so long that the individual "household" has become an expression of nature, has received an inheritance from it through the household and reveals the shared primitive roots of the human race. Even the narrator, who is not a Bowden, becomes part of the now unified flock ("we") by the universality of the household. Just as Addams argues in *Hull-House* that the desire to perform domestic labor is the physical trace of the "starvation struggle" (92) left on our bodies, so the narrator in *Pointed Firs* learns that domesticity is the body, a universal case for the individual soul: "a man's house is really but his larger body, and expresses in a way his nature and character" (192).

The repeated description throughout the text of the house as a shell, as a body that encases the individual soul, underlines what is at stake in such an understanding of domesticity. The narrator writes of how she lives in Mrs. Todd's "quaint little house with as much comfort and unconsciousness as if it were a larger body, or a double shell, in whose simple convolutions Mrs. Todd and I had secreted ourselves" (86). In the colonial period, the home was frequently described as a shell in which woman resided, protected and excluded from the world, and so this simile associates the home with preindustrial society.[34] But there is also a biological implication. The self (individual) is a secretion of the universal body (home). In this "double shell," a double body that stands in interchangeably for both domesticity and nature, Mrs. Todd and the narrator's differences are bridged; they are united together.

While the narrator learns from her involvement in the community that domesticity is nature, that it is the universal body of humanity, such involvement is in the end shown to be less efficacious in overcoming differences than are the narrator's own cultivated perceptions as a wealthy, leisured, traveling lady. Cultivation, as in Addams, coincides with but contains domesticity. The necessities of the situation reveal that involvement can be only temporary; domesticity finally cannot override difference. Thus, in the narrator's second return to Dunnet Landing for William's wedding, she again uses her shell metaphor, describing her "odd feeling of strangeness," in "the little rooms" of Mrs. Todd's house: "It was like the hermit crab in a cold new shell" (284). While the narrator does readjust to the rooms, her readjustment shows that for her the shell (both nature and domesticity) is a temporary body into and out of which she can slip. The narrator is mobile, moving to domestic spaces (shells) but also beyond and in between domestic spaces. And as the story of Joanna Todd's "Shell-heap Island" warns, domesticity by itself can lead to monomania, insanity, and death (a pile of cast-off shells).

What supersedes domesticity (the body), then, is the perception of domesticity that the narrator brings to the situation because she is leisured, wealthy, and nondomestic. Her understanding of culture entails a universality that goes beyond biology, beyond the body. Repeatedly, in the midst of mundane activities and a generally muted narrative, come highly charged comparisons between the people and activities of Dunnet Landing and high culture. Returning to the Bowden reunion, for example, we can see how the narrator's understanding of the universality of domesticity is framed by her larger understanding of high culture: "we might have been a company of ancient Greeks going to celebrate a victory, or to worship the god of harvests in the grove above. It was strangely moving to see this and to make part of it. The sky, the sea, have watched poor humanity at its rites so long; we were no more a New England family" (163). The reference to the "ancient Greeks," a reference repeatedly used when the narrator wants to associate Dunnet Landing with the universality of high culture,[35] links the reunion to a civilization that has long been connected with timeless thought. The reunion is a kind of instinctual drive and reveals a biological inheritance, but such a drive and biology come from the ancient Greeks and so transcend culturally the mortality of the body. Similarly, the reference underlines the narrator's own transcendence of the merely domestic or natural. She can empathize with the residents of Dunnet Landing in part because of her cultivated and educated experiences elsewhere. The reference is meant to reveal how the perception of universality, the perception of a cultivated tourist, is sufficient for dealing with the divisions depicted in the book.[36]

In a similar way to Addams, then, Jewett's story depends on conflicted assumptions about civilization. It is through an involvement in domesticity and primitive labor that the narrator is able to come into real relation with the residents of Dunnet Landing and to bridge the differences that modern civilization has created. The first chapter of *Pointed Firs*, "The Return," is thus freighted with the sense of the return to the beginnings of history and an unalienated and innocent world. It requires education, leisure, and cultivation, however, to perceive that Dunnet Landing represents the primitive past of the human race and to move beyond that racial and biological history. It is a knowledge of the ancient Greeks (just as in Addams it is the cosmopolitanism of modern Greeks who know about the ancient Greeks) that enables one to move beyond the primitive body of humanity's racial past.

The fact that the narrator is a leisured tourist (as opposed to the residents of Dunnet Landing) is therefore figured paradoxically as the greatest force linking her to the citizens of Dunnet Landing. While her knowledge of high culture reveals this force at work, the way she figures herself telling the story does so even more clearly. The cipherlike quality of the narrator works much like the idea of pure artistic value in Addams. The narrator, with no name and no history, is figured as a thoroughly cultivated and neutral witness, a kind of perfect tourist: while observing the villagers' "normal" talk and activities, she reveals nothing about herself that would interfere with that talk or those activities. Taking in a view, then, is the form in which the narrator's perception of the community occurs; she transcends difference and social conflict by observing them.

In the logic of the text, then, the most profound moments of transcendence occur when the narrator and the villagers observe views together, particularly domestic ones. For example, when the narrator tours Green Island with Mrs. Blackett and Mrs. Todd, the three women at first view the scenery separately, suggesting the differences between them. But this separate viewing gives way when the "house [is] just before us," and, for no given reason, the narrator then switches to a description of a unanimity of viewing: "There was just room for the small farm and the forest; we looked down at the fish-house and its rough sheds, and the weirs stretching far out into the water. As we looked upward, the tops of the firs came sharp against the blue sky" (59). As the description continues, the narrator switches back to what the "I" can see, but this only emphasizes the moment where all perceived together, looking downward and then upward to see, in a theologically weighted moment, what lies below and above. Later in this section, Mrs. Blackett shares the "quiet outlook" from her bedroom with the narrator, and even the separation that language registers breaks down: "I looked up [from the view to Mrs. Blackett], and we understood each other without speaking" (84).

Returning again to the Bowden reunion, we can understand an odd image that follows the narrator's cultivated celebration of the universality of domesticity. She writes of the Bowden family and herself that "We could see the green sunlit field we had just crossed as if we looked out at it from a dark room, and the old house and its lilacs standing placidly in the sun" (164). The house in question is lit up in contrast to the surrounding darkness. It becomes a focal point that unifies all, that enables all to see together. From the midst of nature, which itself is understood as a "room" in a house, they see "the" house itself that unifies them; they see together. The narrator describes the scenery in terms of what "we" see, even as a shared metaphor of what "we" see ("as if we looked out"), suggesting that the unanimity expressed by the event of the reunion is also a unanimity of perception, feeling, and emotion. All separation is nullified in the reunion; each becomes all: "Each heart [was] warm and every face [shone] with the ancient light" (156), and it is through the unanimity of what "we" see that this is expressed.

The cipherlike quality of the narrator, then, is part of the same way in which the "I" just as easily becomes the "one," "you," or "we" in the novel, or how narrative agency shifts continually from the specific to the general. That is, in the book the tourist's perception of reality as a "view" enables transcendence of difference; because the narrator is not an "I" with a personal history but a purely observing "eye" means that she can imagine beyond the limitations of personality. In fact, the last chapter of the 1896 edition is called "The Backward View." In this chapter, the narrator views not only the death of the New England past ("the islands and the headland had run together and Dunnet Landing and all its coasts were lost to sight" [306]), but even her own death ("So we die before our own eyes; so we see some chapters of our lives come to their natural end" [303]). The ability to understand objectively, through seeing "timeless" cultural representations (in this case a chapter in a book), enables the narrator to transcend even her own mortality, to encompass the natural within the cultural.

We can return now to the three questions of why Jewett might have seen "misunderstanding" between city and country as so threatening and why she felt that following Plato's words and introducing one to the other would provide the solution to this misunderstanding. Like Addams, Jewett had grown up with representations of a homogeneous American democracy based on rural, small-town life; and also like Addams, she had recourse to these representations in attempting to understand and address contemporary issues. But even in using these representations of social order, Addams and Jewett invoked newer models. While the house, with women at the head, could be imagined by these upper-class, white, progressive feminists as a site where national unity could be achieved, it was a new kind of house, a house that reflected these women's ideas about education and leisure. Unity based on the home became more importantly unity based on transhistorical cultural values—values that educated women particularly understood. These women imagined themselves as professional mediators at a kind of national soiree, able, because of woman's past of domesticity but more crucially because of her present cultivation, to introduce the disparate and frequently opposed social groups that made up American life to each other and to show these groups their transcendent commonalities. Jewett's regionalism, then, is part of a new movement to revise the meaning and use of the home, to insert women into the world of professional work both through their past and especially through their present ability to transcend that world. This new movement, as Hull-House reveals, shaped social work as woman's work and helped shift the meaning of women's work more generally.

At the same time, as this chapter makes clear, if the separated and combined force of past domesticity and present cultivation helped the first generation of aspiring professional women shape new kinds of work for themselves, such a combination did not reverse the hierarchies of national, professional culture. To separate and link two dominant discourses of idealized agency—those of domesticity and culture—is to be progressive in two different ways. First, the combination enables Jewett and Addams to carve out new understandings of the social and new vocations for themselves and other women. But second, the combined discourses depend on using historically specific ideas about social evolution that finally seeks to erase what cannot be erased—their classed and raced historical specificity.

This dynamic is captured perfectly in Jewett's local history, "The Old Town of Berwick" (1894). Writing of village life after the Revolution, she says, "The importance of the village, and its connection with the world outside, can be measured by the manner of its housekeeping; and no one can enter Judge Chadbourne's house or the Hamilton house at the Lower Landing . . . without seeing at once that people of refinement and cultivation had planned them and lived in them with elegance and hospitality. The best life in such a town as this was no more provincial in early days than it was in Salem or Boston, and the intercourse and sympathy between people of the same class in New England was more marked than at any other period."[37]

On the one hand, Jewett breaks down the divisions between the national and the regional, the domestic and the world, to imagine a new relation between them. She recounts Berwick's history because while it is "so locally important and interesting," it also registers the history of the nation more generally.[38] Life in Berwick was no more provincial than that in other parts of New England. Similarly, it is through "housekeeping" that one can understand "the world outside." On the other hand, Jewett rethinks the divisions between nation and region, the domestic and the world, through the category of "refinement and cultivation." And while the category is meant to be inclusive because it transcends divisions, it quickly becomes clear that it is exclusive. The "intercourse and sympathy" between the region and the nation, the home and the world is that "between people of the same class" and the same "New England" stock. It is an exclusive, class and race specific idea of cultural transcendence. And it was legible as such to aspiring African American professional women. In the next chapter, we will examine the way middle and upper-class African American women at the turn of the century also used regionalism to break down divisions between the national and regional, the home and the world. These African American women, like Jewett and Addams, worked to authorize themselves within the "culture of professionalism," but they did so not by claiming an idealized agency associated with an exclusive, class and race specific idea of cultural transcendence but by insisting on the specificity *as well as* the generalizability of their agency. They contested the exclusivity of Addams and Jewett's professionalism, working to redefine expertise as situated rather than transcendent.

Chapter 2
Situated Expertise
Josephine St. Pierre Ruffin, Pauline Hopkins, and the NACW

To depict the growing friendship between Dora Smith and Sappho Clark, two of the heroines in *Contending Forces* (1900), Pauline Hopkins describes the way the northern-born Dora leads the southern-born Sappho through the landscape of Boston. The diction Hopkins uses to comment on this exploration is curiously repetitive: "These *free* days were the gala days of [Sappho's] . . . existence, when under Dora's guidance she explored various points of interest, and learned from observation the great plan of life as practiced in an intelligent, *liberty-loving* community. Here in the *free* air of New England's *freest* city, Sappho drank great draughts of *freedom's* subtle elixir."[1] Such an emphasis on freedom is curious, considering that the novel repeatedly demonstrates what it calls "the force of prejudice" (*CF*, 83) in New England where "The Negro . . . [is] held in contempt by many" (114). Nonetheless, Hopkins links the development of Dora and Sappho's friendship to their "freedom" to wander through Boston's "place[s] of public resort" without "fear of insult" (116). While Hopkins describes Sappho and Dora's walks through Boston's libraries, museums, and churches as enabling them to claim "kinship with the great minds of the past whose never-dying works breathed perennial life in the atmosphere of the quiet halls" (116), such kinship with transcendent culture is not what fosters their friendship. Instead, the "freedom" they find in Boston nurtures their friendship, a friendship the novel later shows to have profound implications for creating a national black political community that could counter the "force of prejudice" (83) experienced by Hopkins's characters in both the North and the South. In order to describe the beginning of this national black community, in other words, Hopkins depends on regional pride about New England, specifically about the city of Boston.

In the last chapter, I argued that middle- and upper-class white women writers' use a kind of double-layered idealized agency in their regionalist writings in order to create new kinds of work for themselves within the culture of professionalism. Relying on a progressive notion of civilization, they show that their authority rests not simply on the universality of primitive domesticity, nature, and the body but on the greater universality of educated cultivation and the mind. Their reliance on assumptions about progressive civilization enables them, on the one hand, to displace Victorian domesticity and reshape woman's social role while on the other hand limiting the application of this new social role to cultivated women. Women and men from putatively primitive cultures or who are associated with the "racial" past of nature and the body represent human universality but only to the neutral and educated viewer who sees beyond their specific and limited embodiment. Jewett and Addams's progressive history, however, was not the only one women relied on to authorize themselves within the culture of professionalism. In this chapter, I want to show a different way women's "past" of domesticity as well as their "present" of cultivation was imagined and described. Such a description challenges, even as it relies on, a version of idealized agency that Jewett and Addams, and professionalism more generally, invoke.

In her groundbreaking work on late nineteenth- and early twentieth-century black women novelists, Hazel Carby has shown that the Victorian cult of domesticity defined transcendent "true womanhood" (the chaste white lady) through its exclusion of immanent black womanhood (the sexualized black slave). To understand the historical import of Victorian domestic ideology, Carby argues, one has to understand the "dialectical relationship"[2] between definitions and constructions of black and white womanhood.[3] Building on Carby's argument, we can say that the use of Victorian domestic ideology *as history* within the culture of professionalism also depends on an examination of this dialectical relationship. At the turn of the century, middle and upper-class black and white women intellectuals alike relied on the Victorian domestic ideology of the past and newer conceptions about women's educated cultivation.[4] Black women intellectuals, however, called into question the claims to universal transcendence on which domesticity and cultivation relied. They worked to authorize themselves within the culture of professionalism through a kind of expertise that would be not only abstracted and transcendent but also specific and situated. Instead of the disinterested neutral expertise that Jewett and Addams constructed out of their combination of ideas from the past and the present, black women professionals complicated such ideas to create what can be described as a situated expertise.[5] In this chapter, I focus again on the form of regionalism to show the overlap and difference between white and black women's construction of their expertise. In Pauline Hopkins's novel *Contending Forces* as well as in the rhetoric and work of the first long-standing black women's national organization, the National Association of Colored Women, regionalism registers how black women authorized themselves within a professional discourse that sought to erase their past and present.

As I suggested in the last chapter, regionalist rhetoric was important in describing and debating national identity at the turn of the century. Nations are "imagined communities," Benedict Anderson has famously argued, their identity or "aboriginal essence" negotiated through "History emplotted in particular ways."[6] Regionalism at the turn of the century was a powerful way of emplotting the history of the nation from a specific vantage point for specific ends. In the last chapter, I showed how white women's racialist regionalism was used to shape ideas about women's role in ameliorating social conflict in the nation. At the same time, the racist regionalism of popular and elite white male thinkers authorized a view of nationhood that worked to strip African Americans of their humanity and their citizenship.[7] It is precisely the dominance of the regionalist form in this period and its impact on national debates that motivated black writers to employ it. If regionalism was used most typically, on the one hand, by white women to authorize exclusive kinds of work and, on the other hand, by white men to create exclusive kinds of citizenship, then it seems reasonable that black women intellectuals would imagine that it was necessary to criticize and redefine such regionalisms to authorize their own work and to insist on their status as citizens.[8]

Such a use of dominant discourses by black intellectuals has been a source of much scholarly debate. Even more so than that of white thinkers, black thinkers' work is held to standards in which value is judged in relation to exteriority to ideology. These standards have traditionally helped to enforce the dismissal of intellectuals already ignored because of institutionalized racism and sexism.[9] Even in recent critiques of idealized agency, scholars tend to focus on whether black thinkers' works were pure or contaminated by mainstream ideas of the time. The trope of regionalism that Hopkins and other black intellectuals relied on, for example, continues to trouble critics. While scholars acknowledge the complex manner in which regionalism could be and was deployed by black writers, they generally conclude that such deployment demonstrates an accession to white power and hegemony. Carby, for example, in her rich and illuminating essay on *Contending Forces*, notes that Hopkins uses "the mythology of a regional tradition of liberty in New England" to "encourage among her readership a resurgence of the forms of political agitation and resistance of the antislavery movement" (*RW,* 129). Carby asserts, however, that this use of regionalism consists both of "severe critiques of the position of blacks in the North and moments of unashamed sycophancy" (130).[10] In a similar vein, Dickson D. Bruce Jr. argues that while regionalism became the dominant form in which African Americans wrote at the turn of the century, the form was finally conservative and assimilationist. Richard Brodhead argues even more forcefully that regionalism was "a genre for the [white] elite" that served "the agenda not of dismantling prejudice but of feeding an appetite for consumable otherness."[11]

Such indictments of regionalism implicitly expect African American writers to stand outside of mainstream conventions or institutions. The result is that analysis of the specific fashion in which these conventions and institutions are refracted in black intellectuals' writing tends to be subordinated to melancholic reflections on the kind of writing that could (or should) have been. I want to displace such reflections and focus on how regionalism worked in Hopkins's text, how it enables her to respond critically to contemporary professional ideas of transcendent expertise, and what it might tell us about how she imagined authorizing and constructing work within the discursive norms of the time.

Regionalism, I argue in this chapter, serves to help Hopkins maintain claims to situatedness or specificity as well as to generalizablity or transcendent universality—the latter categories being those on which professional expertise typically depended.[12] Admittedly, because Hopkins adopts a narrative form used so often against blacks in turn-of-the-century America, the situated expertise she creates does not function in a simple or consistent manner to authorize black women's voices. Nonetheless, regionalism enables her to delineate and criticize how the nation's imagined community is constructed through an erasure of the history and work of blacks in the U.S. *and* to conceive a new kind of black imagined community and hence new kinds of work. In other words, regionalism works as a lever in Hopkins to expose the abstracted, transcendent claims of nationalism and through it those of domesticity and professionalism, of so-called private and public life. At the same time, Hopkins's regionalism creates similarly abstracted claims, though through a reliance on specificity.

To explain Hopkins's complex use of regionalism in *Contending Forces*, I want first to examine how other African American women deployed regionalist rhetoric in order to criticize the abstracted nationalism that disenfranchised their community and to authorize new kinds of work for themselves. Specifically, I will focus on how the National Association of Colored Women (NACW) paradoxically deployed regionalist rhetoric to construct national organization.[13] Historians have shown that the women's club movement in the U.S. in the late nineteenth and early twentieth centuries registers how ideas about gender and women's role in society were changing.[14] I am arguing that the NACW served as a kind of professional organization that worked to shift ideas about race, gender, and modern expertise. Members of the NACW were often themselves professionals and expressed ambivalent attitudes toward domesticity and family life.[15] More important, however, the NACW provided black women—professionals and nonprofessionals alike—with a national, organized community from which they could speak out authoritatively within the culture of professionalism. To form this organized community, the NACW relied in its early years on a regionalist rhetoric, which calls into question the transcendent and abstracted logic of domesticity and professionalism. Reading the rhetoric of Hopkins's novel alongside that of the NACW enables us to see how black women at the turn of the century created a situated expertise for themselves that enabled both their work and their political activism.

On March 24, 1894, the first edition of *The Woman's Era*, the journal published by the Woman's Era Club of Boston, appeared in print. Edited by the club's president, Josephine St. Pierre Ruffin, this edition insists on establishing equality between the regional and the national, the local and the general, even as its explicit aim is to create a national community of black women. The brief "Publishers' Announcement" specifies that *Woman's Era* is "the organ of the Woman's Era Club . . . published monthly in Boston" but also says the journal is "devoted to the interests of the women's Clubs, Leagues and Societies throughout the country."[16] In this announcement, the journal self-consciously functions to create an imagined community of women's clubs through simultaneity and literacy.[17] As Fannie Barrier Williams argues in her 1900 history of the black women's club movement, the paper "gained a wide circulation and did more than any other single agency to nationalize the club idea among the colored women of the country";[18] however, the paper nationalizes the club idea without subordinating the local communities that operated in personal and individualized ways.

This equality between the local and the national is further explored in, and explained by, Ruffin's fascinating article on the new endeavor in this first edition. She writes in her "Editorial Greeting":

> The need of such a journal has long been felt as a medium of intercourse and sympathy between the women of all races and conditions; especially true is this of the educated and refined, among the colored women, members of which class may be found in every state from Maine to Florida, but in nearly all of these places an important factor, and one that receives little or no recognition, and the one more than all others which prevents her from making the most of herself and taking her legitimate place among the advanced women, is the limitation of her surroundings and circumscribed sphere in which she must move. The impossibility of mingling freely with people of culture and learning, and so carrying on the mental growth begun in schools and colleges, shuts her in with her books but shuts her out of physical touch with the great world of art, science and letters which is open to all other ambitious women. In fact the stumbling block in the way of even the most cultured colored woman is the narrowness of her environment.[19]

In this passage, Ruffin describes culture as the "great world" outside the home, a world that enables a universal "mental growth." But she argues that while culture is "open to all other ambitious women," it is closed to "even the most cultured colored woman." Jewett and Addams implicitly criticize the narrowness of domesticity and claim the universality of culture, but Ruffin relies on assumptions about progressive civilization much like theirs to criticize the narrowness of both domesticity and "culture" in a racist society. Black women, she writes, are forced by segregation to exist in a "circumscribed sphere," the use of the word *sphere* suggesting a kind of enforced domesticity. Culture cannot overcome this (enforced) domesticity. Racial segregation "shuts [the black woman] in with her books but shuts her out of physical touch with the great world of art, science and letters." Repeatedly in this passage Ruffin appeals to the general and universal—to the category women and to culture—but then she insists with equal force on the specific or local, on black women's life and on the limitations of culture. She asserts that *Woman's Era* will create "intercourse and sympathy" between "advanced" women of all races but then without grammatical modification, marks out how black women across the nation "especially" need the journal because they have been isolated and limited in their work and lives. In Ruffin's argument, claims to what is shared and universal are not to be relinquished, but claims to specificity are not either.

In the issues that follow this first one, *Woman's Era* continually combined nationalism and localism in order to keep alive the claim to both the generalizable and the specific. There were articles on broad national concerns from colonization to domestic science and from women in business, to contemporary literature; and beginning with the very first edition of *Woman's Era*, there were repeated calls for a "Congress of colored women's leagues and clubs of the country"—in short, calls for nationalization.[20] There were, however, also articles on local concerns dealing with the personal lives and social and political activities of the Woman's Era Club and its members. One of the most important features of this first edition, and one that Ruffin and her staff experimented with and expanded over the years of the journal's publication, is a section devoted to reports by local black women's clubs throughout the nation.[21] These reports focus on the location, history, aims, and organizational structure of individual clubs and are clearly designed both to model and encourage the development of other local clubs and to foster solidarity between the clubs. As the Woman's Era Club's account of itself asserts in the first edition of the journal, the reports provide "interesting reading to sister clubs already formed and in embryo."[22] The journal creates its nationalism through its localisms, its abstractions through its particularities.

On June 1, 1895, little more than a year after the first edition of *Woman's Era* appeared, Ruffin issued the official call for a national conference of black women's clubs, a call that had been carefully prepared for in both the reports of individual clubs and in articles on the topic—prepared for, as Williams's 1900 history suggests, through the very existence of *Woman's Era*. This call again combines nationalism and localism. Arguing that a national meeting has been "a burning desire in the breast of colored women in every section of the United States," Ruffin, as editor of the journal and as president of the Woman's Era Club in Boston, writes that "we, the women of the Woman's Era Club of Boston, send forth a call to our sisters all over the country . . . to meet with us in conference in this city of Boston."[23] She continues: "Boston has been selected as a meeting place because it has seemed to be the general opinion that here, and here only, can be found the atmosphere which would best interpret and represent us, our position, our needs, and our aims. One of the pressing needs of our cause is the education of the public to a just appreciation of us, and only here can we gain the attention upon which so much depends."[24] In this carefully-prepared-for founding moment of the first long-standing national black women's club, Ruffin emphasizes the local site of

Boston. "[H]ere, and here only ... and only here," she repeats, can black women nationalize.

At one level, such localism is clearly linked to what Ruffin sees as the importance of deploying sympathetic representations of the nascent movement. At the end of Ruffin's call to action, she notes that while this conference has long been dreamed of and anticipated by black women everywhere, it was "precipitated" by the attack of "a southern editor ... upon the moral character of all colored women."[25] While his attack makes clear the need for counterrepresentations, for black women to "stand before the world and declare ourselves and our principles," the South is not the place to fight this battle; rather, the North, with Boston as the representative Northern city, must become the battleground because it provides the most fair or just "atmosphere" in which to gain "the attention upon which so much depends."[26]

Still, such an emphasis on the local site seems odd. One assumes that in a call to national action and unity, Ruffin would work to subordinate regionalist rhetoric. And such regionalist rhetoric seems even more out of place in Ruffin's presidential address to the national conference on July 29, 1895, an address in which she insists that above all else there must be "union and earnestness" and the quick settling of "any differences" between black women.[27] In this speech, however, Ruffin explains the importance of meeting in Boston even more fully, framing her explanation in both nationalist and regionalist terms: "This conference will not be what I expect if it does not show the wisdom, indeed the absolute necessity of a national organization of our women. ... This hurried, almost informal convention does not begin to meet our needs, it is only a beginning, made here in dear old Boston, where the scales of justice and generosity hang evenly balanced and where the people 'Dare to be true' to their best instincts and stand ready to lend aid and sympathy to worthy struggles. It is hoped that from this will spring an organization that will in truth bring in a new era to the colored women of America."[28] Here Ruffin explicitly links good publicity to the environment of Boston. And Boston will provide good publicity because of its history, as the phrase "dear old Boston" suggests. Ruffin suggests this city is the local environment that will foster the national aspirations and national organization of black women, just as in the past, Boston's local struggles for democracy and abolition came to have national implications. The local site and its history will enable black women to "band ... together" for protection and to become "an army of organized women," to fight a war for justice. Because of Boston's history, black women will be able "to break ... [their] silence" and thus to gain the "opportunity ... not only to do more but to *be* more."[29] Again, the result, though created by the specific site, will not be local but national: it will "bring a new era to the colored women of America," a new era that nevertheless builds on the possibilities created by the past.[30]

To counter the racist charges made by whites against black women, and to imagine and create unity, then, Ruffin uses a kind of regionalist logic. Such logic insists on the history of the region as a nurturing environment, defines the region as separate from the nation, and then imagines the region as a consolidating point for a larger effort of nationalization. At the same time, this regionalist nationalism is carefully linked to a feminist politics that describes the importance of separatism (described as sectionalism or regionalism) within a larger fight for racial equality. "For many and apparent reasons," says Ruffin, "it is especially fitting that the women of the race take the lead in this movement"; however, she adds, while "[o]ur woman's movement . . . is led and directed by [our] women," it works "for the good of women and men, for the benefit of all humanity *which is more than any one branch or section of it.*"[31] There is a kind of logic of separate spheres here articulated through the notion of different branches or sections of humanity, but while insisting on the sections, Ruffin also imagines their potential cross-sectional unity.

Such a use of a paradoxically regionalist nationalism and a black feminist universalism also informs the talk given by Victoria Earle Matthews on July 30, 1895, the second day of the National Association of Colored Women's first meeting. Like Ruffin's calls to organization, Matthews's talk, "The Value of Race Literature," uses regionalism to delineate the importance of sympathetic representations of the race for unifying them nationally.[32] And like Ruffin, too, Matthews links her regionalist nationalism to her black feminist universalism. Matthews begins her talk with a scathing critique of the canon of American literature. In an impressive early form of image criticism, Matthews works to demonstrate how literary and nonliterary representations of blacks created by respected white authors foster "senseless prejudice."[33] Just as Ruffin describes the damage done by depictions of black women's morality in the mainstream press, so also Matthews argues that such representations provide "indubitable evidence of the need of thoughtful, well-defined and intelligently placed efforts on our part, to serve as counter-irritants against all such writing . . ." (*RL*, 177).[34] However, for historical reasons, Matthews says, such "counter-irritants," which she calls "Race Literature," must remain "*apart* from the general American Literature" (170, emphasis added), figuratively in the nation's regions or margins. Stating that the "distinct[ness]" of black literature arises from the "conditions which govern the people of African descent in the United States" (170), Matthews argues that such conditions create and necessitate a separate race literature: "Our history and individuality as a people, not only provides material for masterly treatment; but would seem to make a Race Literature a necessity as an outlet for the unnaturally suppressed inner lives which our people have been compelled to lead" (173).

Matthews's desire to call into being a separate race literature entails one central goal: to unify the black community. Race literature, she asserts, will enable the achievement of this goal in two interrelated ways: it will consolidate the community both to outsiders who read its literature and, more important, to itself. She argues "that the surest road to real fame is through literature" (177). Race literature will make us better known wherever real lasting culture exists, will undermine and utterly drive out the traditional Negro in dialect" (173). In short, it will subvert one-dimensional, stereotyped depictions of blacks, thereby enabling outsiders to see African Americans within the framework of universal culture and history. More important, however, to Matthews, race literature "will be a revelation to our people" (173) because it will establish a historical narrative of African Americans for themselves: "Race Literature does mean . . . the preserving of all the records of a Race" (183) for "the generation that shall come after us" (185). Race literature will enable the world to recognize the historical specificity of African Americans that render them part of a common humanity, while preservation of that literature will also unite the African American community through its specificity. Separatism paradoxically enables a kind of universalism at two different levels, at the general level of the "lasting culture" of all humanity and at the particular level of African American humanity.

Like Ruffin, Matthews concludes that it is women who are of particular importance in this process. Linking women to cultural production and biological reproduction, she argues that "woman's part in Race Literature, as in Race building, is the most important part and has been so in all ages. . . . All through the most remote epochs she has done her share in literature. When not an active singer like Sappho, she has been the means of producing poets, statesmen, historians, understandingly as Napoleon's mother worked on Homeric tapestry while bearing the future conqueror of the world" (184). Matthews uses regionalism as a kind of trope ("Race Literature" will remain "apart from the general American Literature" [170]) to argue that a historicized separatism—constructed or supported by women—is necessary for establishing a unified and generalizable political community. While she suggests that in the future there may be an American literature that is an "amalgam" (172) of black and white literature, such a future has not yet arrived. For now, the black community, and especially black women, must and will be united nationally by nonnational fictions—fictions that are located in the logic of the region.

Ruffin and Matthews's use of what I have called a regionalist nationalism and a black feminist universalism at the founding moment of the first black women's national organization makes sense not only generally as a response to racist regionalisms deployed by white women and men but also and specifically as a response to white women's national organizations of the time. An appeal to abstract nationalism became a favorite means at the turn of the century by which white women excluded black women from political and social organizations. Because national white women's clubs sought the support of white southern women (or used the need for that support as an excuse), they increasingly restricted black women's participation.[35] In addition, white women used the absence of black national organizations to argue that black women could not be represented in white women's national organizations.[36]

Hopkins herself reported at least three times to the *Colored American Magazine* on these struggles over community and authority that ensued in the white General Federation of Women's Clubs (GFWC) when the NACW applied for membership.[37] Her articles on this subject foreground how nationalist arguments were used to rationalize the GFWC's racism. She records that the president of the GFWC refused to listen to arguments for the inclusion of black women's clubs, stating, "The Civil War is past; the old wounds have been healed; the North and the South have been reunited, and we cannot afford to take any action that will lead to more bitter feeling."[38] Hopkins counters this argument with a regionalist one: "All this is but renewing the old conflict. Thrice before in the history of our country the 'spaniel' North has grovelled before the South, but, thank God, the time came when the old New England spirit of Puritanism arose and shook its mane and flung off the shackles of conservatism. So it will be this time. . . . The claim of the North to govern has been in the past that civilization here is nobler than in the South, and we believe this to be still an axiom."[39] Hopkins argues that New England has the noblest civilization (despite its repeated groveling) and so must govern the South and the nation. At the same time, she ends the essay with an appeal to "the perpetuity of the Union."[40] The national to Hopkins must be created through the regional.

It is no surprise, then, given Hopkins's knowledge of and involvement in the black women's club movement, that *Contending Forces* deploys a regionalist logic, like that we have seen in Ruffin and Matthews, to imagine black women's authority within the nation. While critics have complained about what they see as the loose or disorganized structure of the novel,[41] I argue that its very looseness represents a regionalist logic that responds to the work of other black women intellectuals of the time, particularly those of the NACW. The novel begins with an excursion into the past, showing how national unity was institutionalized in the United States through racial violence and exclusion. When the novel moves into the present, Hopkins's characters resist that national history by acting through a regionalist rather than nationalist narrative, even as they create a new nationalist one. The story is thus not so much driven by plot as by location. As is typical of many regionalist narratives, Hopkins has her characters gather in and-or explore a variety of characteristic sites within Boston. Such investigations of local sites, however, become a means by which Hopkins's characters can analyze, criticize, and revise national institutions and the racist myths that support them. While the novel investigates many different locations within Boston, Hopkins focuses particular attention on the home, the public hall, and the public park, on sites that highlight how sentimental myths about the division of the private and public spheres have enforced nationalist racism. The novel argues for a rethinking of that divide—a rethinking that will enable black women especially—but also black men, to change the meaning of the nation.

The novel begins by historicizing the rise of nationalist racism in the United States. In 1790 when the British government moves to abolish slavery, Charles Montfort, a wealthy slaveowner, decides to leave Bermuda and resettle on a southern plantation in the United States where slavery is still legal and where his fortune will remain secure. Beginning her novel in this period and with the Montfort family's story helps Hopkins investigate and rewrite nationalist myths of origins,[42] describing slavery rather than democracy as crucial to the nation's development. According to Hopkins, Montfort's greed destroys him and his family, for "Nature avenges herself upon us for every law violated in the mad rush for wealth or position or personal comfort where the rights of others of the human family are not respected" (*CF*, 65). The metaphor of the family that Hopkins uses here is important. Nationalism, Anderson points out, is expressed through "the vocabulary of kinship . . . or that of the home" (143). The Montfort family's immigration to America, based as it is on violating the rights of the larger "human family," becomes the occasion for Hopkins to criticize the way the nation constructs itself by distinguishing its white members from other members of the "human family."[43]

More specifically, in Hopkins's America a nation-family that threatens to divide along class lines is united by organized race hatred.[44] Because Mr. Montfort plans to free his slaves once his fortune is secure, the usually antagonistic upper- and lower-class whites join together in the "committee on public safety" (37) to kill him. Public life, Hopkins suggests through her depiction of this "public" committee, is created in the early republic by means of organized, cross-class violence against blacks (and against whites who do not toe the race line). Despite the class antagonism that threatens to divide them, in other words, whites in Hopkins's America are united politically, as a "democracy," by their organized racism. Commenting on the hanging of a man who tried to help a slave woman escape, a lower-class character remarks that the "committee on public safety" "wuz calkerlatin' ter have a celebrashun to which all the *leading citizens o' this county would 'a' been bid*" (37, emphasis added; see also 54–55, 62). Citizenship—inclusion in the nation's family and home, is created by public organization—organizations that work "democratically" across class lines by excluding blacks.

Hopkins's revision of myths about the origins of the nation does not focus solely on the creation of democratic public organizations; rather she gives equal attention to the interaction of public with private life in order to show what the wrongheaded belief in their separation entails. Political and personal desires coalesce in her story. These personal motivations center on the figure of Mrs. Montfort, the idealized genteel lady, head of a gracious—and we soon learn imaginary—private sphere. An odd set of scenes in *Contending Forces* demonstrates the inextricability of political and personal desires. In one scene Mr. Montfort whips the lower-class Hank Davis who has asked him for a job as an overseer. Davis is particularly enraged by this whipping because "[he] had received personal violence of a character that was most galling to the spirit of any free-born Southern man—an ordinary cowhiding, such as he would mete out to his slave" (59). Davis wants revenge but can only act on that desire when the upper-class Anson Pollack authorizes the "committee on public safety" to kill Montfort (60–64); and Pollack only gives such authorization after Mrs. Montfort rebuffs his sexual advances (though she maintains a ladylike silence about Pollack's advances to her husband). While Montfort's liberality with his slaves provides the occasion for Davis and Pollack to unite, Hopkins does not underplay the personal desires that are part of this political attack. Thus, in an overdetermined scene after Montfort has been killed, Davis flogs Mrs. Montfort: "This woman's husband had flogged him—he would have sweet revenge. Those lily-like limbs . . . should *feel the lash as he had*" (68, Hopkins's emphasis). Because Mrs. Montfort is ambiguously black and-or white,[45] this displaced punishment drives home how class hatred is contained by racism. It also suggests, however, that the individual family is the site of the nation-family's conflicts. This image of the prostrated black and-or white woman is one that recurs throughout the novel, and such prostration is enabled (though not caused) by the naive belief that the private sphere is indeed private. Mrs. Montfort's ladylike silence to her husband on the dishonorable behavior of Anson Pollack is a mistake that helps destroy the Montfort family, even if the origin of their problems lies in Mr. Montfort's violation of "the rights of others of the human family" (65). The private sphere, Hopkins makes clear, is not separate from the public sphere, nor should it be imagined so.

The institutionalization of a racist nationalism, based on myths of both the public and private sphere, is the historical "irritant" Hopkins wishes to counter in the rest of her novel. Because the "committee on public safety" had such exclusionary notions of "the human family" (65), and because the individual family is the site on which public conflicts enact themselves, when the novel moves into its present-day regionalist exploration of Boston, the home (as the location of family) becomes the first and most crucial institution and site Hopkins criticizes and revises. The chapter that provides the transition from the eighteenth-century Montforts to their nineteenth-century descendants, the Smiths, is therefore titled "Ma Smith's Lodging-House." This house is depicted as a typical site in Boston's black community: it reveals the force of necessity, that "every avenue for business [is] closed against [blacks]" (86) and so demonstrates how blacks have had to create their own businesses to survive. At the same time, the home enables Hopkins to criticize the nation's continuing sentimental belief in the split between public and private, masculine and feminine.[46] It particularly helps her analyze how this split is used to support a racist nationalism.

Hopkins depicts the home not as a private refuge where the mother creates children but as a thoroughly blended space, a "lodging-house," where public and private spheres, men and women, lower and upper classes are mixed together. In other words, as opposed to sentimental depictions, the home is described explicitly as being involved in the very conflicts that structure the public sphere. The home therefore holds within it both "family" members who accept and "family" members who resist American myths of personal identity, myths that work to divide the "family." Because of this penetration of nationalist myth into the home, Hopkins suggests *not* that the house should more effectively seal or protect its borders but that the house must become self-conscious about itself as a blended space.

John Langley is the tenant who best demonstrates the penetration into the home of divisive American narratives of personal identity. His life story combines details from famous American stories of self-making, particularly those of Benjamin Franklin and Horatio Alger, but underlines the false suppositions that support those myths. Orphaned as a child, the homeless Langley works his way from the South to the North, educates himself, and becomes a successful lawyer and politician. He boards in Ma Smith's house and is engaged in a seemingly respectable fashion to Ma Smith's daughter, Dora Smith. Underneath this quintessentially American story, however, lies another one. Langley is secretly using the lynching of black men for his own political gain and the rape of black women for the attainment of his sexual desires. In his moment of revelation, Langley realizes what his life has been: "He saw himself a half-starved beggar in the city streets, a deserted child claiming kindred with none.... He heard talk of a country to the north which seemed to his childish imagination a fairyland. He determined to go there; so he started on his wearisome journey at an age when the loving mother trembles to have her darling exposed to the perils of the busy streets without a strong hand to guide him through its dangers.... He had prospered. He had accomplished the acquisition of knowledge at the expense of the non-development of every moral faculty" (*CF,* 335).

Langley is not actually self-made, Hopkins makes clear; rather he has picked up a myth of personal identity from the "busy streets" of America, one that depends on the suppression of "every moral faculty." Hopkins adds, "This man was what he was through the faults of others" (336). Nonetheless, this myth represents one of the primary threats to the black community. In fact, the novel's title, embedded in a speech by a black political activist, refers to this threat: "*the contending forces that are dooming this race to despair*" are the "lack of brotherly affiliation . . . [and] the power of the almighty dollar which deadens men's hearts to the sufferings of their brothers, and makes them feel that if only *they* can rise to the top of the ladder may God help the hindmost men" (256, Hopkins's emphasis).[47] Nationalist fictions of identity enforce capitalist individualism, an ideology that divides and thereby conquers the black community.

To counter both the myth and the threat Langley brings from the "busy streets" into the home, Hopkins revises the supposedly autonomous sentimental home in a number of ways. First, she rewrites the sentimental mother. Ma Smith does not simply work to "influence," or determine, her family's moral behavior, as good sentimental mothers do; rather she influences her family and her lodgers, and she influences them in a manner that is described as self-consciously organized and formalized "Ma Smith's great desire, then, was to make . . . [her lodgers] as happy together as possible, and to this end she had Dora institute musical evenings or reception nights that her tenants might have a better opportunity of becoming acquainted with each other. She argued, logically enough, that those who were inclined to stray from right paths would be influenced either in favor of upright conduct or else shamed into an acceptance of the right" (102). Ma Smith's home is a social space that encompasses more than her family, and her influence as a mother thus works with a variety of people. In addition, her influence works through the way she "institute[s]" the socialization of her "tenants." In an assumption that recalls those of settlement workers of the time, there is implicitly the condescending idea that the lower classes can be guided and monitored through their acquaintance with the better classes.[48] As we have seen, however, such monitoring is seen as necessary, given the divisive effects on the black community of the myths of the autonomous private sphere and of the self-made man. Ma Smith's social evenings are a form of communal protection created by her to counter the myths of the larger society.

Besides revising the sentimental mother of the home, Hopkins revises the activities that occur in the sentimental home. Housework is still crucial (sometimes even done by men [*CF,* 171–72]), but this housework is thoroughly politicized. Not only do the women of the "sewing circle" (141), which gathers in Ma Smith's "pretty parlor" (142), work to raise money for their church, but also they spend much of their time discussing "events of interest to the Negro race which had transpired during the week throughout the country" (143). The events, or "facts," are "tabulated upon a blackboard which was placed upon an easel, and occupied a conspicuous position in the room" (143). Hopkins inextricably links the domestic activity of sewing and the public activity of fund-raising and analyzing national news; the prosaic, domestic image of sewing women is combined with the powerful nondomestic image of the Fates, weaving the text of humanity's future. Together, through sewing, tabulating, and discussing, Hopkins suggests, the women can rewrite and redirect the racist and nationalist narratives of the autonomous home and the self-made individual.

If Hopkins's analysis of the private home has led her to revise it as a thoroughly blended space, her analysis of the public hall leads her to a similar revision of it as also blended. As the novel's prehistory has suggested, the political and the familial are intermixed at a number of levels. In the chapters on the response by the "American Colored League" (ACL) to a lynching in the South, Hopkins locates another institution and myth that support nationalism and divide the black community: the national political party and its use of ideology about the private sphere, specifically of family, to enforce unity. She counters this myth of family with a kind of regional politics, one that enables a new analysis of the family's relation to the political party.[49] The public meeting of the ACL is located in the local site of New England: "From the South the cry was: 'Can nothing be done?' 'Where is Massachusetts? Has our old friend turned against us at last?'" (240); and the Boston church at which the ACL's public meeting occurs is described as being decorated in "American flags supplemented by wide bands of mourning. Pictures of the anti-slavery apostles peered out at the audience from the folds of the national colors" (243–44). The "supplementary" "bands of mourning," the New England abolitionists partially enfolded by the "national colors," are nonetheless at the center of the discussion despite their visually and textually marginalized (or regional) position.

In the debate that ensues over the action the ACL should take, the Republican representative, the white Senator Clapp, argues against local agitation by claiming that all concerns must be subordinated to those of the national party. A figure who represents the mixing of politics and sex in a venomous, duplicitous, and debilitating brew (as his title and last name respectively suggest), Senator Clapp makes an alternatively nationalist and universalist political appeal against black agitation. He starts his speech by appealing to familial emotions in his discussion of the party, of white and black, southern and northern "brotherhood" (245). He then "thank[s] God that sectionalism is dead" (246), that the race problem "is national, not sectional" (247), and that "there is an unwritten law, *not peculiar to any section*, which demands the quickest execution . . . of the fiend who robs a virtuous woman of her honor" (248, emphasis added). Clapp's appeal to brotherhood, his call for national party unity, is seconded by Langley, whom Clapp has bribed with an offer of political preferment. Langley tells the gathered crowd that he is "willing to leave the punishment of criminals, the suppression of mob violence, with the national government" (252).

But the community counters these arguments about the importance of brotherhood, of national party unity, with "suppressed murmurs of discontent" (254). This communal discontent is articulated through the personal narrative of an ACL member, Luke Sawyer. Sawyer undermines the legitimacy of the claims for national political unity in two ways. At one level, his story reveals the falseness of the affective appeal to family that the national party is making. Against Clapp's use of the fraternal language of "brotherhood" (245) to enforce nationalism, Hopkins has Sawyer narrate a story that demonstrates how a white *brother* uses his position as a *brother* to rape his black brother's daughter and then to kill that brother when he protests. At a second level, Sawyer's story debunks the appeal the national party makes to the idea of universal good. He tells how he has witnessed the lynching of black male citizens and the rape of black female citizens. Such black citizens are excluded from the universal good.

At the same time that Sawyer provides this critique of the national party system and its use of familial metaphors, Hopkins has two other figures at the meeting underscore his ideas.[50] First, Will Smith, like Sawyer, voices the argument made in the 1890s by an individual crucial to the development of the NACW, Ida Wells, that rape "is the crime which appeals most strongly to the heart of the home life" (*CF,* 271). As with the national party's appeal to brotherhood, Smith argues, whites use family life to disenfranchise black manhood and womanhood. "Lynching [for the supposed crime of rape] was instituted to crush the manhood of the enfranchised black" (270–71), he says. Such an analysis leads Will to a critique of nationalism itself. He derides both the fictional nature of political unity and the black exclusion, even from that fiction by calling America "the social and political structure which you *designate* the *United* States of America" (268, emphasis added). This model of critique, in which national unity is described as a constructed fiction of unity, assumes the ability of those who are actually excluded from it (the members of the ACL, for example) to speak out against its fictionality. The section consolidates itself as a sectional voice to respond to and counter the coercive and violent national voice and fiction of familial unity.

The second figure who supports Sawyer's analysis is Sappho. Sawyer's testimony reveals to the reader that Sappho is actually Mabelle Beaubean, the woman who was raped by her father's white brother. Sappho has never revealed her past to anyone, and so, in a figured repetition of Mrs. Montfort's prostration in the novel's beginning, when Sappho hears her story narrated, she faints and is carried from the room. Langley then guesses her identity and later uses that information in his attempt to seduce her, an attempt that prostrates her yet again (318–19). Sappho's repeated collapse and Langley's use of her prostrations enforce the idea that politics and "home life" (271) are inseparably blended and that the national party is attempting to silence the black political voice through its use of this blending. The fainting, speechless woman and the docile, speechless "section" (in other words, the black community) are equivalent figures—figures who, Hopkins makes clear, could be victimized if they continue to remain silent.

The ending of the novel is precipitated by Sappho's escape from the potential victimization her silence could enable as it did Mrs. Montfort. This escape is located in the last crucial site in the cityscape that Hopkins investigates: the public park. The public park in the United States at this time resonated with the utopian mythology of the New World, of the belief that nature can ameliorate class conflict and foster an ordered and united democracy.⁵¹ At the same time, this public park is the Boston Commons; it can be associated with the origin of American democracy, an origin Hopkins has already called into question in the novel's prehistory. Hopkins makes clear that while utopian mythology about the New World can be expressed through the public park that mythology—as it stands now—depends on violent and willful ahistorical abstraction.

It is in the public park that Hopkins depicts Will Smith and Sappho first beginning to speak of their love for each other (a love that like that of Dora and Sappho becomes significant for imagining national black political community and activism): "The wind whispered amidst the leafless branches of the huge old trees on the Common and Public Garden as they passed them on their way homeward. Once Will took her hand in his; she let it stay a moment" (140). At Easter, the period of rebirth, the Public Garden becomes the site where Will proposes marriage to Sappho. But Will makes a fatal error here. Ignoring Sappho's modest attempt to discuss her past, Will demonstrates that he has accepted the ahistorical myth represented by the public park. He interrupts Sappho midsentence by saying, "I do not care for the past . . . all I ask is that you love me above all other men as I adore you above all other women" (*CF*, 312). Will's refusal to listen to Sappho's story of her past and Sappho's reluctance to push him to listen, a scene carefully set in the public park, reveals the problem of buying into the wishful exclusion of history at the heart of America's imagined community. Hopkins also has John Langley secretly watch this proposal and later threaten Sappho that he will reveal her past to Will if she refuses to become his mistress. The insertion of Langley in this scene set in the Public Garden provides us with an even more sinister reading of succumbing to the wishful exclusion of history in American mythology—the historical violence that precedes, as well as the continued violence that follows, such wishfulness.

Hopkins counters the American myth of the garden with a structurally regional response. That is, the national myth gets rewritten by the individual voicing of the group's experience. Just as Luke Sawyer used his personal narrative to counter the violence being done to the black community by the national party, so Sappho—after her confrontation with Langley—returns at night to the public park to review her history and counter the violence being attempted on her. Her solitary return is an act of repetition: she "walk[s] again through the paths where a few hours before she had known such happiness" (340). But if this walk repeats the past, it is also an act of regional resistance. Refusing to perpetuate the nationalist narrative of prelapsarian innocence, a specific and solitary woman announces her past—a past of rape, of "the curse of slavery" (343)—in the public park. To Hopkins, Sappho's individual announcement of her past in this public space repeats the past in order to create a different future. This announcement makes Sappho into the "active singer"

(*RL*, 184) that Victoria Earle Matthews describes the historic Sappho being in "The Value of Race Literature." This Sappho's refusal to mythologize the past will enable other black women to renounce the nationalist narratives that have created and enforced their oppression. Sappho's disruption of nationalist myths will eventually serve to rally black women together: "[T]he strong, chastening influence of [Sappho's] present sorrow, and the force of character it developed," Hopkins writes in this chapter, "fitt[ed] her perfectly for the place she was to occupy in carrying comfort and hope to the women of her race" (*CF*, 347). The public park no longer resonates with the wishful ahistoricism of New World mythology. While it still represents utopian desires, these desires include an understanding and acknowledgment of a violent history perpetrated on groups of individuals.

Specifically, such utopian desires are represented by a black woman, who by announcing her history not only undermines the nation's myths but also unites black women and prevents another repetition of her (and their) repeatedly figured prostration. For Hopkins, I would argue, Sappho represents the real significance of the national black women's club movement and its regionalist logic: the creation and voicing of a situated expertise.[52] Critics have puzzled over Hopkins's ambivalent portrayal of the figure of the club leader Mrs. Willis in a novel written in dialogue with the development of the NACW. And indeed Mrs. Willis is not the novel's heroine because, like Langley, her work is shaped too much by American myths of personal identity. She is a club woman only because it is through that work that she can gain "the prosperity she desired" (147), and only after she has exhausted her opportunities for speaking to white women (146–47) does she turn her attention to the "advancement of colored women" (147). Mrs. Willis is therefore willing to rely on wishful nationalist ahistoricism, advising Sappho, for example, never to speak of her past to anyone (156). Hopkins acknowledges that Mrs. Willis's "selfishness" results in "glorious fruit in the formation of clubs of colored women banded together" (147), and the narrator even comments that "There are men and women whose seeming uselessness fit[s] perfectly into the warp and woof of Destiny's web. All things work together for good" (157). Nonetheless, for Hopkins, it is Sappho who is the book's heroine because she decides to insist upon her history despite the powerfully silencing and ahistorical myths of nationalism. It is Sappho who transforms nationalist myths with her regional voicing to create a different nation, who as an "active singer" is "fitt[ed] . . . perfectly for the place she was to occupy in carrying comfort and hope to the women of her race" (347).

In the concluding passages of *Contending Forces,* Hopkins imagines uniting the black community by figuring the two opposed camps of contemporary black political thought, as well as northern and southern blacks, becoming members of the same family. The marriages of Sappho and Will Smith, and Dora Smith and Dr. Arthur Lewis signify to Hopkins's reader not only that public and private lives are inseparable but also that the philosophies of the northern-born W.E.B. Du Bois and the southern-born Booker T. Washington can be united. Such a dream of familial unity seems particularly wishful in light of the fact that, three years after *Contending Forces* was published, Washington apparently had Hopkins fired from the staff of the *Colored American Magazine* for not being, said Du Bois, "conciliatory enough."[53] But these marriages are consistent with the novel's didactic and pedagogic insistence on creating a unified, national black community that blends its private and public actions and lives.

Because it is the myths of the United States that make individuals feel "that if only *they* can rise to the top of the ladder may God help the hindmost man" (256), however, the unified, national black community of *Contending Forces* is imagined through regionalism. Hopkins's use of regionalism, her investigation of the local site of Boston, allows for a critique of nationalist myths and their affective claims at the same time that it enables her to envision a new imagined community, a national community figured through regionalism and its affective claims. Hopkins's complex use of regionalism has implications for understanding how African American women, at the moment they sought to establish the parameters of their literary canon,[54] authorized their voices through and against the canons of American literature that excluded them. More broadly, however, Hopkins's regionalism read in relation to the NACW's has implications for understanding how African American women intellectuals authorized their voices at the turn of the century through and against professional discourses that sought to erase them. Regionalism in their writings and speeches is a form by which a notion of situated expertise can be articulated and claimed. Such an expertise calls into question transcendent professional discourse even as it creates its own transcendent professional discourse through its insistence on historical distinctions and differences.

Fannie Barrier Williams's 1900 history of the NACW explicates quite clearly the double-pronged aim—of critique as well as articulation of a different kind of professionalism—of situated expertise. Black women, she writes, were inspired by the national white women's club movement, but she says, "The club movement among [black women] is something deeper than a mere imitation of white women." First of all, black women's national organization was a logical outcome of the "training" they had received in organizing their own churches and secret societies. Furthermore, Williams argues, black women have decided that "progress includes a great deal more than what is generally meant by the terms culture, education and contact." While black women are interested in studying "literature, music, and art"—study Williams implicitly associates with white women's clubs—Williams says that for black women "race problems and sociological questions directly related to the condition of the negro race in America are the principal subjects for study and discussion."[55] In both acknowledging the links between and distinguishing black women's more politicized national club work from white women's "cultured" work, Williams criticizes one kind of authority and expertise while historicizing and claiming another kind. This other kind of expertise "includes a great deal more" than claims to cultivation, though such claims are not excluded. Hopkins's and the NACW's regionalist rhetoric, in short, expressed the manner in which African American women authors and activists could construct their situated expertise to emplot, and hence transform, the nation's history and their work in that nation.

Chapter 3
Naturalist Sentimentalism and Cultural Authority in Frank Norris and George Santayana

In the last two chapters, we have seen how women intellectuals at the turn of the century combined the discourses of domesticity and professionalism in order to create new kinds of work for themselves. White American "new women" like Jewett and Addams mixed Victorian domestic ideology with ideas about educated cultivation to justify their entry into the professions. African American new women like Hopkins and Ruffin deconstructed the notion of transcendent expertise on which domesticity and professionalism depended to create a situated expertise for themselves. Powerful as these discursive changes were, they met with resistance from other professionals, who worked to stabilize both intellectually and institutionally the opposition between domesticity and professionalism.[1] This rearguard action represents these professionals' anxiety about opening up expertise too broadly. At the same time, it also reveals their own self-consciousness about professionalism's conflicting claims. Imagined as democratic, scientific, and disinterested, the professions were nonetheless "interested"—implicated in late nineteenth-century corporate capitalism and its culture of consumption. For many of its proponents, professionalism's market interestedness demonstrated the contradictions at its core, contradictions that overlapped with those of its putative opposite—domesticity. The Victorian domestic woman and the varieties of new women highlighted problems that were, in any case, impossible to evade.

In this chapter, I will use the establishment of modern literary professionalism to explore the ways intellectuals sought to shore up the domesticity-professionalism opposition. In particular, I focus on how a new coordination between professionals and the university could be used to limit claims to expertise by outsiders and to protect a contradictory notion of expertise itself. In literary professionalism, this coordination is evidenced in the gatekeeping manifestoes by university-trained writers and critics who institutionalized exclusive ideologies about expertise. Literary professionalization in the U.S. at the turn of the century, as I shall show, involved chest-thumping public assertions about the literary professional's trained, gender-, and race-specific ability to observe dispassionately the workings of nature and society and therefore to change America and the world. At the same time, however, this confident rhetoric is often inextricable from a rhetoric of failure. Such mixed rhetoric attests to the difficulties professionals faced in living up to their promise to transcend and transform an "incorporated" America. The tension between confident assertion and obvious failure in literary professionals' writings manifests itself crucially through their critique of another failed discourse of transcendence and transformation—Victorian domesticity—and what these experts associate with it—sentimentalism and women. At the same time, the tension is also evident in the thematics of fatality that appear in these writers' work—of the suffering, dead, or suicidal man-artist, driven to his death by the forces that women literally and figuratively embody.

This thematics and aesthetics has proven remarkably resilient in American cultural and social criticism. In this form of criticism, women, domesticity, and sentimentalism are conflated. They represent interchangeably the velvet glove of ideology and moralism that hides the iron fist of capitalist exploitation and liberal bad faith.[2] Lost in the ideal unreality of the home and family, so this symbolic logic goes, women are conservators and defenders of the status quo, while men, experiencing the reality of the world, are forced at least to acknowledge the brutal truths of structural inequality and conflict. This tradition of social and cultural criticism, a tradition that shaped and still shapes the study of American literature, is rooted not only in a struggle over the gendering of cultural authority but also in an attempt to protect a professionalism riven by its own contradictions. The variety of appeals this tragic narrative has for American intellectuals, and its labile gendering, make it well worth historicizing.

I will argue in this chapter that this tragic narrative is closely linked to the development of realism, but more particularly naturalism. Critics have shown how realism and naturalism were crucial in the late nineteenth and early twentieth centuries to the development of a definition of literary professionalism and to its coding as white and male.[3] My last two chapters have demonstrated how such arguments need to be complicated. Many social groups used and challenged such exclusive claims to professionalism at the turn of the century. Nonetheless, this chapter shows how the gendered and racially exclusive claims to literary expertise of a canonical kind of naturalism became crucial to the story we tell about literary professionalism more generally. I am interested in the striking contradictions of this form of naturalism and what they might tell us about the construction and institutionalization of cultural expertise at the turn of the century. Naturalism authorizes itself, on the one hand, through an inextricably linked attack on "feminine" sentimentality and an appeal to science, *and*, on the other hand and paradoxically, through its own deeply felt "feminine" sentimentality about itself. We have tended to ignore this latter characteristic of naturalism, to overlook the ways in which a form that constructs itself as masculine works simultaneously (by its own logic of gender) to feminize itself. But in the relation the naturalist text posits between the American author and his public—often depicted as that between the trained male producer and the cultivated but dilettanteish and amateur female consumer—this sentimentality is clearly evidenced. This woman represents the irresistible force of the market, a market whose ubiquity demonstrates both the vulnerability of the transcendent professional and the need to protect his authority. The effectiveness of this contradictory and tragic narrative form, what I call naturalist sentimentalism, can be gauged by our continued repetition of versions of it today. Its contradictions, ironically enough, seem to enable its continued deployment.

To demonstrate how this contradictory defeminization and refeminization work and how working together they stabilize the domesticity-professionalism opposition, I examine the literary criticism of H. H. Boyesen and Frank Norris as well as Norris's novel *The Octopus* (1901). These two writers exemplify the new coordination between literature and the university at the turn of the century.[4] Critical of capitalism and its mystifying ideologies, aware that their professionalism does not remove them from what they criticize, these academically trained and/or university-affiliated intellectuals articulate their expertise by scapegoating women and by sentimentalizing the plight of the professional. They shore up the binary of domesticity-professionalism, in short, through a domestic logic they disavow. The important effect their naturalist sentimentalism had on American literary professionalism can be demonstrated by exploring George Santayana's influential adaptation of it in "The Genteel Tradition in American Philosophy" (1911).[5] More clearly than Boyesen's or Norris's earlier naturalist sentimentalist writings, Santayana insists on the binary of domesticity-professionalism, elaborating it also as one between femininity and masculinity, sentiment and science, subjectivity and objectivity—even as he simultaneously acknowledges that these oppositions are untenable. The messy, tragic impasse that results becomes the means by which Santayana can prove his own dispassionate, professional objectivity. Santayana's objectivity is a kind, I argue, still embraced by a variety of modernist literary professionals who seek to stabilize their authority through their critiques of capitalism and its "feminizing" effect, a feminization that they imagine—sentimentally enough—can be escaped only by those who stand outside and observe. It is the ideological and institutional stabilization of the domesticity-professional binary evident in Boyesen, Norris, and Santayana[6] that shaped both modernism and the traditional stories we tell about it. It is time to rethink those stories and the contradictions that inhere in them.

Norris's famous manifesto for what he alternately calls romantic or naturalistic writing,[7] "A Plea for Romantic Fiction" (1901), begins with a dramatic expulsion of a feminized sentimentalism from the topic of analysis: "Let us at the start make a distinction. Observe that one speaks of Romanticism and not of sentimentalism. One claims that the latter is as distinct from the former as is that other form of art which is called Realism. Romance has been often put upon and overburdened by being forced to bear the onus of abuse that by right should fall to sentiment; but the two should be kept very distinct, for a very high and illustrious place will be claimed for Romance, while sentiment will be handed down the scullery stairs" (*LC*, 75).

In this essay, written after Norris had "established his image as a *very* serious writer" and was "in demand as an expert,"[8] as one biographer puts it, Norris categorizes and ranks, in the best scientific fashion, different literary genres. While realism, Norris makes clear, "is very excellent as far as it goes" (*LC*, 76) and can be combined with romance-naturalism to create great art, sentimentalism—in one of the numerous and inconsistent personifications of form in the essay—is the scullery maid who must be hustled down the back stairs. Sentimentalism has crossed both gender and class boundaries. She has been seen upstairs and thereby has been linked to romance-naturalism. Such a linking has allowed her to escape the abuse that she deserves and that "King Romance" has instead received.[9] In this image of Christlike sacrifice, the elite masculine form of naturalism-romance has suffered for the sins of a lower-class feminine form.

Analyses of Norris's writing and of naturalism more generally have followed Norris's advice on handing sentimentalism "down the scullery stairs." Norris's essay suggests that there is a relation between sentimentalism and naturalism, albeit a scandalous upstairs-downstairs one that must be hidden; however, U.S. criticism has tended to ignore that relation. In traditional versions of U.S. literary history, for example, critics narrate a story in which only two serious forms compete at the turn of the century—realism and naturalism. As the story goes, realism's optimistic view of man's ability to act and think freely evolved in the late nineteenth century into naturalism's pessimistic view that man is predetermined to act in certain ways.[10] While realism's optimism and naturalism's pessimism have been problematized in recent criticism, the pairing of the two and their status as serious forms have remained constant. A discussion of either form has entailed and continues to entail a discussion of the other. Meanwhile, the scullery maid of sentimentalism tends to appear only as a figure of those unfortunate lapses in judgment that even the most serious authors (and forms) are prone to.[11]

There are many good reasons that realism and naturalism have been paired in American literary studies, not least of which is, as the case of Norris suggests, that realist and naturalist authors defined their work in relation to each other. Nonetheless, one must ask why it became important for American naturalists to position themselves in relation to realism? Why were the two categories of realism and naturalism continuously explored in their works, while sentimentalism disappeared from the field of analysis? And relatedly, why have we followed in these writers' footsteps? Besides the tendency of literary histories to narrate a seamless progression from one movement to the next, there is a politics of classification at work here that is worth exploring.

Mark Seltzer's analysis of the links between scientific theories of sexual difference and the development of the naturalist novel helps us begin to investigate this politics of classification. The naturalist novel, he argues, "registers . . . a displaced competition between rival sexual forces, between what Norris, for instance, calls the 'two world-forces, the elemental Male and Female'."[12] Seltzer demonstrates how naturalism constructed itself through "scientific," abstract accounts of force and generation as "an emphatically 'male' genre" (*BAM*, 29). Particularly, it poses the machine against the mother, in order to "displace . . . the colossal mother" and to "place . . . power back into the hands of the immortal and autonomous male technology of generation" (31). Seltzer explains how this displacement works paradoxically to reinforce the difference between the mother and the machine and to "extend the lines of communication between them" (40). While Seltzer ends by exploring the question of naturalism's relation to realism, his work provides us with an important clue as to why sentimentalism disappeared from analyses of naturalism. If, as Seltzer argues convincingly, the biological mother is displaced in naturalism through "scientific" accounts of abstract force, then the thematics and aesthetics indissociably linked with her by nineteenth-century sentimentalism must also have been displaced.

This chapter builds on Seltzer's conclusions about the relation of gendered scientific discourses to the naturalist novel and how its "regulative biopolitics" explain and justify "gender inequalities" (41), but I want to extend Seltzer's analysis of the displacement of the "colossal mother" in naturalism to explain how this is worked out specifically as part of literary professionalization and the attempt to stabilize it as white and male. Between 1890 and 1915, as Gerald Graff has demonstrated, literary study in the U.S.—which before that time had been indissociably associated with women's colleges—sought to efface its "reputation for effeminacy" in order to establish itself as a serious discipline within the newly scientized professional university.[13] This effacement meant that for naturalism to construct itself as a serious genre, worthy of scrutiny, it had to work at distancing itself from any association with femininity, a category that encompassed the form perceived as feminine—sentimentalism. Many naturalists worked assiduously to make a distinction between (masculine) expertise and (feminine) amateurism. By pairing realism and naturalism, writers at the turn of the century could bypass the possibility that the "amateur" sentimentalism of the "feminine fifties" had had an effect on these forms, which they worked to define as worthy of serious, academic study.

At the same time that this process of gendering expertise was at work, however, realists and naturalists were negotiating the contradictions of professionalism itself. The notion of literary expertise presented peculiar challenges. Critics and authors were working to make the writer fit in with their scientized and democratic conception of reality as involving heredity and environment, nature as well as culture. They therefore argued against the notion of the writer as a uniquely talented and inspired genius. Rather, they insisted that literary expertise—whether that of the author or the critic—depended on inherited proclivities, but even more crucially on training. In short, it could be rationally explained and created. But the issue of training complicated democratization in two central ways. First, if the trained expert knew best, then why did the public get to decide what they would or would not read? Why did the untrained public have a say in authorship?[14] Second, if the professional stood out because of his training, how was this democratization? In line with their dissociation of their work from women and the feminized form of sentimentalism, many important naturalist intellectuals deflected attention away from these paradoxes of expertise by scapegoating women and sentimentalism. Describing feminized sentimentalism as representing both a compromised accession to the amateur taste of the rabble and an elitist resistance to democratization, these naturalists could evade *and* explore their own bad faith. The influential critical writings of Boyesen and Norris demonstrate how the contradictions of literary professionalism—as evidenced in conflicting attitudes about expertise and democracy—work together to construct naturalist sentimentalism.

Boyesen's essay "The American Novelist and His Public" (1886, 1894) provides an early example of the naturalists' democratized conception of the author as a trained professional, the logical problems that ensue from it, and how women and femininity serve to resolve those problems in the essay. A professor at Columbia as well as a novelist, Boyesen argues against the notion of literary genius in this much-cited essay: "It is said that poets are born, not made. The same assertion might be hazarded, with equal truth, of lawyers, engineers, doctors, and clergymen; in fact of any man eminent in his profession . . . Marked inherited ability in a definite direction is . . . no sure guarantee of greatness. Circumstances must do the rest. The man is the resultant of his environment and his heredity. . . . [The idea] that a young man could be trained to be a novelist, as he might for the legal or medical profession, is, therefore, not so absurd as it has been represented to be."[15]

This argument has contrary impulses. On the one hand, Boyesen asserts that, given the right opportunity, any "young man" can become a successful author. Using arguments that were crucial in the development of realism and naturalism, he says that inherited ability is important, but equally crucial are the circumstances in which the potential author finds himself, most crucially the training he is able to receive. The relation of heredity and environment in the formation of the artist can be understood rationally so that anyone could potentially become one. On the other hand, however, while Boyesen democratizes art, imagining a potential artist in all individuals, he also immediately sets limits on his own democratic impulse. The trained artist is likened to "any man eminent in his profession" (*AN*, 41). The idea of the artist as genius, set apart like an aristocrat by "marked" or "inherited" characteristics, is dismantled; however, a new aristocracy of meritorious hard work and "eminence" is put in its place.

This conflicted attitude toward democracy, evident in Boyesen's depiction of the professional artist, also informs Boyesen's depiction of the artist's relation to the market. The artist must sell his wares to "the public," who "makes its authors in its own image and likeness." The "successful" artist must therefore satisfy the "average taste" (43). As is consistent with his democratic notion of the artist, Boyesen at first argues that this is not a problem, is in itself "no serious matter" (44). His sanguinity breaks down, however, when he describes who in fact constitutes the main audience for the American artist, as opposed to his European counterpart. He writes that the "American public, as far as the novelist is concerned, is the female half of it" and more particularly those young girls "with an abundance of time at their disposal, and a general disposition to employ it in anything that is amusing" (44). While European writers have not been harmed by writing for the "average" (masculine) taste, writing for young girls is "permanently injurious" to the American novelist. Boyesen argues that "To be obliged to repress that which is best in him, and offer that which is of slight consequence, is the plight to which many a novelist, in this paradise of women, is reduced. Nothing less is demanded of him by that inexorable force called public taste, as embodied in the editors of the paying magazines, behind whom sits, arrayed in stern and bewildering loveliness, his final judge, the young American girl. She is the Iron Madonna who strangles in her fond embrace the American novelist; the Moloch upon whose altar he sacrifices willingly or unwillingly, his chance of greatness" (49).

This is a familiar argument from the late eighteenth century onward in both Britain and America, that young leisured women, living off the wealth their fathers produce, are the primary audience for the novel—an argument that Lora Romero points out has never been verified in any convincing fashion and yet is continuously insisted upon in the history of the novel.[16] Truth claims aside, however, what is striking in this passage is how an at first unstable object of blame finally stabilizes itself in the figure of the young girl. Blame moves from the "inexorable force" of "public taste" to "the editors of the paying magazines" before it settles finally and permanently on the "young American girl," or the "Iron Madonna."[17] The focus on the young girl enables Boyesen to express and displace what otherwise might be seen as a very direct critique of the American "public," of the ways in which, in consumer capitalism, the "average taste" decides who is an author, not the meritorious trained expert.

The young girl also serves to highlight the extraordinary vulnerability of the American novelist in Boyesen's analysis. "Willingly or unwillingly," the author's hard work, his training, is sacrificed to the unworthy, leisured, and all-powerful "Moloch" of a young girl. The professional author is portrayed as the virtuous victim of a bewildering and forceful seduction. As a result of this seduction, the author is unable to write about the "vital things of life," about "politics" and "large questions and problems" (46). His work should describe the "strong forces which are visibly and invisibly at work in our society, fashioning our destinies as a nation" (46). It should be "bound by the laws of reality" (50) and "penetrate . . . into the heart of reality" (51). Instead, he writes "ingenious and entertaining yarns" (50), discusses "dress with elaborate minuteness, and enters, with a truly feminine enthusiasm, into the mysteries of the toilet" (45). The Iron Madonna forces the professional novelist not only to write domestic rather than realist or naturalist narratives but also to become himself feminized, an Iron Madonna. In other words, while Boyesen's conception of the author as a professional is a realist and naturalist one, dependent on the notion that heredity and environment form people, and while he opposes realism and naturalism to domestic sentimentalism, his polemic paradoxically depends on feminizing the virtuous genres of realism and naturalism and telling a quite sentimental story about the threats they face from young girls, threats that the professional writer who deploys them also faces.

In Norris's critical writings of the 1890s, we can see the same contradictions as in Boyesen, the same displacement of these contradictions onto the young American girl, and the same resolution in the narrative form of naturalist sentimentalism. In Norris's criticism, written in the years after he had studied literature at both the University of California and Harvard, there is a different focus than in Boyesen's. While Boyesen's democratically trained literary professional is threatened by the market (in other words, by untrained female readers), Norris's democratically trained literary professional is threatened by training itself, which on the one hand opens up expertise to too many people and on the other hand isolates the expert from the real, lived world of his audience. Throughout his critical writings, Norris defines literary authorship as professional work and hence as not only democratic (*LC*, 11–15, 71–72, 94–97) but also scientific, disinterested, and outside market determination (10, 47, 90–92). But while Norris consistently insists that being a poet is "a question of training" (15; see also 9, 11, 13, 52) and the notion that "poets are 'born not made' . . . is sheer nonsense" (14), the fractures between a claim to trained, authoritative expertise and democratization become clear, as with Boyesen, in discussions of women. The notion of training democratizes too much and too little for Norris, even as it remains central to his conception of authorship.

In an essay that reveals these problems clearly, "Why Women Should Write the Best Novels: And Why They Don't" (1901), for example, Norris argues that while women have the "leisure . . . education . . . [and] temperament" to become writers, "It is, of course, a conceded fact that . . . the producers of the *best* fiction are men and not women" (35, emphasis added). Such a "fact" is explained at first as being social in its roots. Norris argues that because "the majority of women still lead, in comparison with men, secluded lives" (36), their writing is shaped by "literature" and not "life" (35), hence their writing fails. Norris's "'life'—'literature' antithesis," as Donald Pizer calls it, was one he inherited from his writing teacher at Harvard, Lewis Gates (*LC,* xvii) and is crucial to Norris's criticism and novels, and to naturalists and realists' formulation of their writing more generally. It is also always inextricable, as Pizer further points out, from a "masculine-feminine rhetoric" (23). Pizer argues convincingly that Norris relied on this gendered life-literature antithesis "to insure the masculinity of the artist" in an era when the artist was popularly associated with "effeminacy and even homosexuality" (23–24). But while anxiety about sexuality is a crucial part of Norris's life-literature antithesis, it is more specifically an anxiety about the virility of professional expertise.

At first, Norris's argument about women writers' failure to produce good novels appears consistent with his democratic and progressive notion of training. Women's failure simply represents the effect of social conditions they do not control. Leading "secluded lives" in the private sphere, women are only allowed to have the vicarious experience of literature, not of life. In addition, their heredity works against their producing great literature. Besides their lack of "experience," Norris writes, women have "more specialized" (*LC,* 36) brains than men. They therefore "try to do too much, to polish too highly, to develop more perfectly" and are finally reduced to "hysteria" (36). And, Norris asks, "who shall say how many good, even great, novels have remained half written, to be burned in the end, because their women authors mistook lack of physical strength for lack of genuine ability?" (36).

This curious conclusion, which imagines women novelists burning their too polished, too perfect drafts, seems to satisfy Norris. Nonetheless, it raises the question of how any woman could have "genuine ability" given both her environment and her heredity, her secluded life and her specialized brain. The answer can be found in Norris's original claim that authorial ability is simply a question of training and that such training should include academic work. He writes: "From almost the very first the young man studies with an eye to business, or to a profession. In many State colleges now-a-days all literary courses, except the most elementary . . . are optional. But what girls' seminary does not prescribe the study of literature through all its three or four years, making of this study a matter of all importance? And while the courses of literature do not, by any manner of means, make a novelist, they familiarize the student with style and the means by which words are put together. The more one reads, the easier one writes" (34)[18]. While men are trained in college for business, women are trained to read and understand literature. As a result, some have "genuine" literary ability, an ability that exceeds the business training of men.

In fact, it is women college students and the academic writing they produce that enable Norris to explore his larger anxieties about expertise itself, and so, characteristically, it is these women for whom he reserves his greatest spleen.

Arguing against the literary training he himself received at Berkeley, he writes: "The 'co-eds' take to the 'classification' method even better than the young men. They thrive and fatten intellectually on the regime. They consider themselves literary. They write articles on the 'Philosophy of Dante' for the college weekly, and after graduation they 'read papers' to literary 'circles' composed of post-graduate 'co-eds,' the professors' wives and daughters and a very few pale young men in spectacles and black cutaway coats. After the reading of the 'paper' follows the 'discussion,' aided and abetted by cake and lemonade. This is literature! Isn't it admirable!" (7). This description registers a competitive anxiety about these greedy consumers and excessive producers of literature and lemonade who are attempting to assume the mantle of professionalism. But it is also self-reflective and reveals Norris's own hesitation about the contradictions of the professionalism he elsewhere claims. Most clearly, it critically highlights the problems of professionalism's claim to democracy. For if one argues that the problem with literature produced and eagerly consumed by women and effeminate men is that it is the result of elite training (and so based on literature and not life), and at the same time that what characterizes the professional male author is his training, one demonstrates the male author's feminized removal from life, and the way his derivative texts can be eagerly consumed by a femininized rabble. Women's removal from life resonates, as it does in Boyesen, with problems in the conception of professional authorship. To shore up the (masculine) expertise under threat of feminization from its own logical contradictions, Norris explicitly attacks the privileges and protections of domestic "femininity" but then promptly assumes them for the professional, male writer.

Thus, for example, in his famous manifesto for what he called romantic or naturalistic writing, "A Plea for Romantic Fiction," cited earlier, Norris both insists sentimentalism is a degraded form and appropriates it. Adopting the persona of the scientist who objectively classifies and categorizes disparate phenomena, Norris nonetheless tells a sentimental story about masculine romance-naturalism. Lower-class, feminized sentimentalism must be expunged from the field of serious literature, even as Norris appropriates its narrative reliance on Christlike sacrifice for naturalism. Masculine naturalism is "forced to bear" critical abuse for the sins of sentimentality.

Eve Sedgwick has argued in her suggestive rereading of sentimentalism that this "feminine" form may really be at the core of the self-pitying struggles over "masculine identity" from the 1880s to World War I, where "the exemplary instance of the sentimental ceases to be a woman per se, but instead becomes the body of a man who . . . physically dramatizes, *embodies* for an audience that both desires and cathartically identifies with him, a struggle of masculine identity with emotions or physical stigmata stereotyped as feminine." Specifically, she argues, male sentimentalism is worked out "in the explicit context of the displayed body of Jesus."[19] Such an analysis helps us understand both Boyesen's and Norris's figurative description of realism and naturalism as wrongfully bearing the sins for feminine sentimentalism. Building on Sedgwick, we could argue that the case of Boyesen and Norris further suggests that sentimentalism is at the core of struggles over the identity of literary professionalism in the U.S. at this time, struggles that entailed shoring up a white, masculine professional identity that was threatened not only by women and ethnic or racial others but also by its own contradictions. Norris's most famous novel, *The Octopus* (1901), dramatizes these struggles over professional identity and the attempt to shore it up, both in its explicit critiques of sentimentalism and in its seemingly unconscious use and appropriation of sentimentalism.

The Octopus poses itself as both a tough-minded, scientific account of the workings of corporate capitalism and a protest against the effete literary traditions that have supported that economic system. Based on the Mussel Slough incident of 1880 in which California ranchers were killed when they protested the monopolistic practices of the Southern Pacific Railroad, *The Octopus* has been linked to the muckraking journalism of the Progressive period. Norris focuses with special care in his reformist novel on how sentimental, domestic ideology enables and enforces the brutal functioning of corporate capitalism. This is worked out particularly through a battle between the forms of naturalism and sentimentalism in the novel. The novel attacks sentimentalism and its notion of separate spheres through its own notion of a universe governed by abstract and impersonal force. Like other realist and naturalist writers, Norris insists that the objective reality of "force"—alternatively nature and the market—is all there is. At the beginning of the novel, the railroad, driving its way violently into a pastoral idyll of a shepherd and his flock, embodies a larger narrative refusal to imagine transcendent spaces outside of the workings of force, as sentimental texts do. The moment such transcendent notions are invoked in the text, Norris negates them with "factual" accounts of the power and ubiquity of naturalist force. But these negations paradoxically lead structurally to a recurrence to similar kinds of sentimental, transcendent appeals. In his ambivalent portrayal of the novel's literary professional, the poet Presley, Norris acknowledges the impasse in his own professional discourse. His solution is to remove the central characters who survive the workings of force from the domestic world altogether and place them in the world of male imperialist adventure.

The novel's critique through negation of sentimentalism appears most dramatically in its attack on the personal power of the sentimental mother.[20] The novel shows that personal power signifies little in the face of naturalist reality. The best example of this can be seen in Norris's depiction of Hilma Tree, the novel's sentimental girl and then mother par excellence. In the tradition of sentimentalism, when Hilma Tree marries Annixter, she creates him morally. Annixter describes her effect on him to the poet Presley: "she's made a man of me . . . [A]s soon as I woke up to the fact that I really loved her, why, it was glory hallelujah all in a minute, and, in a way, I kind of loved everybody then."[21] When Hilma becomes pregnant, her sentimental influence expands to include the ranching community generally. At a picnic, sitting on a rise above everyone, "as on a throne, raised above the rest, the radiance of the unseen crown of motherhood glowing from her forehead," her impending motherhood leads the rough ranchers around her to bare their heads in honor of her and to refrain from using foul language (*TO*, 504). Annixter, "living in this influence of a wife, who was also a mother," is described as "trembling on the verge of a mighty transformation" (497). To negate this version of the mother's "sentimental power," immediately following this picnic, Norris has the abstract force of Nature (embodied by the railroad) kill Annixter and the ranchers whom Hilma has influenced, while Hilma herself miscarries her child.[22]

This direct attack on sentimental accounts of the (mother's) personal power is echoed most dramatically by the novel's infamous ending. After most of the main characters have been killed, Presley reflects on the greater good that is done despite "the welter of blood": "But the WHEAT remained. Untouched, unassailable, undefiled, that mighty world-force . . . moved onward in its appointed grooves . . . Falseness dies; injustice and oppression in the end of everything fade and vanish away. Greed, cruelty, selfishness, and inhumanity are short-lived; the individual suffers, but the race goes on. Annixter dies, but in a far distant corner of the world a thousand lives are saved" (651–52). Force wins out not only over "the Mother" (496), but also over the personalized narrative form of sentimentalism.

But this ending, which has received so much criticism, need not be read only as the triumph of impersonal naturalist force over personal sentimental power. In these last two paragraphs of the novel, thousands of lives "are saved," while "Annixter dies." Why this invocation of one specific individual, namely Annixter, at the moment when abstract impersonal force triumphs? Annixter is being figured here in the same manner as naturalism was in Boyesen and Norris's criticism—as Christlike—though Annixter is specifically sacrificed in order to save the people Cedarquist describes as the "hungry Hindoo" (648). While the "white man's burden" is a crucial part of the ending of *The Octopus*, and one I will return to in a moment, I want to focus on why Presley—the novel's literary professional—juxtaposes Annixter's individual death to the larger abstract force of nature.

Before as well as after Annixter's marriage to Hilma, Presley and Annixter have a special relationship. They are "the best of friends" and "never met without a mutual pleasure, taking a genuine interest in each other's affairs, and often putting themselves to great inconvenience to be of trifling service to help one another" (27). In addition, both men are described in relation to each other as being college educated: Presley "had graduated and post-graduated with high honours from an Eastern college, where he had devoted himself to a passionate study of literature" (9), while Annixter, "like [Presley,] . . . was a college graduate" (24). Annixter's and Presley's college education marks them in the novel, as it does Vanamee (the third main character whom Norris develops), as men "of wide reading and great intelligence" (35). Despite Norris's continual attacks on academic study as opposed to life, he nonetheless imagines a college education as crucial in creating "intelligence" and in shaping men's most profound intellectual and emotional ties.

Annixter's death enforces and renders more poignant these college men's close relation. When Annixter dies on the verge of his "mighty transformation" (497), the novel posits that it is Presley's, not Hilma's, duty to memorialize Annixter and his development. Norris makes this point by first depicting Presley as switching places with Annixter: "When [Hilma] spoke, it was with the old-time velvety huskiness of voice that *Annixter* had learned to love so well" (628, emphasis added), then by describing Presley as being "made" into a man by Hilma, just as Annixter was. What is noticeable about this "making," however, is that Hilma is simply the catalyst for it: "Then suddenly all the tired heart of him went out towards her. A longing to give the best that was in him to *the memory of her* . . . leaped all at once within him, leaped and stood firm, hardening to a resolve stronger than any he had ever known" (629–30, emphasis added). Presley is "hardening" into manhood, but it is through a "memory" (629), a memory of the "old-time" (628), obsolete sentimental mother. So, despite the erotics of the scene, Norris does not suggest that Presley will marry Hilma. Instead, Presley says to her, "I am going away and it is quite possible I shall never see you again"(631).

Just as Presley becomes Annixter (though Annixter for whom Hilma is a "memory"), so also the dead Annixter is transformed into Hilma—into the sentimental man (mother). Presley sees Hilma as "strengthened and infinitely ennobled by his [Annixter's] death" (629) and advises her that her sorrow for Annixter 'will only be a great help to you. It will make you more noble, a truer woman, more generous" (630). In other words, Annixter's influence now "makes" Hilma, and by implication it will "make" Presley, and the "hungry Hindoo" (648). Like any number of sentimental heroines, Annixter's influence works from beyond the grave. Hilma, of course, says she does "not understand" (631) Presley's vision of Annixter's sentimental power. But she does understand why he is memorializing Annixter thus: "I do not know why you should want to be so kind [to me], unless—yes, of course—you were my husband's dearest friend" (631). It is Presley's job to memorialize Annixter, not Hilma's, for Presley was Annixter's "dearest friend," not his mother-wife.

So, in this scene of memorializing, Presley assumes Annixter's place, and Annixter assumes Hilma's place. Presley becomes a man, and Annixter becomes a kind of sentimental man-mother, the memory of him influencing others for good from beyond the grave. Presley and Annixter become more closely tied to each other through bonds of love, while Hilma disappears except as a marker for a certain kind of obsolete rhetoric that is relied on but improved. Sentimentalism is thus negated and then refigured, refigured not in the man's bond to the wife or "the Mother," but in his bond to another college-educated man.

With this in mind, the ending of the novel seems less incoherent. The last lines of the novel assert that the specific case does not matter; only abstract force and the whole matters. But, in fact, the novel knows how to make this point only through the specific, personal, and sentimental. For example, if Vanamee can preach the greater good of force by the end of the novel, it is only because his dead lover is replaced by a personal, reborn one who murmurs to him "I love you, I love you" (639). Similarly, Presley's understanding of the greater good, which Vanamee has explained to him, comes when he can memorialize Annixter in terms of the sacrifice necessary to save the "hungry Hindoo," himself, even Hilma.[23] The personal and the sentimental have not been deleted from the text; rather the representation itself is changing from depicting suffering woman to depicting suffering man. More important, control over sentimental representation has moved from a woman and mother (the unprofessional) to a man and poet (the professional). The struggle of naturalist writers against sentimentalism is being worked out here through the opposition between the figures of the mother and the trained, professional poet.

This leads us into *The Octopus*'s second main critique of sentimentalism—namely, its unprofessional aesthetics. In Norris's view, just as sentimentalism imagines a sphere outside of the market, so does it also imagine itself as working in an aesthetic and moral realm outside of capitalism. But, Norris argues, sentimental aesthetics are actually deeply implicated in creating and reproducing the exploitative relations of capitalist production. This attack on sentimental aesthetics is articulated most clearly in Norris's satirical account of the leisured and cultivated society ladies in San Francisco. Similar to Boyesen, Norris depicts these women as disrupting the real work of politics. These ladies are first described as "a file of hens" (309) invading the sanctuary of a male club on "Ladies' Day." This invasion of hens into a "masculine haunt" (309) interrupts the conversation the men are having about strategies to outmaneuver the railroad (305–307). Specifically, the ladies disrupt the men's political conversation in order to view a painting of "a girl in a pink dress and white sunbonnet" standing against the Contra Costa foothills and to engage in the pretense of professional examination that reveals their actual amateurism: "The ladies and young girls examined the production with little murmurs of admiration, hazarding remembered phrases . . . expressing their opinions in the mild technicalities of the Art Books and painting classes" (311).

Because these women disrupt the work of real life with their educated *and* dilettanteish aestheticism, the book depicts them as enabling the railroad's oppresssion of the people. They embody the city itself, "a Midway Plaisance," in

Cedarquist's description, where art lulls the public into "indifference," allowing the railroad to crush its opposition (303). But equally bad, in Norris's account, is these women's conviction that they have the education to define what is good art. Through his displacement of the sentimental girl-mother, Hilma, as well as through the men's discussion of the railroad, Norris shows that "a girl in a pink dress and a white sunbonnet" (311) has nothing to do with the real story of California. Nor does she have anything to do with the stylistics of "naked" (60) naturalist force. It is not simply that art distracts the public from the struggle with the railroad but that bad art of the kind admired by educated women distracts the public from that struggle.

In the novel's most outraged scene, in fact, Norris depicts these educated, society ladies' desire for what is "tasteful" as coterminous with the murderous force of the railroad. The ladies become the insatiable market desires that drive the railroad. Presley is invited to an elaborate dinner put on by society ladies where tasteful art and tasty delicacies are the only topics of discussion. He finds himself comparing the ladies at this dinner to the recently dead "Harran, Annixter, Osterman, Broderson, Hooven" (608), imagining that "all these fine ladies with their small fingers and slender necks suddenly were transfigured into harpies tearing human flesh" (608). Norris upholds Presley's vision of these ladies by juxtaposing them and their chatter about taste to Mrs. Hooven's death by starvation on the streets of San Francisco (592–603). The juxtaposition suggests that the insatiable desires of dainty women for what they think are tasteful and tasty objects fuels and disguises the market forces that crush the masses.

Despite this critique of sentimentalism, however, the novel itself concludes that social reality *is* divorced from aesthetics. At the end of the novel, when Presley meets Shelgrim, the railroad's titan, he finds not "a brute, a terrible man of blood and iron [but] instead . . . a sentimentalist and an art critic" (574). The opposition between the "brute" and the "art critic" is Presley's, but in the discussion of aesthetics that follows between Presley and Shelgrim, the narrator again upholds Presley's view. Shelgrim does not criticize Presley's popular poem "The Toilers" because of its socialist protest against the railroad; rather he criticizes the poem for being derivative, inspired not by life but by art. Says Shelgrim, "I like the picture [of 'The Toilers'] better than the poem. . . . There's only one best way to say anything. And what has made the picture of 'The Toilers' great is that the artist said in it the *best* that could be said on the subject" (574). To Shelgrim, art is good or bad, depending on whether it is original or derivative, whether it is expressed well or badly. Aesthetics is one question, and specifically a question for experts who know what is original or derivative; social reality, specifically laissez-faire capitalism, is an entirely different one, though, again, one on which only those with knowledge can deliver judgment. Presley is depicted as converted, first by Shelgrim's analysis of aesthetics and then by his discussion of laissez-faire capitalism. Shelgrim is expertly right about each and right about their separation.

Presley's conversion is confirmed by the narrative's trajectory. If in the beginning of the novel Norris dramatically upsets a pastoral idyll to criticize the sentimental notion of a transcendent sphere outside the determination of the market (49–51), by the end of the novel, the railroad is itself sentimentalized, a market force envisioned as transhistorical and transcendent, separated from mere humdrum social reality. As Shelgrim puts it, "Railroads build themselves. . . . Men have only little to do in the whole business" (576). Or as Presley and the narrator conclude in an optimistic rendering of Shelgrim's abstracted notion of market force in the last lines of the novel, "The larger view always and through all shams, all wickednesses, discovers the Truth that will, in the end prevail, and all things, surely, inevitably, resistlessly work together for good" (652).

Norris's critique of and reliance on the thematics and aesthetics of sentimentalism is part and parcel of the text's ambivalence about the professionalism it insistently claims. The novel describes itself, as I have argued, both as an unsentimental account of the workings of corporate capitalism and a protest against the effete literary traditions that shore up the injustice of that economic system. If Norris's naturalist account recurs to sentimentalism, however, his analysis of the literary professional, Presley, shows why that recurrence is necessary. Like many other naturalist kunstlerroman, the novel ends in a stalemate over the problem of art and the artist in consumer capitalism.[24] In *The Octopus*, this stalemate is worked out not only, as we have seen, through the depiction of the public as protected, insatiably destructive, dainty ladies but also through an analysis of the problematics of training. While Presley's views are repeatedly supported by the narrator, and while he is explicitly contrasted to the text's sentimental ladies, Norris nonetheless suggests that Presley's literary expertise has removed him from "Life," much as domesticity has removed the bourgeois society ladies from it.[25] Particularly, he is removed from the laborers he imagines he can help through his writing. When Presley's writings about life achieve popular success, Norris makes clear it is because they are either shallow or misunderstood. In addition, even Presley's attempts to live life are described as laughable failures.

At the beginning of the novel, Presley's college education, as I have said, is used to demonstrate that he is a man "of wide reading and great intelligence" (35) and hence to link him to the other college men in the book. At the same time, this college education reveals, in Norris's logic, that Presley is an elitist Easterner whose desire to produce literature—like the coeds Norris attacked in his critical writings—comes from literature and not from life. This means, writes Norris, that Presley is "nervous, introspective," "merely irresolute," "morally . . . of that sort who avoid evil through good taste, lack of decision, and want of opportunity" (8–9). He fundamentally cannot engage life, let alone represent it, for "his mental life was not at all the result of impressions and sensations that came to him from without, but rather of thoughts and reflections germinating from within" (8). The metaphors of impregnation and germination are ones that Norris relies on to describe Presley's artistic process (45) in the beginning of the book. In this case, the metaphor functions to feminize Presley, as a sort of ridiculous Madonna, his conceptions occurring outside of (and without insemination by) actual reality. But as the book progresses, Presley begins to find "Life" more engaging than "Art" and abandons his poetry temporarily (40–41, 307). Because he lets go of art and experiences life, when he returns to his poetry, he succeeds for the first time with "the People" (372). But it is a momentary success. This is evidenced not only by Shelgrim's critique of this first successful poem Presley has written but also later in the novel, by the failure of the "literary" (552) speech Presley delivers to the people after many of his friends have been killed by the railroad. The people cheer wildly for Presley, but he knows that they have responded enthusiastically only because they are an excited mob and not because they have understood him.

Similarly, when he tries to act to change reality by bombing the house of the railroad's representative, he fails in a most pathetic way. This failure is underlined by the fact that this bombing did not originate in his own impulses but was imagined and planned by the cowardly anarchist Caraher, who himself never acts. The failure of both Presley's attempt to represent life in his poetry or even to live life highlight the problems at the heart of the book's claim to an objective and expert presentation of reality. To want to represent real life, to be trained to represent real life, finally to represent real life, the book shows, is to make life unreal. It is to be divided irremediably from life and from "the People." There is no solution offered at the end of the novel to resolve the professional artist's dilemma, except the resolution offered by an imperialist escape from the problem of the "domestic" altogether. This escape itself implies, however, a domestic logic of its own, as Amy Kaplan and Laura Wexler have argued in different ways.[26] With "the memory" of Hilma and Annixter inspiring him "to give the best that was in him" (*TO*, 629–30), Presley heads out to India, where he will perhaps find redemption in an engagement with the real that he has failed either to write about or to discover at "home."

At one level, then, the book explicitly insists that representations of reality must be created by trained professionals, that this will result in objective analyses of reality and end the sentimental belief in locations outside of reality. At another level, however, the text neither trusts the public to understand these expert depictions of reality properly nor the expert to create them. The result of this impasse is twofold. First, by aggressively shifting the object of representation, and the authority to represent and to criticize, from women to men, from the "unprofessional" female to the "professional" male, the masculine naturalist novel hopes to evade the impasse. At the same time, the naturalist novel acknowledges, through its own stalemate over representation, the failure of this move to address the problems it has posed. For that reason, it feminizes the professional male, attempting to place him in a realm outside of critique. One way to do so is to remove him from the problem of domesticity altogether, to send him outside the bounds of feminization to the frontier beyond, in the case of Norris to the frontier of imperialist adventure. So the novel ends just as Presley departs for India. But even such a vision of masculine imperialist escape from the domestic is itself indebted to domestic ideology.

This complicated dynamic of naturalism—of insistent defeminization and equally insistent refeminization—has been crucial to the formation of modern American literary studies more generally and particularly to the kind of social criticism it embraces. We can see this best in the essay that created a set of terms for this tradition of social criticism, an essay that remains influential today—George Santayana's "The Genteel Tradition in American Philosophy" (1911). This talk, delivered by a Harvard professor at the University of California just before his flight from America to a semipermanent exile in Europe, relies on and productively elaborates contradictions we saw in Boyesen and Norris. It too works to criticize previous claims to cultural authority and to map out a new kind of professional expertise despite Santayana's documented distaste for professionalism.[27] It too poses the problem with old forms of expertise and the promise of new ones through an opposition of domestic sentimentality and naturalist force. But when that opposition proves untenable because of the contradictions that inhere in it, Santayana does not propose escape into empire as Norris does. In an earlier poem on which "The Genteel Tradition" is based, "Young Sammy's First Wild Oats" (1900), Santayana did find the solution to American feminization in imperialism.[28] In "The Genteel Tradition," however, Santayana lets the impasse construct a different form of escape from the problem—namely, a kind of cultural authority based on disinterestedness or objectivity that describes itself as disengaged from what it analyzes.

Early on in the essay, Santayana uses a striking analogy to define the "genteel tradition" and how it has shaped cultural expertise in America. He argues that the American mind is divided into "two mentalities," which "may be found symbolized in American architecture: a neat reproduction of the colonial mansion—with some modern comforts introduced surreptitiously—stands beside the sky-scraper. The American Will inhabits the sky-scraper; the American Intellect inhabits the colonial mansion. The one is the sphere of the American man; the other, at least predominantly, of the American woman. The one is all aggressive enterprise; the other is all genteel tradition."[29] This famous analogy works to create an absolute divide between two kinds of work and thought, emblematized by gendered space, in order to articulate its critique of the American intellectual. On the one hand, there is America's past as a colony of England and its inheritance of elitist traditions. The "colonial mansion" inhabited by women best embodies this because it imagines itself separated from the modern world in a superior and protected space but is really engaged in that world in a "surreptitious," or vicarious, and hypocritical fashion. On the other hand, there is America's present of capitalist innovation and aspiration. The "sky-scraper" inhabited by men and itself a representation of phallic masculinity best embodies this to Santayana because it is the unequivocal sign of engagement with the modern world.[30]

This passage beautifully condenses realists' and naturalists' critique of Victorian, sentimental, domestic culture. But this famous analogy that seems at first to present us with an absolute opposition between domesticity and modern business—between the derivative, vicarious feminine culture of the past and innovative, active masculine professional endeavor of the present—is more complicated than it first appears. It is, after all, rather striking that to criticize feminized domestic discourse, Santayana relies on the notion of the separate spheres of men and women—a separation he has shown is more imagined than real, given the colonial home's "surreptitious" reliance on modern conveniences. It is equally surprising that to describe innovative capitalist enterprise, he uses the image of the skyscraper. For while the "sky-scraper" is meant to embody male engagement with modern reality and slyly modernizes and concretizes the transparent eyeball lifted into the ether of Emerson's "Nature," it also clearly establishes male engagement with reality as a kind of transcendence of history, a being above and beyond the messiness below.[31] Elitist separation from reality is not as easily stabilized in the figure of women's sentimentalism as it first appears despite the way the "two mentalities" have been appropriated by American cultural criticism.

The shakiness of the colonial home-skyscraper antithesis is part and parcel of Santayana's larger ambivalence about modern capitalist reality and the intellectual's proper relation to it. For if Santayana is critical of the intellectual's feminized separation from this reality, evidenced by the "genteel tradition," he is equally critical of modern American reality—of its banal, pragmatic materialism, of the conformity it insists upon, of its complacent and disturbing triumphalism (*GT*, 42–43). As a result, Santayana continually oscillates in his history of the "genteel tradition" between describing it as operating outside American realities and as a product of those realities. He states that there was no moment when the genteel tradition, or the "hereditary spirit" (39), did not obtain in America. In the early years of the nation, he asserts, it was the result of "the pressure of external circumstances" (42), of "a small nation with an intense vitality, but on the verge of ruin" (41). Calvinism is the logical philosophical outcome of this situation (41). This analysis of the genteel tradition as coextensive with the determining force of American history breaks down, however, when he analyzes romanticism and transcendentalism. He offers at first a story of the romantics' alienation from their intellectual and historical circumstances, their heroic resistance to it, and their refusal to sell out: "They could not retail the genteel tradition; they were too keen, too perceptive, and too independent for that. But life offered them little digestible material, nor were they naturally voracious. They were fastidious, and under the circumstances they were starved" (43). He argues that these intellectuals escaped the "mediocrity of the genteel tradition" in their work. They fed only on their own minds, and their "manner . . . was subjective" (44), so they were protected from American reality and from "retail[ing]" the "genteel tradition." But he then promptly reverses course and argues that at another level their noteworthy resistance to selling an impoverished reality (what "life offered them") meant that they became, along with the Calvinists, the "chief fountains of this [genteel] tradition" (61). In short, by resisting the genteel tradition, these romantics became part of it.

Similarly contradictory is Santayana's analysis of his prime target in "The Genteel Tradition," what he calls "current academic philosophy" (40; see also 38, 39). At times, he criticizes academic philosophy as utterly removed from its environment and context, "slightly becalmed . . . float[ing] gently in the backwater" (40; see also 39, 61–62). At other times, he attacks "the academic mind" (62) because it is far too invested in reality, in "white-washing and adoring things as they are" (61) and in working to establish an "illegitimate monopoly" (61) over American thinking. Relying on Thorstein Veblen's term for corporations, the "vested interests," Santayana describes academic philosophy as doing the ideological work of corporate capitalism, of "defending some vested illusion or some eloquent idea" (49). He criticizes academic philosophy rather contradictorily for being both outside of and utterly invested in American capitalist reality.

The compelling feature of Santayana's cultural history, then, is that it represents an irresolveable and tragic paradox: the American intellectual is damned if he engages with reality and damned if he resists it. Either way, he will fit or be fitted into the genteel tradition. The fact that Calvinism and transcendentalism—one the passive expression of, the other the active resistance to external circumstances—are the two "chief fountains" of the genteel tradition, and the fact that academic philosophy, whether embracing or disengaging itself from capitalist reality, is part of the genteel tradition, suggests that the dilemma that Santayana is interested in exceeds the problem of America's "two mentalities" (39) of timid intellectual traditions and creative business life, of feminized and masculinized culture. The real dilemma that concerns him is the inescapable fate of the American intellectual, of his necessary feminization by American capitalist reality, whether he accedes to it or not.[32]

Nonetheless, Santayana does not end "The Genteel Tradition" on the note of tragedy. Like Norris, he works to find the greater good in this dilemma. Unlike both Norris and the younger Santayana, who ten years earlier found the solution in imperialist escape, the older Santayana finds a way out in the impasse itself. The older Santayana's solution involves both sides of the life-literature antithesis that tormented the naturalists. He insists both on nature and a disavowal of nature, both on reality and a disavowal of reality in favor of representation. He begins the conclusion of the essay with a move that gestures to an escape much like Norris's. Arguing that philosophical naturalism will successfully undermine the genteel tradition, he writes: "This revolution, I should think, might well find an echo among you [Californians], who live in a thriving society, and in the presence of a virgin and prodigious world. When you transform nature to your uses, when you experiment with her forces, and reduce them to industrial agents, you cannot feel that nature was made by you or for you, for then these adjustments would have been pre-established" (62). Like the greater good Norris finds despite "the welter of blood" in *The Octopus*, Santayana's nature reveals the greater good despite the dilemma that capitalism poses for the artist. Even when the westward-stepping Anglo-Saxon reduces to "industrial agents," this "virgin and prodigious world," nature remains beyond human history.

Nature's transcendence of history proves, however, the possibilities of human transcendence: the "non-human beauty and peace [of nature] . . . stir[s] the sub-human depths and the super-human possibilities of your own spirit" (62). So Santayana goes on to add that even more important than nature's transcendence of history is man's own transcendence of history through his mind: "[T]he peculiarity of man is that his machinery for reaction on external things has involved an imaginative transcript of these things, which is preserved and suspended in his fancy; and the interest and beauty of this inward landscape, rather than any fortunes that may await his body in the outer world, constitute his proper happiness. . . . Let us therefore be frankly human. Let us be content to live in the mind" (64). As with his paean to naturalism, Santayana aggrandizes subjectivism's transcendence of life, of whatever "fortunes . . . may await his body in the outer world." He insists on the "inward landscape" of fancy, on precisely the representation of and exteriority to reality that he castigated as part of the genteel tradition. The closing lines of his talk render perfectly through parataxis the central contradiction of the essay: "Let us therefore be frankly human. Let us be content to live in the mind."

Robert Dawidoff has argued that Santayana's work is characterized by its "cosmopolitan detachment," by a liberalism that works "to see without wishing to take on the responsibility of changing what is seen through."[33] And indeed the contradictions of Santayana's essay, enacted in his paratactic conclusion, do create the effect of detachment. Critical of Victorian domestic ideology and recognizing implicitly the connection between its logic of separation and transcendence and professionalism, critical also of the reality that domesticity and professionalism seek to transcend, Santayana ends up revising the ideal cultural expert as detached from both. To Santayana, the naïveté of critique *and* acceptance, of investment in any polemic at all, show how corporate and consumer capitalism seduces, feminizes, and betrays the artist. Detached observation is the only solution.

The terms of the impasse Norris and Santayana chart, as well as Santayana's solution to it, have been crucial to modernist literary professionalism. More particularly, it has been formative for those different strands of analysis linked to a liberal critique of corporate and consumer capitalism, which work "to see without wishing to take on the responsibility of changing what is seen through." In one version of this kind of critique, the critic follows in the track of naturalist sentimentalism by evading the paradoxes of professionalism by scapegoating women and sentimentalism. This serves to inoculate the critic and the texts s-he prefers from the suggestion of having themselves been feminized or seduced by such an "interested" reality, even as they acknowledge its power. From Boyesen's "Iron Madonna" (1886) to the mothers and society ladies of Norris's turn-of-the-century naturalism, from George Santayana's "two mentalities" (1911) to Van Wyck Brooks's explicitly racialized revision of Santayana's mentalities" as "Highbrow" versus "lowbrow" in *America's Coming of Age* (1915) and Vernon Louis Parrington's influential repetition of Santayana in *Main Currents of American Thought* (1930), from Thomas Beer's "Titaness" in *The Mauve Decade* (1926) to Ann Douglas's use of the same figure in *The Feminization of American Culture* (1977, 1988, 1998) and *Terrible Honesty* (1995), women and sentimentalism have revealed to American intellectuals the tragic corrupting power of corporate and consumer capitalism.[34] The peculiarity of this narrative is that by alternately blaming real and symbolic women, the thinker thereby posits masculinity and professionalism as located in spaces outside of such all-pervading and all-powerful corruption—in other words, they sentimentalize masculinity and professionalism.

Santayana's argument has also enabled a kind of analysis that criticizes such sentimentalism while also building on it. In this form of cultural analysis, the critic scapegoats any kind of polemic whatsoever, recognizing how all texts are equally invested in the economic and social system, equally feminized by American corporate and consumer capitalism, whether they are critical of it or not.[35] The critic's recognition of this tragic situation enables him to explicate judiciously the "moral sentimentalism," as Peter Carafiol puts it, of polemical or political forms of criticism that imagine themselves outside this dilemma. But while such new historicist criticism highlights the moral sentimentalism of much political criticism, it depends on a kind of moral sentimentalism itself. It imagines, as Carafiol argues, that only an "objective" outside view can provide a genuine critique.[36] Or, as Mark Seltzer puts it, new historicists often enact "melodramas of uncertain agency." These melodramas depend on continuously staging for the reader the opposition of agency and nonagency in order to highlight the evacuation of any agency or any differences in agency in corporate capitalism (*BAM,* 199–201).[37] I would add that such melodramatic criticism interestingly enough positions itself also as a kind of reasonable realism, detached from the "melodrama of uncertain agency" that it continually produces. It imagines itself as treating all cultural production impartially, equally inside their time and place, even as it describes itself (sentimentally) as outside the emotionally charged, polemical postcolonial, and feminist critiques of it that it "objectively" diagnoses. The naturalist sentimentalism of much recent criticism, in short, represents a new version of the turn-of-the-century literary professional's shoring up of expertise through the feminine and sentimental ideology it imagines it disavows.

Reading Norris and Santayana together helps us understand why naturalist sentimentalism became so important to literary professionalism more generally. It was a narrative form that rationalized and scientized cultural expertise through a critique of corporate and consumer capitalism. Naturalist sentimentalism posed its critical and defensive account of capitalism in part by scapegoating those who succumbed to the seductions of the market either more than the professional did or more naively than the professional. Such scapegoating distracts from the investments that this professionalism itself made. It used its own tragic self-recognition as a way to limit expertise and protect itself. In the case of Norris and Santayana, the life-literature antithesis, the profound distaste for, as well as aggrandizement of, the professional, worked to create the "objectivity" that authorized the cultural expert. The contradictions their work displays became institutionalized in the notion of an always-threatened literary professionalism that must be shored up by the demonstration of more disinterestedness. To adapt Nina Baym's famous formulation, naturalist sentimentalism narrates stories of beset professional manhood, beset by the "interested" and subjective polemics of outsiders.

In the remainder of the book, I will continue to examine the effect of this surprisingly successful attempt to stabilize the domesticity-professionalism antithesis in modernism. In particular, I will focus on one opposition—that, as we have seen in Norris and Santayana, was particularly important to stabilizing professional authority—the opposition between subjectivity and objectivity. This opposition carries with it the others (domesticity-professionalism, life-literature, masculinity-femininity), and it is, as I have shown, a profoundly difficult one to sustain. What happens, for example, if women intellectuals, instead of interrogating these binaries try to appropriate them? What effect might this have on these binaries? Or indeed, how might appropriation enable or stymie a woman professional?

In an essay written in 1900 on the power and promise of Frank Norris's work, Willa Cather writes approvingly of Norris that he has "abjured tea-table psychology . . . and subtle dissections of intellectual impotencies, and . . . the whole literature of nerves."[38] Comparing him to other "young . . . American writers" (*WP*, 2: 748), Cather continues: "Most [young American writers] observe the world through a temperament, and are more occupied with their medium than the objects they watch. And temperament is a glass which distorts most astonishingly. But this young man [Norris] sees with a clear eye and reproduces with a touch, firm and decisive, strong almost to brutalness" (2: 748). Norris's clear vision—undistorted by "temperament"—shows his allegiance to an objective world of "Things as They Are" (2: 747). His clear-sighted objectivity reveals that "He has the kind of brain stuff that would vanquish difficulties in any profession" so that he is able to depict "American life, the real life of the people" (2: 749). His is a "realism of the most uncompromising kind" (2: 746). This means, for Cather, that he can expect neither "popularity for his book," nor "pressing commissions from the fireside periodicals" (2: 746).

Cather's analysis of Norris's professionalism closely resembles Norris's own views. She praises Norris for his objectivity. His vision is undistorted by subjectivity—by temperament or intellectualizing. It is even "algebraic" (2: 749). His ability to be objective reveals his "brain stuff," his professional capabilities, which are equated with forcefulness, masculinity, democracy. Cather sees subjective writing, by contrast, as necessarily impotent, feminized, elitist—creating literature of the "tea-table" and of the "nerves." Such literature, while elitist, also panders to the popular taste. Norris's professionalism enables him to stand above such pandering. Like Norris and Santayana, Cather activates a domesticity-professionalism, literature-life, feminine-masculine set of binaries. Also like Norris and Santayana she does so to protect an ideal of professionalism that is riven by contradictory notions of its relation to the market and democracy. The reason for and the effect of activating these binaries in Cather and other women intellectuals' work, however, are strikingly different. These differences are the subject of the next chapter.

Chapter 4
"Going over to the Standard"
The Paradoxes of Objectivity in Ida Tarbell and Willa Cather

Since the 1930s, two sets of questions have been inextricably linked in criticism of Willa Cather's writing: whether her work is politically engaged and how that engagement or disengagement relates to her personal life.[1] While the description of Cather's political and personal investments and their relation to each other have changed over the years, the structure of the debate has been remarkably consistent for over seven decades. Whether critics praise or denigrate Cather's work, they have tended to use her personal life explicitly or implicitly as proof for their analyses of her politics. Certainly biography has long played and continues to play an important role in literary criticism generally, despite the much-touted death of the author. But in criticism about Cather, biography tends to be insistently personal and ahistorical, avoiding analysis of the specific ways in which Cather was shaped by and negotiated the institutional constraints and discursive norms of her time.

Part of the focus on the personal in Cather's work has to do with Cather's fairly successful attempt to erase the records of her life history that would help scholars situate her. Deeply embittered by the sex and gender politics of 1920s and 1930s literary criticism, Cather apparently hoped that by destroying as many personal records as possible she could evade her reduction to lady novelist status, or worse yet, "deviant" lady novelist.[2] As a result of these erasures, we are left with a biography, in which she seems to emerge directly from her childhood, an indigenous American genius. Her work is thereby read as disengaged from specific institutions or social pressures. Such individualistic readings are enforced by the logic of the closet. By the terms of that logic, critics read Cather's life as one of hidden, suppressed, personal secrets that need to be exposed, protected, or both.[3]

But if part of the focus on the personal in Cather studies has to do ironically enough with Cather's understandable attempt to minimize the significance of her biography, this chapter argues that such a focus also has to do with professionalism and its attempt to imagine itself outside the market—even as it is imbricated in it. This chapter rethinks the critical tendency to rely on biographical claims to anchor readings of Cather by analyzing not how personal life shapes textuality but how historically shaped forms of textuality incite us to read for personal life. An important reason Cather's personal relation to her fiction is so stridently debated, I argue, is that her work attempts to achieve and defend a notion of professional objectivity and impersonality, which itself paradoxically highlights "personality." This contradictory dynamic represents the continuing negotiations and struggles of professionals with corporate and consumer capitalism and the gender and racial implications of that struggle.

Impersonality served important ends for Cather, given the social politics of her time (not to mention ours), presenting her with the possibility of evading reduction to the status of deviant lady novelist. It was, in addition, a highly valued modernist technique and enabled her to enter into the pantheon of serious American writers.[4] While the social politics and aesthetics of modernity are crucial parts of the appeal of impersonality to Cather, I specifically examine how her high valuation of objectivity and impersonality is enabled by and coincides with that of professional journalism, a field in which she worked for two decades, writing and editing a massive body of nonfiction and fiction. I show how the conflicts and contradictions of professional journalism shaped Cather's high valuation of impersonality and her subsequent experimentation with it in her fiction. At the same time, this impersonality, I argue, shapes the way audiences read and continue to read from impersonality and objectivity to the personality behind it. By directing the reader to the personal, this journalistic impersonality enforces the historic tendency in Anglo-American criticism to read women's text reductively as only personal, only subjective, only autobiography.[5] In short, what Michael Schudson has called the journalistic "ideal of objectivity" enabled Cather's work but also proved self-defeating. Cather's destruction of the records of her life suggests that she increasingly recognized this dilemma. On the one hand, that action conforms to her notion that her work was professional and should be evaluated impersonally; on the other hand, it reveals her sense that her work would not be read impersonally unless she erased all signs of the personal.

The first section of this chapter examines the development of the relation between impersonality and personality in professional journalism by charting the conflict Progressive journalists, like Cather,[6] experienced between their notion of professionalism and the corporate and consumer capitalism that, ironically enough, enabled the development of their professionalism. I show how the notion of journalistic objectivity developed out of a critique of capitalism. Progressive journalists, like Hamilton Holt and Will Irwin, argued that "commercialism" had a powerfully compromising effect on their profession. Adapting Peter Novick's analysis of historical objectivity in the same period, we could say that these professionals' insistence on and development of impersonal objectivity worked as a kind of prophylactic against the nagging fear that they had sold out, had "gone over to the Standard," in Ida Tarbell's resonant phrase.⁷ Objectivity demonstrated to Progressive journalists that their work was not commercial but professional, not dependent and interested but independent and disinterested.

More specifically, I focus on how Progressive journalists like Holt and Irwin (and Cather and Tarbell) theorized objectivity as a methodology whereby they balanced competing forces for their readers, thereby transcending mere self-interest.⁸ In these early years of professional journalism, rhetorical balance directed the reader toward the personal integrity of the journalist whose expert skills enabled him or her to balance, rather than choose between, competing forces disinterestedly. At one level, this dynamic suggests a certain conscious openness to subjectivity, to the realm of the personal, which we have seen is linked by many modernists to Victorian femininity. And this kind of ambiguity and slippery gendering of professional journalism is indeed evident in the period.⁹ In the work of the Progressive journalists I will be focusing on, however, their professionalism combines old and new forms of masculine authority, the impersonality of the scientist, and the personal integrity of the gentleman—a combination that Samuel Haber argues that the professions rely on generally.¹⁰ While this kind of journalism activates the domesticity-professionalism binary, describing its objectivity as masculine in contrast to feminine subjectivity and self-interestedness, it also insists that personal integrity (what could potentially be seen as feminine and subjective) is masculine. Personal integrity is described as neither limited by enclosed domesticity nor by self-interested consumerism, as women of the past and present are. The professional's personal integrity is constructed, in short, as normatively white and male.

How did the professional journalist's ideal of balanced objectivity, and its dynamic of white, masculine impersonality-personality work for women journalists? This question could be answered in a variety of ways.¹¹ In this chapter, I am focusing on two Progressive, white women journalists who appropriated the logic of this normative white masculine professionalism to authorize their work. I compare how Tarbell and Cather, who both worked for the Progressive magazine *McClure's*, productively adapt the theories and practices of journalistic objectivity in their writings. Objectivity and impersonality seemed to offer these women a methodology whereby authoritative knowledge could potentially be dissociated from femininity and particularly from the denigrated characteristics of a self-interested feminine subjectivity, which modern journalism excoriated. But while Tarbell and Cather attempt in different ways to escape the figural association of women's writing with subjectivity, the journalistic objectivity they rely on in combination with the gendered social and aesthetic politics of the time returns them to it. As a result, these women's social criticism is rendered incoherent by the terms they themselves use. At the same time, their audience is enabled structurally to reduce them to (an imagined) feminized "interestedness."

There is at the start one central difficulty in comparing Tarbell's and Cather's writings: namely, the substantial differences in the aim and effects of their nonfictional and fictional writings as well as the differences over time as each author continues to experiment with and negotiate the contradictions of journalistic professionalism. Nevertheless, my focus on their similarities enables us to see both the contradictions in journalistic professionalism that shape their ideals of objectivity and the paradoxes that thereby ensue for them as women.[12] In each writer's expression of her vocational ideals, particularly in the antifemininity that marks those ideals (and which is also an antifeminism and often a poisonous racism and ethnocentrism), we can see Tarbell's and Cather's critique of how commercialism compromises professionalism. Their ideals of professionalism, which assume a normative white masculinity, manifest themselves in the content and form of two of their most important critiques of commercialism, Tarbell's *The History of Standard Oil* (1904–5) and Cather's *The Professor's House* (1925). Their balanced objectivity points to their personal integrity, which in turn highlights precisely what they hoped to escape: the specificity of what (in the logic of the professionalism they adopt) is their "interested" femininity.

Historians have long noted that the 1880s and 1990s were crucial years in the development of modern, professional journalism.[13] The advertising revolution that occurred in the post–Civil War period enforced trends noticeable already in the 1830s—namely, the development of affordable magazines and newspapers for a broader audience, greater independence of such magazines and newspapers from political parties, and new respectability for journalists. Under the linked but often conflicting pressures of increasing commercialization, democratization, and specialization, journalism became professionalized.

But while journalism professionalized at the turn of the century, some historians have argued that objectivity did not become a discursive norm until after World War I. Michael Schudson, for example, argues that journalists at the turn of the century saw themselves as both scientists and as storytellers. Because they saw no conflict between empirical, fictional, or didactic narratives, Schudson says, their work cannot be likened to modern, professional journalism.[14] He argues that it is only in the 1920s and 1930s that objectivity became a normative ideal. Disillusioned by the role they themselves had played in disseminating governmental propaganda, journalists formed their "ideal of objectivity," seeking to create "a method" that would separate facts from values in "a world in which even facts could not be trusted."[15] Schudson cites Walter Lippmann's *Liberty and the News* (1919, 1920)—with its critique of the "manufacture of consent" and its call for professional training—as the most forceful expression of the modern, professional journalistic ideal of objectivity.[16]

I rely on Schudson's definition of the ideal of journalistic objectivity as an attempt to imagine and create a methodology that would separate facts and values in a world in which "even facts could not be trusted"—and specifically as a set of techniques whereby facts are seen as true if they have been submitted "to established rules deemed legitimate by a professional community."[17] Nonetheless, I want to complicate his periodization. If the "ideal of objectivity" becomes normative in the post–World War I era, it was already being formed by Progressive journalists who most keenly felt the contradictions between their developing professional ideals and the demands made on them within corporate and consumer capitalism.[18] Lippmann's famous postwar book crystallizes arguments that appeared a decade earlier in the writings of Progressive journalists. These journalists argued, on the one hand, that they were disinterested experts, with independent standards of their own, and therefore professional. On the other hand, since they themselves realized that their success depended on selling their wares to advertisers and to the public, such an argument was difficult to sustain. The solution to this early dilemma of commercialism (as in Lippmann's later one) was their own insistence upon professional methodology of objectivity. Against commercialism's self-interestedness and exaggeratedly biased claims, they posed their professional objectivity, which to them meant the method whereby they disinterestedly balanced competing interpretations and beliefs for readers. Their ability to balance opposed views enacted and proved to them their own objectivity. Two famous examples of these reformist journalists' development of a balanced notion of objectivity demonstrate this dynamic: Hamilton Holt's lecture *Commercialism and Journalism,* published as a book in 1906, and Will Irwin's "muckraking"[19] series, "The American Newspaper," appearing in *Collier's* (1911).

In *Commercialism and Journalism,* Holt, then the managing editor of the well-respected, Progressive magazine *Independent* begins with the question "Is journalism a profession or a business?"[20] Like contemporary historians of journalism, Holt links the expansion and democratization of the press to the rise of advertising. Like them also, he argues that this link has made the media vulnerable to control by advertisers (*CJ,* 37–75). Advertising, he argues, "is at present moment by far the greatest menace to the disinterested practice of the profession upon which the diffusion of intelligence most largely depends" (34). Along with the old limitation of how the editor's "personality" impinges upon editorial policy, journalists now also face the new limitation of the editor's fearful desire to retain advertisers and subscribers (37). In addition, Holt criticizes the production of news itself. The "press agent," he says, "manufactures" (40) the news if he has none, with the result that he also "manufacture[s] public opinion" (55), a phrase that Lippmann adapted so effectively more than a decade later. These factors could contribute to making journalism a "business" rather than a profession, and this difference is described as the compromised body of a woman. In the "swollen advertising pages" (76) of magazines and newspapers, says Holt, one sees the effects of "editorial prostitution" (75).

To face the threat such prostitution poses, Holt models and argues for balance in both form and content. Two-thirds of Holt's book lays out the problems that commercialism poses for professional journalism, but the last one-third focuses on positive trends that counter the effect commercialism is having on journalism. Holt particularly examines editorial resistance to unethical forms of pressure. He suggests that resistance is one of the natural benefits of a competitive economic system. While commercialism may be the "greatest menace to freedom of the press," Holt argues that in commercialism lies the "seeds of its own destruction." Commercial journalism has created the competitors that will destroy it in the "weeklies and monthlies that have thrived by fighting commercialism" (98). He cites the integrity of various magazine editors, including Samuel McClure of *McClure's,* Ida Tarbell and Ray Stannard Baker of *McClure's* and later of the *American* (94), and the editor of his own magazine, the *Independent* (78). From these "great" editors (94), Holt concludes that the solution to the problem of commercialism lies in the "old, old remedy" of "personal integrity" (103–5).

This solution of personal integrity is interesting for two reasons. First, it depends on a belief in the balanced nature of competition. Competition is defined as a principle of equalizing two sides. Force A will be countered not necessarily by B but by Anti A. Greater commercialism (in other words, personal interestedness) leads to the counteracting force of greater professionalism (in other words, personal disinterestedness). Second, the book enacts the principle of competitive balance formally. If the first sections of Holt's book have shown what Holt calls the "seamy side" (78) of the relation between commercialism and journalism, the last sections counteract that account by demonstrating the other side of this relation. The thematic and formal balancing represents a logic of consensus, of a normative critique and acceptance of the status quo. The solution to personal interestedness, Holt suggests, relying on the content and form of his argument, lies in the counterweight of the professional journalist's personal disinterestedness.

The most famous Progressive analysis of the conflict between journalism and commercialism, Will Irwin's "The American Newspaper," which appeared in serial form in *Collier's* (1911), not only analyzes and solves the problem with commercialism in the same way as Holt but also presents its argument in the same balanced form that Holt uses. Like Holt, Irwin spends a substantial amount of time in this series discussing the conflict between commercialism and professional journalism—explicitly in six of his fourteen essays, implicitly in all of them.[21] His first essay opens with the question Holt's does: "[I]s journalism a business or a profession? In other words, should we consider a newspaper publisher as a commercialist, aiming only to make money . . . or must we consider him as a professional man, seeking other rewards before money, and holding a tacit franchise from the public for which he pays by observance of an ethical code?" Posing the "condemners" of journalism against its "defenders," both of whom are "special pleaders," Irwin argues that "truth and justice lie somewhere between their extreme views."²² Such an argument depends on his sense that "special" pleading is a problem because it is linked to commercialism and that balancing out such pleading will lead to objective truth. The consensual or normative view, rather than that of the "special pleader," is also the balanced and objective one.

Irwin's argument is a more carefully developed variation of Holt's, since he acknowledges from the beginning that his distinction between business and professionalism is debatable. Nonetheless, he discovers the solution to the problem of commercialism—in a similar fashion to Holt—in the equalizing principle of competition. Balancing even more carefully than Holt both the content and form of his argument about the negative influence of commercialism on journalism, Irwin argues in the final essays in his series that magazines prove that personal integrity in journalism pays "in cold cash."²³ He cites *McClure's, Ladies' Home Journal*,²⁴ and *Collier's* itself²⁵ as examples of the "magazine standard,"²⁶ a standard that proves that "nothing profits... like truth," like "commercialized sincerity."²⁷ While the phrase "commercialized sincerity" makes us think first of Holt's "editorial prostitution," Irwin sees it as a balancing force against its opposite—commercialized insincerity. In the final essay, he insists that one cannot necessarily be hopeful about the future of journalism in general, but that nonetheless, "In the profession itself lies our greatest hope. In spite of all commercial tendencies, its personnel and intelligence are improving year by year." The "noble dissatisfaction of the men over the condition of their craft," Irwin continues, is a sign that "the system will cure itself."²⁸ Ida Tarbell's "temperately and accurately written" *History of Standard Oil* for *McClure's* exemplifies these changes.²⁹ As in Holt, critique and acceptance are balanced out in a logic that points us to the personal integrity and disinterested professionalism of the journalist. The newspapers' commercialized insincerity has gone too far and so will necessarily be countered by the magazine's commercialized sincerity and journalists' noble dissatisfaction. And as in Holt, the content and structure of Irwin's series itself provides a form for that idea.

The history of *McClure's*, the magazine that played a formative role in both Tarbell's and Cather's careers, highlights some of the complexities this paradoxical solution of "commercialized sincerity" entails and suggests how this paradox became important thematically and formally to both women's writings. *McClure's* is perhaps the magazine most associated in its time with Progressive reform and, as we have seen, to its contemporaries, with professional integrity. For a decade, it was also an astonishing commercial success. Samuel McClure, the magazine's founder, says in his autobiography (1913), ghostwritten by Willa Cather, that he had not originally envisioned the magazine as reformist, a statement confirmed in the autobiographies of his most famous writers—Ray Stannard Baker, Lincoln Steffens, and Ida Tarbell. Instead, he simply wanted to publish stories that were "interesting," and hence sold well.³⁰ While McClure never really defines "interesting," by looking at the magazine, one can make a few guesses about its meaning. Most striking was the innovative emphasis on the personal and biographical.[31] Lengthy biographies of famous individuals fueled subscription rates in the early years of the magazine. Tarbell's biography of Napoleon, which ran from November 1894 to April 1895 and was amply illustrated with portraits of Napoleon and his family, doubled subscriptions.[32] Her biography on Lincoln from August 1895 to December 1895, which included the earliest daguerrotype of Lincoln yet seen by the public, doubled circulation again.[33] Muckraking, for which *McClure's* was to become admired as exemplary of journalistic professionalism, can itself be read as a form of celebrity biography. McClure, for example, says that when the magazine chose to study the development of trusts in the U.S., Standard Oil was chosen because "it was the creature largely of one man, one figure, one personality—John D. Rockefeller. So that the Trust would lend itself almost to the simplicity of biographical treatment." Rockefeller, McClure continues, "is the Napoleon among business men,"[34] an analogy that suggests he at least saw Tarbell's series on Standard Oil as depending on the techniques used in her Napoleon biography, which had established the financial viability of the magazine.[35] And indeed, crucial to *The History of Standard Oil* is Tarbell's analysis of the personal character of Rockefeller, his business genius and successes, as well as his lack of integrity, his hypocrisy, even his physical repulsiveness.[36]

For the purposes of this chapter, however, there is a more important way in which the commercial success of *McClure's* depended on the personal. As the magazine became associated with the highest professional standards and with social reform, as the journalists made visible the inner lives of celebrities and trusts alike, the reputations of its writers were also established. The character, in both senses of the word, of the *McClure's* reporters became crucial to their work. As they laid bare business and government corruption, they revealed to their audience that they could not be corrupted, that they were autonomous professionals, and this enabled them to sell their magazine even more effectively. In a letter McClure wrote to Tarbell in 1903 while *The History of the Standard Oil Company* was being published, he demonstrates how Tarbell's personal and professional integrity has made both her and the magazine famous and successful: "Your articles are the great magazine feature of recent years. The way you are generally esteemed and reverenced pleases me tremendously. You are today the most generally famous woman in America. You have achieved a great distinction. People universally speak of you with such a reverence that I am getting sort of afraid of you."[37] To McClure, Tarbell's articles are "the great magazine feature of recent years," a fact made equivalent in the sentence to the esteem and reverence in which she personally is held. Being of great personal distinction is indistinguishable from selling copy.[38]

We can see another angle on this issue if we recur to Holt's and Irwin's work. It is striking that in both of these muckraking accounts of journalism, the work of *McClure's* and Ida Tarbell is specifically cited as examples of the journalistic professionalism inhering in the "magazine standard." Ida Tarbell, and the magazine she works for, prove that personal integrity is a viable solution to commercialism in that, paradoxically, it sells well. Holt and Irwin thereby call into play the "myth" that developed in the wake of the publication of *The History of the Standard Oil Company*, the myth of "The Gentlewoman and the Robber Baron," as a Tarbell biographer puts it.[39] In this myth, which was turned into a successful Broadway play, the lady's gentility wins out against the robber baron's rapacity.[40] The story of the trust is one about two different kinds of character, and it therefore also becomes a story that sells. However, this story of Tarbell's character, relying as it does on feminine rather than masculine authority, proved to be a double-edged sword for her.

While Tarbell's and the other muckrakers' character was important to the saleability of *McClure's*, I do not want to argue that the "character" of the muckrakers at *McClure's* was simply a commercial proposition, though McClure seems to see it that way—and, as Willa Cather more directly asserts was the case—as I shall discuss below. On the contrary, in 1906, Baker, Steffens, and Tarbell resigned from the magazine because they were convinced that their personal integrity was being compromised by McClure's desire to expand his empire. As Tarbell later described it, the writers felt that McClure wanted to engage them in "a speculative scheme as alike as two peas to certain organizations the magazine had been battering."[41] These writers then pooled their money to resuscitate the *American*, but this venture was short-lived. The magazine lost money and was taken over by Crowell Publishing Company in 1911. As early as 1912, the writers were worrying about how their work was being censored, and by 1915, all of them had resigned.[42] While their careers were not destroyed by their resignations, and all continued to support themselves through their writing, they took financial and professional risks in leaving *McClure's*, risks that did not pay off.

This dramatic conflict between commercialism and professionalism at *McClure's* is also of interest because it was crucial to the trajectory of Cather's career. It was the staff's mass resignation from *McClure's* in 1906 that led McClure to hire Cather to work for the magazine, where she became managing editor in 1909, a job Tarbell had also held.[43] While much has been made of Cather's ambivalence about journalism and Sarah Orne Jewett's advice to her that precipitated her resignation from the magazine in 1912, it is striking that the conflicts at *McClure's* that led to her hiring and the complicated ethics of her position have not been discussed much. Cather, however, did comment on this conflict and the larger issues that underlie it in a story published many years later, "Ardessa" (1918). Here, Cather analyzes how commercialism undermines the integrity of journalism, including that of professional journalists, so that no ethical position is available within the narrative. There are, however, ethical possibilities in the narrative's structure and in the narrator's position. While criticizing journalism, the story depends on the profession's response to commercialism, on the notion of balanced objectivity that points finally toward the integrity of the narrative and its narrator. This is worked out through a situating of the narrator outside femininity and outside (feminizing) non-whiteness.

"Ardessa" analyzes the transformation of the American magazine industry from its genteel Victorian past to its modern, professional, commercialized present. In her account, Cather indicts the current close relation between commercialism and journalism—a relation she charts out through the contest between the lady on the one side and the Jewish "girl" on the other. The story focuses on "a red-hot magazine of protest . . . called 'The Outcry' " founded by Marcus O'Mally, a millionaire from the West.[44] O'Mally, Cather tells us, has no particular ambition to change the world; rather he simply is motivated by social ambition (*A*, 105). Cather further muddies the notion of the magazine's social reform mission by arguing that O'Mally simply taps a market desire for puerile forms of voyeuristic self-loathing. He knows "what everybody secretly wanted" (105), which is to "read about their own wickedness" (106), and he exploits that desire shamelessly. Most crucially, however, O'Mally's skill at playing the "publicity game" (105) enables him to "manufacture celebrities" (106), as Cather puts it in the language of Holt and Lippmann, or, more precisely, to manufacture and sell the celebrated integrity of his writers: "Other people . . . had discovered that advertising would go a long way; but Marcus O'Mally discovered that in America it would go all the way—as far as you wished to pay its passage. Any human countenance, plastered in three-sheet posters from sea to sea, would be revered by the American people. The strangest thing was that the owners of these grave countenances, staring at their own faces on newsstands and billboards, fell to venerating themselves, and even he, O'Mally, was more or less constrained by these reputations that he had created out of cheap paper and cheap ink" (106).

Cather's analysis of muckraking as market-driven, prurient scandalmongering and muckrakers as carefully hyped, self-satisfied egotists is supported by the history of journalism "Ardessa" narrates. Space, as in the later Cather, describes historical change. When the story begins, the commercial and creative domains of journalism are divided not just ideologically but also physically in the layout of the office: "The business and editorial offices of 'The Outcry' were separated by a long corridor and a great contempt" (112). Similarly, the people who work in those different spaces are divided. In the business offices are Jewish immigrants: specifically, the "impudent . . . rapacious young Hebrew" (112), Miss Kalski, and the "thin, tense-faced Hebrew" (110), Becky Tietelbaum. In the editorial offices are the ladylike stenographer, Ardessa, and the magazine's writers.

If Cather relies on anti-Semitic descriptions of mercenary Jews in order to describe the modernized business offices, she relies on modern stereotypes about the obsolescence of femininity to describe the editorial offices. Ardessa is the central figure in the editorial offices, and Cather writes of her: "Ardessa was not young and she was certainly not handsome. The coquettish angle at which she carried her head was a mannerism surviving from a time when it was more becoming. She shuddered at the cold candor of the new business woman, and was insinuatingly feminine" (105). Cather enforces the notion of Ardessa's obsolescent femininity by describing her also as "cloistered" in the editorial offices, where she provides what she thinks is "a graceful contrast to the crude girls in the advertising and circulation departments across the hall" (107). Residing in a kind of separate sphere analogous to the Victorian home, Ardessa furthermore works in an outdated fashion. Because she had been the stenographer for the "ailing publication" (106) that preceded the "Outcry," she has "long been steeped in literary distinctions and in the social distinctions which used to count for much more than they do now" (107). She does not actually work; rather she is a kind of hostess "gratifying . . . her own vanity" (108) by " 'personally' receiv[ing]" the writers whose work is no longer popular and who will never be published again in the "Outcry." Her femininity is inextricable from her obsolete, personalized, elitist work habits.

Also separated from the business offices and situated in the editorial offices are the "great men" on the staff. They too are feminized by Cather, described like Ardessa as separated from the world outside that they pretend to depict. Writes Cather, they are "as contemplative as Buddhas in their private offices, each meditating upon the particular trust or form of vice confided to his care" (107). These celebrity writers, isolated in their "private" offices from the reality they are supposed to describe, imagine they are personally fighting financial and moral evils, never realizing that their protected status depends solely on a carefully marketed integrity created by O'Mally "out of cheap paper and cheap ink" (106). O'Mally's selling of them enables these writers to think they are separated from the commercialism and monopoly capitalism they deplore when they are really quite fully implicated in it.

Ardessa's and the writers' feminized separation from the world is one that cannot be sustained. The historical separation between the business and editorial offices can be only an imagined one in the modern world. Cather dramatizes this point particularly in how her characters are mobilized in the spaces of the office. Midway through the story, Miss Kalski "serpentine[s]" her way out of the business office and "cross[es] the Rubicon into the editorial offices" (112). The crossing and Miss Kalski's "insolent" (112) skill at outmaneuvering Ardessa in office politics, reveal that the supposed divide between the commercial and creative offices is an obsolete one. So also does Ardessa's permanent crossing at the end of the story from her cloistered office into one shared with Miss Kalski and the business manager. It is not just that the editorial and business spheres of the magazine are irremediably mixed, but rather that commercialism is the prime factor. As O'Mally puts it when he informs Ardessa that she must move over to the business office, that is "where we get our money from" (115).

Cather describes this end of separate spheres in journalism as a fall. Miss Kalski's movements are serpentine (112), and she has a "low, siren laugh" (113). Becky's eagerness to work "corrupt[s]" (111) others. Nonetheless, Cather balances this fall by making Ardessa unsympathetic in her outmoded femininity and the celebrity journalists ridiculous in their complacent critiques of a system in which they are implicated. While Becky and Miss Kalski represent commercialism, they are also hardworking and ambitious. Their kindness to Ardessa after she is moved to the business office demonstrates that while they are rapacious, they are also businesslike good sports. In short, neither the old, elitist, feminized magazine business nor the new, commercialized, aspiring, also feminized "Hebrew" one is given preeminent value in the story. Since Cather's raced and gendered criticism of the present is balanced by her class and gendered criticism of the past, and both are equally and derogatorily feminine, the reader is led to believe that value resides in neither the past nor the present of journalism but rather in the balanced objectivity of the narrative and its clear-sighted narrator who shows the shortcomings of both the past and the present. In short, the "character" of the narrator and the narrative are crucial solutions to the impasse the story lays out.

"Ardessa" criticizes the way in which journalism (even putatively reformist journalism) is implicated in consumer capitalism; however, in its analysis of and resolution to this "fall," it relies on the same imagined solution to the problem of commercialism as the reformist journalism it criticizes—an ideal of the balanced objectivity of form and content that directs the reader's attention toward the integrity of the narrative and its writer. This explains the temptation critics face to read the story as an autobiographical roman à clef. Cather worked for a famous reform magazine, and so it is easy to read Cather's life story into the thinly veiled caricatures of McClure and his staff. Those biographical parallels are, of course, compelling. I would argue, however, we also look toward biography because the story is objectively balanced in the manner Holt and Irwin describe. It shows the compromised status of both the present and the past, resolutely refusing either nostalgia or optimism. Only the disinterested narrative and its narrator, therefore, remain uncompromised. In particular, in a story in which present and past are described as self-interested, and the symbolic logic used to make that point feminizes and racializes self-interest, the narrator structurally appears normatively white and male, above the compromised individuals depicted in the story. "Ardessa" suggests how the journalistic ideal of objectivity could represent for women writers the ability to escape reduction to gendered or racialized interestedness and hence to compromised commercialism. But it also provides the framework whereby we are directed to the personal integrity of the writer and, therefore, in this case, to the femininity that belies the writer's white, masculine normativity. In short, the journalistic ideal of objectivity helps enforce the way women are seen only as personal and—by the logic of modern professionalism—interested. In the sections ahead, I examine the complexities of this self-defeating dynamic in both Tarbell's and Cather's theories about professionalism and in the practice of it in their mature writings.

Tarbell's most striking statement of professional ideals appears in a series of essays she published in the *American*, which were republished in book form as *The Business of Being a Woman* (1912, 1925). Written during the heyday of her career, this text is a vocational narrative of sorts. It foregrounds the issues that surround the creation of professional journalism's notion of objectivity—namely, the conflict between disinterestedness and interestedness in corporate and consumer capitalism. It reads this conflict through differing accounts of woman's role in society. On the one hand, it poses the "business" of womanhood in terms of Victorian notions of woman's natural disinterestedness; on the other hand, it criticizes Victorian womanhood's business in true modernist fashion as of necessity corrupted by woman's transhistorical personal interestedness and more specifically by her consumerism. Tarbell's analysis of woman's role directs us to look at Tarbell's own masculine impersonality in objectively demonstrating woman's interestedness, but at the same time, structurally, the analysis does so by calling into question Tarbell's authority to speak.

At first, the book's argument seems simply to repeat the ideas of Victorian domestic ideologues from the previous century, that men belong in the corrupted world of market capitalism and women in the pure home. *The Business of Being a Woman*, however, involves an important expansion of this Victorian analysis of a world separated into public and private spheres. Into the divide between the tainted market capitalism of men and the pure emotions and domesticity of women comes a new distinction between the impersonal and personal. This new distinction at first supports the moral hierarchies of Victorian culture. Tarbell argues that the problem with modern, "uneasy" woman is that such a woman refuses to recognize that she is naturally sympathetic and emotional and that this affectability is "the most wonderful part of her endowment."[45] Similarly, uneasy woman wrongly believes that household work confines her. Uneasy woman needs instead to recognize how privileged she is. After all, says Tarbell, housework poses "an independent *personal* problem" (*BW*, 64, Tarbell's emphasis). Men, by contrast, "work under the deadening effect of *impersonal* routine. They do that which others have planned and for results in which they have no permanent share" (64, emphasis added).

Finally, however, this new distinction between the personal and the impersonal does not support the moral hierarchy of Victorian domesticity that Tarbell invokes. If sympathetic emotionality in Tarbell's argument is woman's "most wonderful" endowment, it is more crucially her worst characteristic.

The book begins with an attack on uneasy woman's "self-discussion" (1). The "revolting" (21) woman's narcissistic obsession with herself, with the personal, is described as a sign of an unnatural perversion (5–6).[46] As Tarbell continues, however, the "revolting" woman simply brings to a head the essential problem with woman per se that transcends Victorian and modern temporalities. Historically, Tarbell argues, woman has always mismanaged the home because in the "necessity of concentrating her whole being on a little group [she becomes] . . . personal" (100). Such a woman denies free expression in the household and is intellectually rigid in her views. As a result, neither her husband nor her children are comfortable in the home and are forced to escape to saloons (100–101). More important, because of woman's personal approach to the household and because she is the prime consumer in America, national business practices have been compromised, resulting in the development of trusts and other forms of corporate malfeasance (65, 100–101).

Even the modern career woman, Tarbell argues, is too personal. Professionalism depends on suppressing emotion. When a career woman denies her natural self, Tarbell asserts, she becomes not only "cold," but also "self-centered, and intensely personal" (43). The greatest career woman's work is second rate, Tarbell continues, because her work is a "personal thing to which she clings as if it were a living being," when instead she needs "to see the big truths and movements which are always impersonal" (45).

Tarbell's criticism of women and their "personal" view of the world is clearly linked to a journalistic ideal of objectivity in two ways. First, and most obvious, the force of her argument lies in its denigration of the personal and subjective in order to aggrandize the impersonal and objective. Objective impersonality can solve the problem of trusts which are created by, and equivalent to, female subjectivity and interestedness. Relatedly, to Tarbell, her argument itself is objective. This means that nominally she presents the possibilities and problems of both the personal and the impersonal, though clearly the latter category finally receives higher value. Similarly, her solution to the problem of being too personal balances woman's natural subjectivity with man's objectivity, a balance encapsulated in her solution to woman's subjectivity and America's problems more generally in "scientific household management" (70).[47] Woman, Tarbell argues, must learn to "see her business as a profession" (*BW*, 221). By balancing the competing forces of subjective domesticity and objective scientific management, both the private and public spheres will be purified (64–68).

If Tarbell's solution is to balance subjectivity with objectivity, she nonetheless depends in the end on the kind of invocation of the personal that I have argued was inherent in journalistic notions of objectivity. Despite her claims to the contrary, Tarbell's impersonal objectivity refers finally to her own personal integrity, her subjectivity. "One of the most disconcerting characteristics of advocates, conservative and radical," Tarbell writes, "is their conscienceless treatment of facts. Rarely do they allow full value to that which qualifies or contradicts their theories" (217). She makes clear here and throughout the book that she, by contrast, has a conscience, which makes her factual—in other words, able to present both sides of the case, to give "full value" to what "qualifies or contradicts" her theories. Even though she is herself famously a career woman who uncovered corporate malfeasance, she treats career women in as unflinching a manner as other women.[48] In order to verify her objectivity, the reader looks toward Tarbell's exceptional personal integrity. What proves Tarbell's argument finally is that she is a woman, with a record of treating facts conscientiously, evidenced not only by her balanced account but also by the fact that she can impersonally delineate the destructive subjectivity of all women, including herself.

The dramatic manner in which Tarbell first elevates, then more emphatically denigrates, femininity ends by ensconcing as primary the very interestedness she seeks to criticize and reform. What is important here is not simply that Tarbell contradicts herself or that like Norris and Santayana she sees women as somehow more implicated in capitalism than men. While those are striking features of her argument, it is more crucial to examine how the reader is positioned to focus not so much on woman's role in implementing a "vicious" industrial system but instead on the personal flaws of woman and the personal integrity and authority of one woman, Tarbell herself (though by her logic, she too is personally flawed). Tarbell's antifemininity and antifeminism perfectly exemplify, in other words, the central problematic within journalistic objectivity: namely, how it is used to shore up professionalism against an interested commercialism but recurs to the personal—to the domain of the interested—to do so.

Tarbell's most famous work, *The History of the Standard Oil Company* (1904–5), demonstrates both the productive power that her theory of journalistic objectivity had for authorizing her social critique and the logical and structural problems that ensue and undermine that social critique. As opposed to Henry Demarest Lloyd's privately printed *Wealth against Commonwealth* (1894), which first systematically detailed the case against the Standard Oil monopoly and which was read by few of his contemporaries, Tarbell's series caused a sensation. While Tarbell relied heavily on Lloyd's sources and research, and was equally polemical, she presented the case against Standard Oil in a very different fashion. Reviews at the time emphasized her balanced objectivity "[H]onest the writer has tried to be to both sides of the story," wrote one reviewer. She has "beaten upon facts rather than upon a gong," wrote another.[49] Or, as Samuel McClure wrote in an editorial in *McClure's* on her series, "Her story has been what it pretended to be, a straight historical narrative backed by documents." She "has made no attempt to work on the emotions of her readers."[50] Tarbell achieved the effect of balanced objectivity that these reviews describe through careful framing and structuring of the narrative's themes.

The History of the Standard Oil Company describes itself, as McClure says, as "straight" history. It begins with the discovery of the uses of petroleum as a revolutionary "method...of illumination" (*SO*, 1: 4) and the oil region's transformation from "wilderness to market-place" (1: 3). Similarly, Tarbell insists in her preface on the notion that as a history the text is driven by the documents. The staff of *McClure's*, she states, had simply been looking for a way to discuss the trust question. While McClure argues that Rockefeller's biography motivates the staff's choice of Standard Oil, Tarbell says Standard Oil was chosen because it was "the most perfectly developed trust" (1: ix) and because "it is one of the very few business organisations of the country whose growth could be traced in trustworthy documents" (1: x). As opposed to Lloyd, who quotes documents briefly and instead primarily summarizes and analyzes them, Tarbell relies heavily on direct and lengthy quotation as well as a long appendix to convince her reader of her accuracy. Also as opposed to Lloyd, Tarbell claims that her documents relay the viewpoints of both the corporation and its competitors (*SO*, 1: xi). Lloyd had been criticized heavily for not confirming his facts with Standard (though, as his biographer notes, few of his "facts" were wrong, and Tarbell relied on many of them).[51] In Tarbell's most dramatic claim to balance, she states that Standard Oil "courteously" offered to give her "all the assistance in their power" (*SO*, 1: xii), and "there is not a single important episode in the history of Standard Oil Company, so far as I know it...which I have not discussed more or less fully with officers of the company" (1: xiii). While the independents confirmed what she found in the documents, so did Standard (1: xii–xiii), the object of her critique.

The structure of the text also enforces this sense of balanced objectivity. The series was organized chronologically into two main parts, and within these two parts, there are always two forces working against each other. In the first section, Tarbell describes the rise of Standard Oil and its general success at eliminating competition despite resistance. In this section, the chapters emphasize the noble foolhardiness of the "Oil Men." The failure of the Titusville oil producers to resist Standard Oil in the early 1870s is associated with their "despis[ing] small things" and being "notoriously extravagant in the management of their business" (1: 112). They lacked the "far vision" (1: 109) of Rockefeller. So, Tarbell concedes, while Standard's elimination of weak competitors "was cold-blooded...it must be confessed that it showed a much firmer grasp on the commercial practices of the day, and a much deeper knowledge of human nature as it operates in business, than that of the producers" (1: 120). As McClure argues in his editorial on the series, Tarbell "has asked no sympathy for the independent oil men," a position that while not true can at least be argued because of Tarbell's various and carefully staged concessions.[52]

In the second section of the book, Tarbell again chronicles two competing forces. This time, however, the Independent Oil Men typically resist in more intelligent ways despite Standard Oil's complex machinations. Here, Tarbell emphasizes how the secretive business practices of Standard Oil begin to undermine its success by demoralizing its workers and making the public believe the company is worse than it is. The company's actions lead to resistant counteractions, just as competition does more generally in Holt's *Commercialism and Journalism*. Describing the founding of the Pure Oil Company by a group of "independents," for example, Tarbell writes:

> Their courageous and persistent struggle no doubt seems to most of them as of purely personal and local meaning. All they asked was to get a fair share of the profits in their business. They knew they did not get it, and they believed it was because there was not fair play on the part of the railroads and the Standard Oil Company. Aroused, they each fought for the particular thing which would give them relief. They only combined because driven to. They have become a strong organisation almost solely because of the persistent opposition of the Standard Oil Trust. . . . It looks very much as if in trying to make way with several small scattered bodies Mr. Rockefeller had made one strong, united one. (2: 190–91)

Competition to Rockefeller's monopoly naturally emerges out of his unethical attempt to crush it. Because of Rockefeller's actions, the necessarily "personal and local" becomes the effectively impersonal "organisation."

Even at the level of the sentence, Tarbell works to stage her narrative in a balanced fashion. In the penultimate chapter of the series, titled "The Legitimate Greatness of Standard Oil," she writes, "Mr. Rockefeller's great creation has really been strong, then, in many admirable qualities. The force of the combination has been greater because of the business habits of the independent body which has opposed it. To the Standard's caution the Oil Regions opposed recklessness; to its economy, extravagance; to its secretiveness, almost blatant frankness; to its far-sightedness, little thought of the morrow; to its closefistedness, a spend thrift generosity; to its selfish unscrupulousness, an almost quixotic love of fair play" (2: 253–54). This, of course, is not a balanced account despite its framing as a concession to Rockefeller's "great," "strong," and "admirable" company. The dichotomously balanced pairings structurally suggest balance, though such balance is undermined by the connotations of the terms associated with Standard. Nonetheless, this passage's structure, swinging rhythm, and location in a chapter on Standard's "legitimate" greatness encapsulate syntactically the larger effect of balance that Tarbell works hard to achieve.

The chapter from which this exemplary moment of "balance" is taken, however, also reveals how such balance points in this period finally toward personal integrity. The implicit moral judgments the passage makes are backed up in this penultimate chapter by Tarbell's careful depiction of herself. She writes, "Something besides illegal advantages has gone into the making of the Standard Oil Trust. Had it possessed only the qualities which the general public has always attributed to it, its overthrow would have come before this" (1: 231). Here she subtly opposes the unbiased professional analysis of a journalist with that of the "general public's" emotional and uninformed one. She does not excuse Standard Oil's actions; however, her criticism, unlike that of the public's, is based on fact, not emotional polemic.

At the same time, she articulates the views of the general public that her professional skill and character dispassionately affirms. Similarly, she deflects any attack on her personal investment in the case against Standard Oil by referring obliquely to her professional skills and character. She writes: "It is not surprising that those who realize the compactness and harmony of the Standard organisation, the ability of its members, the solidity of the qualities governing its operations, are willing to forget its history. Such is the blinding quality of success! . . . They are weary of contention, too—who so unwelcome as an agitator?—and they begin to accept the Standard's explanation that the critics are indeed 'people with a private grievance,' 'moss-backs left behind in the march of progress'" (2: 254). This is a slippery passage, for after all, since Tarbell's family's business was adversely effected by Standard Oil's practices, she could be seen as an "agitator" with "a private grievance." Tarbell counters such arguments by agreeing with them. It is "not surprising" that people succumb to the allure of Standard, and as an expert, she certainly can see that side of the argument as well as the problem with "agitators." Nonetheless, she is a professional and so, unlike many people, is not "willing to forget [Standard's] history" or to misapprehend what is or is not progress. As a fair-minded journalist who has weighed the evidence carefully, she opposes the extremes of public response—either hysteria or private agitation. Her disinterestedness accounts for both and creates a new consensus with which the public can generally agree.

The way Tarbell subtly relies on personal character to enforce her claim to balanced objectivity in the story is thematized more broadly by the concluding chapter of *The History*. In this passionate jeremiad against complacency, Tarbell does not argue for the dismantling of trusts but for more professionalism, which she defines as personal integrity. Invoking the nineteenth-century interpretation of the Civil War as judgment for the sin of the "peculiar institution" of slavery, Tarbell argues that "the people of the United States will pay for their indifference and folly" (284) regarding the "peculiar methods" and "peculiar aids" (274) of Standard Oil. Greater professionalism—comparable to personal integrity—is the solution to the problem of monopoly capitalism: "It is possible," she says, "to be a commercial people [and] a race of gentlemen" (288). The concluding sentences of her series insists on the personal integrity that the text has exemplarily performed: "When the business man who fights to secure special privileges, to crowd his competitor off the track by other than fair competitive methods, receives the same summary disdainful ostracism by his fellows that the doctor or lawyer who is "unprofessional," the athlete who abuses the rules, receives, we shall have gone a long way toward making commerce a fit pursuit for our young men" (2: 292). "Fair" competition, the balanced competition between professionals, refers to their integrity, to their trained sense of personal morality. And with this kind of gentlemanly professionalism, one need not make a distinction between, for example, journalism as a business and journalism as a profession. Personal integrity will solve the conflict between commercialism and professionalism.

As I noted earlier, Tarbell's exposé was a sensation in her time, and, as McClure said, she became "generally esteemed and reverenced."[53] But in the years following the publication of *The History*, Tarbell's reputation began to decline, and now she is known primarily for *The History*, and perhaps among feminists, for her antifeminism. There are, of course, many factors in the decline of her reputation, but I would propose that an important one was how her work staked its objectivity finally on her personal integrity. A part of Tarbell's problem is that she had trained her public to read implicitly for her character, and it was her character, and particularly her character as a "lady," not her arguments, that therefore were scrutinized. For example, in a critical review of Tarbell's flattering biography of the head of U.S. Steel, Elbert H. Gary, a writer for the *Nation* argued that Tarbell had always been rather blindly probusiness. *The History*, he said, was an anomaly in her work explained by her desire for "filial revenge."[54] *The History* is, of course, also probusiness despite the *Nation*'s argument. What is crucial, however, is that Tarbell's work is being criticized in terms of the gendering of her biases. The invalidity of her work is proven by her biography as a daughter. Such a critique makes little sense except in light of her claim to disinterestedness and (gentlemanly) personal integrity.[55] As in Tarbell's own *The Business of Being a Woman*, the *Nation* reads the career woman as far too interested and personal, bent only on protecting her family rather than larger ideals and beliefs. Tarbell's use of professional objectivity is turned against her, and her personal, feminine self-interestedness becomes the site on which the value of her work is debated.

While Cather's articulation of her vocational ideals focuses on literary objectivity, those ideals are shaped by journalistic professionalism. Cather's antifemininity and antifeminism, which also inform her ethnocentrism and racism, are parts of the same attempt to assume and protect a normative white, male professionalism that we saw in Tarbell's *The Business of Being a Woman*. Femininity represents compromised, commercial interestedness, unprotected by impersonal objectivity. This is one reason that in Cather's early years, her angriest literary criticism is directed at women writers who symbolically embody to her the compromised status of any writer or artist in consumer capitalism. At the same time, the personal is what shores up objectivity to Cather. And so, as with

Tarbell, the notion of impersonality, which is meant to foreclose the issue of personal interestedness, ends up focusing our attention on that domain.[56]

Like Tarbell, Cather sees women's greatest gift as that of feeling and emotion, and argues, like Tarbell, that it is precisely this gift that finally compromises women's work. In 1895, Cather writes, "It is a very grave question whether women have any place in poetry at all. Certainly they have only been successful in poetry of the most highly subjective nature. If a woman writes any poetry at all worth reading it must be emotional in the extreme, self-centered, self-absorbed, centrifugal . . . Learning and a wide knowledge of things does not seem to help women poets much. It seems rather to cripple their naturalness . . . Learned literary women have such an unfortunate tendency to instruct the world . . . They must learn abandon . . . A woman can be great only in proportion as God put feeling in her (*WP,* 1: 146).[57]

Like Tarbell on women generally, Cather argues that women writers can be great only if they are their natural emotional selves. At the same time, however, if women produce the "subjective" poetry natural to them and hence "worth reading," such poetry will of course be narcissistic and limited. Similar to Tarbell's analysis of career women, Cather further argues that women who try to escape their personal viewpoint through a trained and impersonal "knowledge of things" are even more problematic than natural women because learned women's subjectivity is translated into didactic moralizing.[58] So, Cather concludes, women are only great if they exploit their God-given subjectivity; however, that subjectivity is precisely what prevents them from being great no matter what they do. As Cather says elsewhere, the irremediable problem with women is that they are "so horribly subjective" (1: 277).

Unsurprisingly, then, and similar to journalists of the time, Cather describes the writing she admires in these early years as objective and impersonal. This objectivity is conceived in a structurally similar way to that of journalistic objectivity. In describing her admiration for Henry James, Cather writes in 1895 that his stories "are sometimes a little hard, always calculating and dispassionate, but they are perfect." Because he is hard and dispassionate, Cather argues, James is the only English-speaking author of the day who is "really an artist." Instead of selling out as other writers have, he is "really keeping his self-respect and striking for perfection" (1: 275). Or, as she writes about James in 1898, "You may not be greatly moved at any time, but the most respectable part of your mentality will be awakened, refreshed, interested, satisfied. You will see a theme perfectly handled, an idea developed with consummate skill and a high artistic conception admirably portrayed" (1: 486).[59] The coldly impersonal represents values beyond the commercial. In coldness lies the purity of aesthetic perfection. Ironically, however, as Cather describes this coldly impersonal ideal, she refers finally to the artist's personality. Objective art makes us think about the artist, about his professional integrity, evidenced by his technical "skill" and "high artistic conception."

In one of Cather's most famous and carefully composed essays on literary aesthetics, objectivity is even more critically anticommercial and, paradoxically, against her assertions to the contrary, even more closely linked to the problematics of journalistic objectivity than in her early work. In her important manifesto "The Novel Demeuble" (1922, 1936), Cather relies on an analogy of the overstuffed Victorian home to describe mass-produced writing and its object-oriented thematics of consumer culture. She specifically attacks "mere verisimilitude" (*NF,* 48), what most people think is "realism" (45), for its unthinking reliance on the materialistic values and temporality of such a culture. Such putative realism, she argues, is as much a manifestation of a commercial society as shopping and journalism, which in this essay are comparable categories. This form of realism "asserts itself in the cataloguing of a great number of material objects" (45) just as "the Woolworth Store windows" are "piled high" with cheap material goods (44). Cather argues that true art cannot be allied with shopping or journalism: "If the novel is a form of imaginative art, it cannot be at the same time a vivid and brilliant form of journalism. Out of the teeming, gleaming stream of the present it must select the eternal material of art. There are hopeful signs that some of the writers are trying to break away from mere verisimilitude, and, following the development of modern painting, to interpret imaginatively the material and social investiture of their characters; to present their scene by suggestion rather than by enumeration. The higher processes of art are all processes of simplification" (40).

While Cather seems to be saying that the artist is an improved journalist and shopper since s-he selects longer-lasting, better-quality events and goods, she is genuinely trying to imagine how the artist could escape consumer culture. The problem is that such escape is difficult to imagine within the logic of her description since she sees the entire culture as pervaded by the values and temporality of consumption. Like the journalists she decries, Cather uses a notion of the skilled professional's personal integrity to theorize escape from such a total system. She asks rhetorically if true realism "is not . . . more than anything else, an attitude of mind on the part of the writer toward his material?" (45). One sees in *The Scarlet Letter,* he says, the "reserved, fastidious hand of an artist, not . . . the gaudy fingers of a showman or the mechanical industry of a department-store window-dresser" (49). In the theories of the journalists we read (and against whom Cather is supposedly posing herself in this essay), impersonal objectivity points to the personal journalist—her-his professional integrity and disinterestedness. Likewise, to Cather, eternal, impersonal art points to the personal author—her-his skilled fastidiousness. Cather's famous statement in this essay that "It is the inexplicable presence of the thing not named . . . that gives high quality to the novel or the drama, as well as to poetry itself" (50) is interesting not just for its reworking of Oscar Wilde but also for its passive construction. The thing is "not named" (by the author), "is created" (50) (by the author), who is in the sentence literally not named but to whose integrity we are nonetheless directed.

The Professor's House (1925) most explicitly of Cather's novels demonstrates how her work is indebted to professional journalism's critique of commercialism and its solution in the ideal of objectivity. More deeply pessimistic than Tarbell's *History*, more ingenuous in its adaptation of the ideal of objectivity, the novel nonetheless subtly insists, as Tarbell's *History* does, on the authority and disinterested integrity of the narrator and narrative above all else. Analysis of Cather's work, and of this novel specifically, often focus on its evasion of categorization, its doubleness, its ambiguity.[60] None of these characteristics are the same rhetorically as "balanced objectivity," but I would argue that in Cather's work they overlap not only as expressions of the conflicts the writer experiences in consumer capitalism but also as attempts at solving those conflicts.

Cather's description of *The Professor's House* the year the novel came out is suggestive for my reading. She writes: "In my book, I tried to make Professor St. Peter's house rather overcrowded and stuffy with new things; American proprieties, clothes, furs, petty ambitions, quivering jealousies—until one got rather stifled. Then I wanted to open the square window and let in the fresh air that blew off the Blue Mesa, and the fine disregard of trivialities which was in Tom Outland's face and in his behavior."[61] As in "The Novel Demeuble," Cather uses the metaphor of the house, no longer the Victorian refuge from the market but rather thoroughly permeated by the detritus of consumer culture, in order to criticize the objects and values of capitalism. Instead of "unfurnishing" that house, however, Cather opens the window to the "fresh air" of Blue Mesa and Tom Outland. Interestingly, though, Cather's metaphor of the open window is not a simple one of corruption versus purity, for if the novel opens up the window, the story remains within the frame of the house. Simple escape is not possible. The image of opening the window yet remaining within the home suggests that Cather narrates a stalemate, a complicated and tense balance between opposed forces.

The world we enter in *The Professor's House* is a fallen one in which everything and everybody seem to have been compromised because of the overarching effects of consumer capitalism. St. Peter's Jewish son-in-law, Marsellus, who has replaced his beloved dead protégé, Tom, emblematizes the commercialism whose corrupting presence invades all spheres of life. There is no ambiguity in the anti-Semitism Cather depends on to portray Marsellus, an anti-Semitism we already saw serving Cather's anticommercialism in "Ardessa." As Marsellus cheerfully admits, he "commercialize[d]" Tom's ideas and has received the "monetary returns . . . [,which are,] of course, large."[62] Particularly damning is Marsellus's unconsciousness of the significance of such an admission. When St. Peter thinks of the ways that Marsellus's entry into his family has "changed and hardened" his wife and daughter, he also acknowledges that "Louie, who had done the damage, had not damaged himself" (*PH*, 157). In the book's logic, the Jew embodies the invasive spirit of commercialism. He cannot be corrupted because he is corruption itself—he has no pride, no standards, no desires outside of commercialized ones. To Marsellus, shopping with women is as valuable and delightful as talking with the great intellectuals of Europe (153–54)—there is no distinction between thought and consumerism, masculinity and femininity. He is the novel's queer character, but his queerness is not associated with the critical and liberatory possibilities of border crossing, but with consumer culture's flattening of important differences and distinctions, its buying and selling of ideas and ideals as well as objects.

While Marsellus emblematizes the total system of consumer capitalism that the novel describes, we are nonetheless continually offered the possibility of opening the window, of finding uncompromised ideas, locations, or moments. Continually the novel suggests that such a discovery has been made by one or another character, but continually it undermines such discoveries.[63] This opening and then shutting down of these windows does not work in a systematic manner but accretively. Just as we are convinced that one character has escaped the total system of consumerism, a detail suggestively outlines her-his self-interestedness. The careful balance Cather establishes between depicting a character's integrity and implying at the same time his or her compromised status points finally toward both the narrator's ascetically disinterested knowledge about all the characters and the narrator's conscientious refusal to insist on one interpretation or the other. Balance thereby transforms the narrator into the central source of ethical authority for the reader, into the only really open window in the novel. To show how this works, I will focus on the pairing of St. Peter and Tom Outland, two characters whose emotional and professional lives are most prominently used to suggest possible qualities of disinterestedness that stand outside consumer capitalism. Despite the suggestion that these two stand outside the market, Cather nonetheless also proposes alternative interpretations to their lives and characters. As a result, the reader cannot finally adjudicate between the interpretive possibilities. Thematically as well as structurally she must look toward the narrator, who lays out the different possibilities with the "reserved, fastidious hand of an artist, not . . . the gaudy fingers of a showman or the mechanical industry of a department-store window-dresser" (*NF*, 41).

Cather subtly and carefully unfolds in the first section, "The Family," a multilayered analysis of St. Peter's emotional life. At one time, his family had apparently been a happy one (*PH*, 121). This is no longer the case. Instead it is now a family divided by competing desires, each member linked to the other only by layers of betrayal. What precipitated the "fall"? To St. Peter it is the innate stupidity or crudeness and hence materialism of his wife and his daughter Rosamond (hardened as they were by the arrival of Marsellus) that makes, as he puts it, Medea's solution to family life seem like the only one (121). While Tom Outland's arrival made "a difference" (44) in his marriage, it did so by simply highlighting the fundamental fault lines. Before Tom arrived, Lillian had been St. Peter's closest companion. He remembers this companionship in coolly evaluative terms. Along with Lillian's "really radiant charm, she had a very interesting mind," or, as he thinks to himself, "it was quite wrong to call it mind—the connotation was false." Rather, he decides, Lillian has "vehement likes and dislikes," "prejudices," and "divinations" (44). But while her emotionalism is somewhat engaging, her "worldliness" (156) is not. In the few moments during their marriage when they were tested by material circumstances, "she became another person, and a bitter one" (255). To St. Peter, Tom allowed him to escape from his companionship with the mildly engaging but finally contemptibly materialistic Lillian into a new love: "Just when the morning brightness of the world was wearing off for him, along came Outland and brought him a second youth" (256).[64] But while St. Peter's interpretation of his contemptibly stupid and materialistic family, and specifically his wife, is the dominant one in the narrative, Cather balances it with highly suggestive and alluring alternative interpretations.

At the opera, for example, Cather suggests that Lillian's stupidity and hardness is a form of self-protection against St. Peter's coolly evaluative scrutiny and rejection of her. Even St. Peter momentarily ceases to scapegoat her in this scene and recognizes "something lonely and forgiving in her voice, something that spoke of an old wound, healed and hardened and hopeless." His response to her forgiveness, however, is to scrupulously avoid touching her, fingering her gloves instead. This gratuitously emphatic rejection makes Lillian's "lip quiver" and literally forces her to look away from him as she has had to throughout her life (88–89). St. Peter's vindictiveness in this scene provides us with the possibility that there is not only another side to the story but also a side that (if our narrator chose) could be elaborated on at length and could undermine what we have learned from St. Peter about his family. This is particularly confirmed by St. Peter's "square-dealing, dependable" (82) daughter, Kathleen. She suggests that St. Peter is profoundly self-interested and that such a quality enables him to betray passively those he loves most—not only Kathleen but even more fundamentally, Tom.[65]

There are, however, not only competing possible interpretations of St. Peter's family life but also competing interpretations of his professional life. At first, it appears that, as opposed to his compromised family life, his work represents impersonal purity and achievement. He has lived in his work life "two lives, both of them very intense" (22)—that of a teacher and that of a writer—and he has done "full justice" (23) to both and therefore gotten "what he wanted" (22). Both his teaching and his writing are described as immutable and timeless in their satisfactions and achievement. His responsiveness to "youth" has been constant, for it has "nothing to do with Time" (22). Similarly, his creative work is described as creating "impersonal emotion" (87), apparently the kind of emotion that is not mutable as his feelings for his family are. Thus, when St. Peter thinks of the high point of his writing life, he thinks of a moment, when alone with an unidentified sea captain, "the design of his book unfolded in the air above him, just as definitely as the mountain ranges themselves." In this moment of aesthetic achievement, it is not the ideas in the book that become clear to him but its design. This design is compared to "inevitable" natural forms, and unlike his family, "the design was sound . . . and it had seen him through" (101).

While the purity and uncompromised satisfaction of St. Peter's professional life seems like a counterweight to his dissatisfying and compromised personal life, Cather provides a totally different interpretation of it as well. From Kathleen's suggestion that he has betrayed those he loves out of self-protection stems the idea that the achievement of his work was not worth the cost of the betrayal. For St. Peter's professional life has, in its turn, been compromised and has compromised him. Symbolic of this is the university for which he works. St. Peter sees himself as having spent his career fighting "the old fight to keep up the standard of scholarship, to prevent the younger professors, who had a sharp eye to their own interests, from farming the whole institution out to athletics, and to the agricultural and commercial schools favored and fostered by the State legislature" (52). Knowledge for knowledge's sake is not the point of the university; rather, "commercialization" (52, 135) is. And St. Peter knows that in his fight against commercialization, he has been "beaten" (52). Likewise, his "creative work" (23) has been commodified. It has earned him the "five thousand pounds, which had built him the new house into which he did not want to move" (27). He resists this commodification of his work by trying to stay in the old house, to regain the "great pleasures [that] don't come so cheap" (27), but the end of the novel makes clear that such retrenchment against change cannot be sustained. St. Peter has just been beaten by the forces of commercialization not only in his personal life but also in his work life.[66]

Like the juxtaposition of work to family life in the first section of the novel, the second section, "Tom Outland's Story," seems, at first, to "open the window" on St. Peter's experiences; however, also like that first juxtaposition, it fails finally to do so. St. Peter links women with domestic or personal betrayal, saying after one buying spree his daughter Rosamond compels him to share with her, "I was thinking . . . about Euripides; how, when he was an old man, he went and lived in a cave by the sea, and it was thought queer, at the time. It seems that houses had become insupportable to him. I wonder whether it was because he had observed women so closely all his life" (152).

Cather's narrative, however, does not fully endorse St. Peter's misogynist view of personal betrayal. The unconventional, all male, homosocial "happy family" (194) of Tom, Roddy, and Henry, with its ideal "housekeeping" (205, 209) on Blue Mesa, is corrupted as easily as the conventional heterosexual one.

The men's desire to find more cliff dwellings—a kind of greed of discovery—leads to Henry's being bitten by a snake and dying, while Tom and Roddy betray each other simultaneously in their different ideas over how to "realize" (243) on their discovery. The story of the brutally murdered, "Mother Eve," further enforces the biblical resonance of the men's experiences on Blue Mesa, showing that temptation and "unfaithful[ness]" (221) inhere in all personal relations. Even in their earliest forms, human society was necessarily fallen.[67] "Primitive" native American life seems to offer yet again the open window, but in the "pure" (206, 239) environment of Blue Mesa, just as in the stifling atmosphere of St. Peter's home, there is, as Father Duchene puts it, "personal tragedy" (221).

Similarly, if the university provides the model for the ways St. Peter's work life is as compromised and compromising as personal life, Tom's work life—even before he invents the Outland vacuum—drives home this point. Particularly, his work life highlights the failure at the center of democratic society. At first, the novel suggests that in the pride of working men for their work and in their solidarity with each other, there is a disinterestedness that transcends consumer culture. The open window of Tom's narrative depends in large part on this suggestion. Tom's first action in this section of the book is to protect the money and life of the careless and seemingly unsympathetic Roddy—whom he barely knows—simply because Roddy is vulnerable. Working men's disinterestedness is further emphasized when Tom tells St. Peter the story of meeting Roddy. Tom lingers not on his own but on Roddy's disinterestedness, and how it embodies a larger quality of his class: "He was the sort of fellow who can do anything for somebody else, and nothing for himself. There are lots like that among working-men. They aren't trained by success to a sort of systematic selfishness" (181). In Tom's narrative, Roddy is the quintessential figure of democracy, genuinely selfless, as are "lots" of "working-men." Roddy is "a conscientious reader of newspapers" who "brooded on the great injustices of the time; the hanging of the anarchists in Chicago . . . and the Dreyfus case" (184). However, Tom's narrative also suggests that the democratic man cannot be trusted. He will sell out the larger nation because of his ignorant and limited selflessness. Roddy reads newspapers and therefore, it is suggested, misunderstands the lesson of modern consumer capitalism, of the mercantile Jew who sells what should never be sold. As Tom says in his argument with Roddy after Roddy has sold the native American artifacts of Blue Mesa to a German, "You've gone and sold your country's secrets, like Dreyfus" (241).

Tom's own disinterestedness, his kindness to Roddy, his anger at Roddy, his contempt for the "vulgar" (202) rabble, and his desire for communal ownership of the Mesa with his fellow countrymen —all suggest that he is a better version of the uncorrupted democratic man than Roddy. Even Tom's belief that the Mesa needs to be analyzed first by "proper specialists" (219) argues for his disinterested love of democracy. Such a view, however, is undermined by

St. Peter's problematic idealization of Tom. Just as Tom at first idealizes Roddy's working-class disinterestedness, so in almost precisely the same language, St. Peter idealizes Tom's "dream of self-sacrificing friendship and disinterested love" that St. Peter thinks Tom shares with the "day labourers" (168), among whom he was raised. St. Peter's analysis of Tom as a "disinterested" working man, however, seems to fail, just as Tom's of Roddy does. We learn from Tom himself that Roddy thinks that their fight "come[s] to money in the end," that Tom's "Fourth-of-July talk" is really a way of saying that Tom believes Roddy has sold Tom's "property" (243-44). And Tom himself realizes that he has betrayed Roddy, using metaphors of buying and selling to describe his actions: "Anyone who requites faith and friendship as I did will have to pay for it. I'm not very sanguine about good fortune for myself. I'll be called to account when I least expect it" (252). And Tom indeed is called to account in the "war to save democracy," a democracy that is so apparently faltering.

The last section of the novel, "The Professor," does not adjudicate between the competing interpretations of either St. Peter or Tom, nor does it shut down the possibility that some individuals do escape the pervasive influence of consumer culture. In the last section of the novel, Augusta—a figure of traditional faith—opens the window in St. Peter's study, saving him from a literal and metaphorical aspyhxiation. This quasi-religious ending has been much debated. I would argue that this debate suggests how the notion of balanced objectivity that inheres in professional journalism coincides with the literary value of ambiguity, for whatever the ending means, Augusta is herself described as a balancing factor. To St. Peter, she is "a corrective, a remedial influence" in his life; she is "the bloomless side of life that he had always run away from" (278). And it is in the balanced and ascetic stoicism that Augusta represents that we are guided as readers away from the plot to the narrator, to the "fastidious hand" that dispassionately shaped its balanced form and content.

The narrative underscores the effect Augusta has through its description of the diary Tom kept at Blue Mesa that St. Peter is editing for publication. St. Peter's description of Tom's diary provides us with the novel's ideal narrative. Tom's diary is impersonal, having "almost nothing about Tom himself" (167) in it, and yet this means that it enables its reader to see him more clearly and deeply than it would otherwise: "To St. Peter, this plain account was almost beautiful, because of the stupidities it avoided and the things it did not say. If words had cost money, Tom couldn't have used them more sparingly. The adjectives were purely descriptive, relating to form and colour, and were used to present the objects under consideration, not the young explorer's emotions. Yet through this austerity one felt the kindling imagination, the ardour and excitement of the boy, like the vibration in a voice when a speaker strives to conceal his emotion by using only conventional phrases" (260).

Tom, like the artist in "The Novel Demeuble," is an improved consumer in his sparing, rather than excessive, use of language. He focuses on objects, but he uses only "pure" words to describe them as objects, concealing, rather than advertising, his emotions about them. This "austerity" guides one away from the corrupted objects and toward the pure and disinterested "imagination" of Tom. Similarly, the novel points us structurally and thematically toward the austere and stoic balancing of conflicting opinion by the narrator. In the end of the novel, what remains for us is to respect a narrative and a narrator that map out with stoic asceticism a balanced account of a world compromised by commercialism. It is a narrative that refuses to invest in any one interested interpretation or another. We have been taught not to rely on St. Peter, Tom, or even Augusta; rather we depend on Cather, who unlike her characters, has stood outside the interested narrative in her balancing of competing accounts and with a "reserved and fastidious hand" disinterestedly presents a fallen world of competing interests.

Both Tarbell's and Cather's work engages itself with a critique of consumer capitalism thematically and formally. Their journalism and fiction narrates the way individual self-interestedness comes to dominate all human interactions within the overarching compulsions of this economic system. Against the subjective self-interest of capitalism they pose their professionalism, but paradoxically such professionalism depends on their personal integrity, on delineating their individual and subjective refusal to be bought. By the logic of their own analysis of the personal as self-interested, they thereby compromise and invalidate their own critiques. More than any of the other women writers I explore in this book, Tarbell and Cather suggest how professionalism for women could as much reinforce the status quo as undermine it. Particularly, their attempt to assume disinterestedness through appeals to a normative white masculinity resulted in their being read even more emphatically as respectively a lady journalist and a queer lady novelist. I do not mean to argue simply that they are to blame for the reduction of their work to the personal, for, given the gendered social and aesthetic politics of their time, this was likely to happen in any case. Nevertheless, their appeal to professionalism helped enforce such reductions.

Their entrenched belief in the ideal of objectivity as their careers wound down makes a particularly depressing spectacle. Two examples will have to suffice, Tarbell's autobiography *All in the Day's Work* (1939) and Cather's novel *Sapphira and the Slave Girl* (1941). Tarbell's autobiography insistently dramatizes her objective impersonality,[68] most strikingly in her description of the way her later work balances out her earlier work. Tarbell explains, for example, how she came to write *New Ideals of Business* (1914), a book which argues that scientific management pays literally and ethically. According to Tarbell, before she wrote this book, she had recorded for the public "the worst conditions" in industrial life[69] (albeit as an objective historian she repeatedly insists, not as a muckraker [*DW*, 241]). Because she has focused on the worst conditions, "My conscience began to trouble me" (280). Under the proddings of her "guilty conscience" (280), Tarbell decides it is her "business as a reporter" "to rake the good earth as well as the noxious," as much her job to "present this side of the picture as to present the other" (280). She favorably compares her desire to balance opposed views with Lincoln Steffens's desire to take a stand. During Steffens's struggle with the issue that "confronted us all—that is, whether we should stick to our profession or become propagandists," Steffens turns to Tarbell and asks, "Should we not make *The American* a socialist organ?" Tarbell says she "flared." "Our only hope for usefulness was keeping our freedom, avoiding dogma, I argued. And that," she concludes with satisfaction, "the *American* continued to do" (298). It is with no apparent irony that a few pages later in the autobiography, Tarbell records how she is forced to quit the *American* when it was sold to Crowell, which wanted a "wholesome . . . commercial success" (300).

If an explicit theme of the autobiography is Tarbell's balanced objectivity, her lack of irony about the selling of the *American* demonstrates that a subtext of her book is how the professional journalist's economic insecurity in consumer capitalism undermines her supposed "freedom" and objectivity. From the description of her birth on the first page to the conclusion of the book, Tarbell records without analyzing how personal and national economic instability shape and constrain individual lives.[70] Her career is narrated as a constant struggle to balance freedom with economic security, a balance that she can achieve only momentarily.[71] It is important to Tarbell to convince her reader that she was never swayed by radicals, conservatives, or her own self-interest; however, she leaves the reader with the impression that while she was never bought by any individual or group per se, she was never free, that to survive she continuously took on projects or joined journals against her free will.[72] Her acknowledgment of how financial insecurity constrained her, as well as her seeming failure to understand this, is dramatically underlined in the end of her autobiography where she discusses her surprise that she continues to work at eighty despite physical and mental exhaustion because "I still [have] security to look after" (*DW*, 398). Objectivity is, as Schudson would say, an ideal in Tarbell's life, an imagined solution to the lived conflicts in her career that constrain her ability to live up to the ideal; it is also an ideal upon whose shoals her work founders in contradiction.

We face a comparable kind of self-annihilating logic in Cather's novel *Sapphira and the Slave Girl*, a novel in which the young Cather is named as a character. This novel clearly rewrites that quintessential sentimental text, Harriet Beecher Stowe's *Uncle Tom's Cabin*. In her critical writings, Cather had repeatedly criticized Stowe, describing her work as the product of the "feminine mind," characterized by its "hankering for hobbies and missions."[73] Central to *Sapphira and the Slave Girl* is Cather's attempt to disrupt Stowe's sentimentalism and her conflation of white women and blacks as transcendent and disinterested Christlike victims of the male market. In Cather's story, power is not associated with white men; rather power is associated almost solely with white women. Images of male castration abound in the novel, set in a town called Capon Springs. Henry Colbert, Sapphira's husband, is a deeply pious but ineffectual and irresolute man who allows himself to be swept along by a stronger (female) will when a moral crisis comes. Sapphira Colbert, by contrast, is coldly calculating, ruthless, and effective. She runs the plantation and controls the slaves' lives, especially manipulating their sexual relations. The action of the book is precipitated by Sapphira's jealousy of a slave girl, Nancy, and Sapphira's attempt to have her nephew rape Nancy. Cather uses Sapphira to suggest, contra Stowe, that white women were not only accessories to white men's rape of black women but also, in their attempt to gain or keep power in a slave economy, were really and symbolically rapists themselves.

Cather's disruption of sentimental notions of white womanhood and its supposedly untroubled alliance with black slaves is powerful and important. However, Cather balances the story of white women's accession to slavery with an account of the virtues of slavery and of white woman's nonculpability that render the novel toothless and confused. While Nancy is forced to flee slavery to escape the rape Sapphira has engineered for her, she nonetheless says, "I don't mind Miss Sapphy's scoldin'. Why, she brought me up, an' now she's sick an' sufferin' . . . I ought-a borne it better," a refrain that is repeated later by Sapphira's daughter who helps Nancy escape and by Sapphira's husband who passively finances the escape.[74] Even slavery itself is suddenly presented at the end of the novel as beneficial. As Henry Colbert puts it, "There are different ways of being good to folks . . . Sometimes keeping people in their place is being good to them" (*SG*, 268), a viewpoint that is rendered conclusive in the novel's epilogue.[75] This suggestion that there are two sides to everything and that the artist must present both and not favor one over the other reveals Cather's continuing link to turn-of-the-century notions of journalistic professionalism. Cather guides us to read, as we did in *The Professor's House*, for the personal integrity of the author who neutrally balances conflicting views of slavery. But more so than even *The Professor's House*, such dogmatically balanced objectivity renders Cather's social criticism incoherent.

While Norris and Santayana used the domesticity-professionalism binary to protect as masculine a professionalism increasingly threatened by its own contradictions, Cather and Tarbell activated it both to protect professionalism and to escape their reduction to a feminized Victorian domesticity. To a degree they succeeded. They authorized their social critiques of corporate and consumer capitalism within the professional logic of journalism, and their work had important results in their time and since. At the same time, however, because Cather and Tarbell argued for the importance of the impersonal even as they depended on the personal and because they aggrandized the normatively white and masculine over the raced and feminine, their works reflexively pointed their readers back to precisely what they were hoping to evade—the personal, feminine, domestic. Going over to the normative white, male standard (to adapt Tarbell's phrase) did not prevent critics from reading Cather's and Tarbell's work reductively. One could argue that whatever Cather and Tarbell wrote would have been read through the lens of the personal because of the dominance of the domesticity-professionalism binary in modern thinking and the way it structurally locates women in the realm of Victorian domesticity. But as I will show in the next chapter on the use of both sides of that binary by Zora Neale Hurston and Ruth Benedict, not only was a more thoughtful use of that binary possible, but also such a use enabled more coherent forms of social analysis and critique.

Chapter 5
Objective Domestic Critique
Anthropology and Social Reform in Ruth Benedict and Zora Neale Hurston

In the last chapter, I showed how Ida Tarbell and Willa Cather rely on contemporary theories of the professional journalist's balanced integrity in a not always successful attempt to stabilize the opposition between Victorian domestic and modern professional culture and relatedly between (interested) subjectivity and (disinterested) objectivity. In this chapter, I turn to two women professionals who, in contrast to Tarbell and Cather, carefully and critically sought to destabilize the binaries of modern professionalism in order to authorize new kinds of professional authority. Ruth Benedict's and Zora Neale Hurston's anthropology and fiction revise the gender and race politics of modernity through a provocative questioning of *and* reliance on domesticity and professionalism, on subjectivity and objectivity. Their work builds on that of predecessors like Jewett, Addams, Hopkins, and Ruffin who in different ways challenged the gendered and racialized discourses of modern professionalism. Benedict and Hurston's work, however, is especially notable for its consciousness of the limitations under which its challenge operates. With historical hindsight, we can nevertheless see how even these women's consciousness is limited in ways not clear to them. Together, Benedict and Hurston demonstrate both the possibilities professionalism provides for relative outsiders to it and the constraints it creates.

I want to begin with a passage from Hurston's work that exemplifies the dynamic this chapter explores. In the Works Progress Administration's funded project, *The Florida Negro* (1938), Hurston writes a fascinating third-person analysis of her own writing. She describes how "Zora Neale Hurston won acclaim for two new things in Negro fiction":[1]

The first was an objective point of view. The subjective view was so universal that it had come to be taken for granted. When her first book, *Jonah's Gourd Vine*, a novel, appeared in 1934, the critics announced across the country, "Here at last is a Negro story without bias. The characters live and move. The story is about Negroes but it could be anybody. It is the first time that a Negro story has been offered without special pleading . . . The author is an artist that will go far." The second element that attracted attention was the telling of the story in the idiom—not the dialect—of the Negro. The Negro's poetical flow of language, his thinking in images and figures was called to the attention of the outside world. It gave verisimilitude to the narrative by stewing the subject in its own juice. (*FMO*, 910)

The contradictory claims Hurston makes here about the objectivity and subjectivity of her writing deserve analysis. On the one hand, Hurston places this evaluation right after a scathing attack on black protest writing, what she calls "Race literature." She poses her work as an antidote to race literature, asserting that "Hurston" writes objectively. She defines an "objective point of view" as one that is unbiased, universal, and therefore also artistic. By contrast, a subjective point of view is implicitly described as didactic, culturally specific, and inartistic. Hurston furthermore links her objectivity to her use of the "idiom" of the Negro, not the "dialect"—dialect being associated apparently with the inartistic depictions of blacks by her literary predecessors.[2] Hurston thus makes objectivity the grounds on which to claim that her fiction is more realistic and hence has more scope and artistry than that of previous writers about race whose work was mired in specificity and "pleading."

On the other hand, if Hurston is asserting a claim that her work provides a new, more authentically objective account of the "Negro," such a claim is undermined by her division of the world into an "outside world" and an inside world, a world of whites and a world of blacks, the latter to which she belongs as a Negro writer. Here, Hurston is claiming the greater truth and authenticity of her work over other writers about black culture because she is an insider and thus knows subjectively the "thinking" of Negroes. She enforces her status as an insider through her use of the colloquial and domestic metaphor of "stewing the subject in its own juice." If, as we saw in the last chapter, subjectivity is anathema to Cather and Tarbell because of its connection to the Victorian past and its feminized, unprofessional, sentimental culture, then Hurston's colloquial metaphor and the claim it undergirds suggest a willingness to claim both authoritative objectivity and subjectivity. She does not hesitate to criticize as well as invoke qualities associated with the degraded narrative forms of the past. What explains her willingness to claim both objectivity and subjectivity, to assert the novelty of her work and yet link it to narrative forms of the past?

At one level, this passage itself provides a provisional answer. Hurston ascribes the contradictory values of objectivity and subjectivity to her audience, the critics of the "outside" world; and indeed, early reviews of Hurston's work claim in the same breath that its significance lies in its unbiased depictions of the Negro and in Hurston herself being a Negro and so able to understand the subjective workings of the Negro mind.[3] Hurston's third-person citation of praise for her work can be read as a canny analysis of and dry commentary on the competing demands the literary market makes on minority intellectuals, demands both to transcend and embody essential difference. Nevertheless, if the literary market provides an answer to why Hurston claims both objectivity and subjectivity, it is only a partially satisfying one. After all, Hurston's views in *The Florida Negro* overlap with her critics' insofar as she poses their positive evaluation of her work against a highly negative account of "race literature." A fuller answer to my question thus requires a more contextualized account of the significance of objectivity and subjectivity to Hurston.

Hurston's seemingly contradictory reliance on claims to objectivity and subjectivity in her fiction and ethnography has, in recent years, become central to debates about her work. At the heart of these disagreements are different convictions about the possibility of escaping professional constraints.[4] Critics have linked the objectivist impulse in Hurston's work to her training in anthropology at Barnard under Franz Boas, but they have disagreed about the significance of that training. Hazel Carby, for example, argues that anthropology provided Hurston with a putatively "scientific objectivity" and a "professional point of view," which became tools "in the creation of her discourse of the rural folk." Such an appropriation of anthropological discourse, Carby argues, represents "'Negroness' as an unchanging, essential entity" and "displace[s] the discourse of a racist social order and maintain[s] the exclusion of the black subject from history."[5] Graciela Hernandez is equally troubled by Hurston's professional training; however, in contrast to Carby, she argues that in her ethnographies Hurston undermines anthropological practice. Through a complex use of self-reflexivity, says Hernandez, Hurston "challenges and debunks a social science paradigm that prizes objectivity as an indicator of 'social truth'." Hernandez argues that Hurston undermines her authority as ethnographer by demonstrating her own inability to capture or contain in writing the power of oral culture.[6]

It is striking, however, that while Carby and Hernandez disagree on whether anthropology constrained Hurston's thinking, like many other critics who have weighed in on this topic, they agree on disciplinarity itself, which they assume is monolithic. Anthropology, in both their accounts, is objectivist, ahistorical, and racist, and Hurston's failure or success is therefore gauged in terms of her ability to distance herself from anthropological paradigms. The problem with such an assumption of disciplinary totality, however, is that U.S. anthropology was not in the least unified as a field during the years when Hurston studied and practiced it. Both Carby's and Hernandez's compelling arguments depend on flattening out the contentious intradisciplinary debates of anthropology during the 1920s and 1930s.[7] As George Stocking has shown, in these years, the aims and status of the discipline were deeply contested by anthropologists themselves. Some of these newly professionalized scholars sought to describe anthropology as an objective science, but many of the most prolific and influential ones—including Franz Boas, Ruth Benedict, Margaret Mead, Robert Redfield, and Edward Sapir—saw anthropology as a humanistic as well as scientific discipline, focused on subjectivity and so necessarily itself subjective.[8] This is not to argue that these anthropologists gave up their belief in or claims to objectivity or that their notions about objectivity and subjectivity were unproblematic. It is to say, however, that their ideas were carefully developed and that Hurston's work responds and contributes to complex debates about these terms within the field.

To reopen the question of Hurston's ideas about objectivity and subjectivity, then, I want to examine Hurston's relation to specific debates in Boasian anthropology of her time rather than to a generalized anthropology imagined as unified. I want to do so by investigating Hurston's relation to a scholar of her own generation, the anthropologist-poet Ruth Benedict. There are good intellectual and biographical reasons for such a shift in focus. Boasian anthropology is generally divided into three stages: (1) the late nineteenth-century critique of evolutionary anthropology, (2) the early twentieth-century study of the geographical distribution of culture elements (historical reconstruction or diffusion), and (3) beginning in 1911, but picking up speed after 1920, a shift from historical study of culture processes to psychological study, what is called culture and personality studies.[9] Benedict and Hurston were students during the third stage, arriving at Columbia and Barnard respectively in 1921 and 1925. Both were unconventional students; they were in their thirties when they began their studies in anthropology with Boas. Their age upon enrollment attests to another similarity between them, namely that both struggled for years to find work that satisfied and interested them, and much of their struggle had to do with the differently limited options available to black and white women at the time.[10]

It is not just the contentious debates within anthropology, however, that we need to keep in mind as we trace out Benedict's and Hurston's ideas about objectivity and subjectivity. It is also important to remember the larger social and political context that shaped those debates. Susan Hegeman has argued that the shift from historical to psychological studies of culture in Boasian anthropology can be seen as a response to what Boas felt was the pressing need for scientists to use their authority to speak out clearly and publicly against the virulent forms of racism and nationalism that emerged during and between the two world wars. In Hegeman's helpful account, Boasian anthropology stabilized itself as a profession by claiming its specialized and neutral knowledge of cultural diversity as well as its "strongly ethical and humanistic respect for the complexity and integrity of cultural others."[11]

This appeal to both scientific and humanistic forms of authority in response to war-time, racism and nationalism has been highly controversial in its time and ours. In its time, it was controversial because it called into question the claims that the "Waspish 'hard'-science establishment" had made about anthropology since the late nineteenth century.[12] By contrast, more recent scholarship argues that culture and personality studies functioned in typically modernist fashion to subordinate circumscribed historical explanations to totalizing and ahistorical ones. They have further asserted that while such studies proposed themselves as relativistic, they were finally culturally absolutist, irrevocably dividing in terms of both time and space the primitive and the civilized, the culturally authentic and the inauthentic.[13] Hegeman, for example, suggests it would have been better if Boasian anthropology had stuck to the path of inductive historical analysis and avoided generalizing polemically about cultural difference, even for ethical and political ends.[14] Without denying the charges against culture and personality studies, I nonetheless will argue that the combination of objective and subjective appeals did not necessarily function to fix cultural differences. In Benedict's and Hurston's most compelling work, such a mixed rhetoric instead enabled these two women to protest against contemporary U.S. social politics, even as they scrutinized the limitations of their claims to both objective and subjective authority. In short, "modernist anthropology" appealed to Benedict and Hurston because they could use it to engage in both social and disciplinary critique for a broad public.[15]

This chapter shows that in the most carefully thought-out work of their mature periods, Benedict and Hurston use ahistorical generalizations about cultural difference as a device to authorize their feminist and antiracist analyses of American society as well as implicitly to interrogate the generalizations upon which their polemics rest. Indeed, these two women subordinated history to psychological accounts of culture in ways that we could call typically modernist. Psychological studies of culture enabled these two women, who studied anthropology relatively late in their lives, to engage in social criticism that escaped the putatively "subjective" moralizing associated with Victorian culture and hence women's intellectual work as well as (especially for Hurston) that of "race literature." They linked their social criticism to the transcendent authority of the profession of anthropology, not to that of a degraded femininity or the feminized other. If this sounds like opportunism, it is also true that Benedict and Hurston recognized the problems in their use of professional discourse and specifically in subordinating history for polemical ends. Because of their focus and their willingness to place subjectivity at the center of human culture, their writings highlighted a historical connection between the modernist professional work they were engaging in and the supposedly feminine forms of subjective social analysis of the past.

Their consciousness of repudiating but also depending on the subjective analysis ascribed historically to women's intellectual work—albeit in a new, "objective" form—is revealed in the metaphors they use about the home and domesticity. For Benedict and Hurston, domesticity represents women's past—a narrow past falsely centered on the purely subjective—and hence they rely on it to represent any historically constrained subjectivity, most particularly any limiting national or group subjectivity. Nonetheless, while they denounce domesticity as professional scientists and artists, they also invoke it to insist on the centrality and power of subjectivity. Crucially, in fact, domesticity represents their belief that finally the one thing that one can examine somewhat impartially—and therefore change—is one's own (inescapably) culturally determined subjectivity. They engage in the paradoxical project of what I will call objective domestic critique—a critique both of women's traditional domesticity and of the nation or group, a critique that cites historical issues but subordinates them to larger polemics. The result is a professional discourse that—through its insistence on the importance of a historical past that it uses, criticizes, *and* dismisses—simultaneously maps out its own limitations in describing the world while nonetheless asserting its ability to create social change.

In order to discuss Benedict's and Hurston's productive dialogue with both the ideas and conventions of Victorian domestic and modern professional culture, this chapter begins by examining their preprofessional responses to the binaries of public and private, objectivity and subjectivity, inherent in the gendered social roles of nineteenth-century domestic ideology and enforced, as I have argued in the last two chapters, by the logic of modern professional discourse. In Benedict's and Hurston's early crises over vocation, there emerges, in different ways, an incipient critique of modern professionalism. Their preprofessional thinking shows that they were troubled by the modernist claim to historical rupture on which much professional discourse relied as well as by the representational politics that inhered in its account of objective and subjective forms of knowledge. The study of anthropology, I argue, helped them to frame their analyses for a broad audience: it provided them with tools with which to criticize clearly and directly race and gender ideology in the U.S., even if they wielded those tools in different ways and to different ends than many of their professional colleagues. I focus on Benedict's *Patterns of Culture* (1934) and Hurston's *Seraph on the Suwanee* (1948) in order to show how they use modernist anthropology to reform ideas about gender, race, and professional knowledge. The paradoxes of "objective domestic critique" enabled Benedict and Hurston to situate themselves in two antithetical traditions and to suggest to a general public the overlapping importance and limitations of each.

I want to emphasize here that this chapter is shaped by its own polemic— that I am focusing specifically on writings by Benedict and Hurston that link the role of public intellectual to the didactic traditions of Victorian social reformist writing and that thereby question the claims of modernist professionalism. While this is my focus, I do not mean to imply that popularizing complex ideas to a broad audience necessarily results in democratic, antiracist, or feminist work. On the contrary, much of Benedict's and Hurston's later work, also written for broad audiences, is characterized by an absence of disciplinary self-critique and hardened analyses of cultural difference.[16] Similarly, I am not arguing here that public intellectuals are somehow more free than academic intellectuals or that the public, however conceived, does not itself construct or constrain its thinkers in certain ways. As I show at the end of the chapter, although both Benedict and Hurston conceived of themselves and were seen by others as public intellectuals, Benedict had more success than Hurston, in part because she was authorized by the academy and in part because racism is not unique either to the academy or to the general public. Nonetheless, I want to show what both Benedict and Hurston were able to achieve by relying on and questioning professional discourse despite the intellectual and practical difficulties they faced and despite their retrenchment in later years to more rigid ideas about their professional authority.

Benedict's and Hurston's writings before they studied anthropology and as they searched for satisfying work attest to the powerful influence that the modernist association of the past with a degraded, premodern domesticity exerted on women intellectuals. In these early writings, Benedict and Hurston appropriate the set of associations typical of modernist professionalism. In very different ways, however, they also begin tentatively to question the gender and race politics that inhere in modernist professionalism. After they study anthropology, they are able to shape their objections about modernist professionalism more clearly and forcefully. And they do so by using the terms of their professionalism, even as they highlight the contradictions of those terms.

Benedict's journal entries before she began studying with Boas record her bitter, decade-long struggle to find a vocation as well as to negotiate the gendered representational politics of modernism. She worked at and (to her mind) failed as a social worker, teacher, wife, and writer. Writing in 1912 on "the Mask" she wears to hide the "real *me*," a person who was, she says "terrorized by loneliness, frozen by a sense of futility" (*AW*, 119), Benedict decides:

So much of the trouble is because I am a woman. To me it seems a very terrible thing to be a woman. There is one crown which perhaps is worth it all—a great love, a quiet home, and children. We all know that is all that is worth while, and yet we must peg away, showing off our wares on the market if we have money, or manufacturing careers for ourselves if we haven't. We have not the motive to prepare ourselves for a "life-work" of teaching, of social work—we know that we would lay it down with hallelujah in the height of our success, to make a home for the right man. . . . It is all so cruelly wasteful. There are so few ways in which we can compete with men—surely not in teaching or in social work. If we are not to have the chance to fulfil [*sic*] our one potentiality—the power of loving—why were we not born men? (120)

These themes of the division of market and home, men's world of work and women's of feeling and emotion, men's and women's essential skills and abilities, women's natural inferiority and inability to compete in the work world—including the realms of teaching and social work supposedly best suited to them—are repeated frequently in her journals from 1912 until the early 1920s (114, 130–31, 145–47). In a logic that highlights the overlap of Victorian and modern ideology, the only sphere in which women can succeed, in Benedict's view, is that of the affections and emotions. She struggles mightily, therefore, to justify their value. Writing in 1913, after becoming engaged to Stanley Benedict, she says: "We turn in our sleep and groan because we are parasites—we women—because we produce nothing, say nothing, find our whole world in the love of a man.—For shame! We are become the veriest Philistines—in this matter of woman's sphere.... In general,—a woman has one supreme power—to love. If we are to arrive at any blytheness [sic] in facing life, we must have faith to believe that it is in exercising this gift ... in living it out to its fullest that she achieves herself, that she "justifies her existence" (130). Benedict's conflicts are evident in this passage. On the one hand, she demonstrates she is well read in modernist debates of the time that argued that the Victorian domestic woman was a parasite who lived off the wealth her husband produced.[17] On the other hand, Benedict objects to the assumptions about women that inform such a notion of her parasitism. And her objection is phrased in traditionally Victorian terms. Only a philistine, one who appraises things in terms of their market value, Benedict argues, would see woman's work in the home as parasitism.

So throughout Benedict's early journals, we find her working hard to justify the immaterial value of the emotions and of subjectivity. As late as the 1920s, for example, she is still writing, "The emotional part of woman's life—that part which makes her a woman—must be brought up out of the dark and allowed to put forth its best.... [T]he high goal remains an inward affair, a matter of attitude" (146). Because Benedict's later writings consistently refute any notion of biological essentialism, some scholars have insisted that Benedict broke with Victorian ideas of womanhood after she studied anthropology.[18] But there is something more complex happening in both these early writings and her later ones. While she is wrestling with Victorian gender roles here, she is also explicitly resisting modernist assumptions about a rupture with the Victorian past and its concomitant degradation of femininity, domesticity, and subjectivity.[19] These early writings by Benedict, disturbing as they sometimes are, nonetheless suggest that she saw that problems inhered for women as much in the ahistoricism of modern ideas as they did in Victorian ideas about domesticity.

The written records of Hurston's years before she began studying anthropology are not as extensive as those we have for Benedict. She too struggled to find a vocation but in a quite different way than Benedict. Benedict's background was middle class, and she worked in middle-class women's professions until she married. After her marriage, she was supported financially, if not emotionally, by her husband. By contrast, Hurston was forced to provide for herself from the age of fourteen when she left her father and stepmother's home. She held a variety of temporary jobs on the fringes of the economic system, from maid to manicurist, struggling against enormous odds to obtain an education. Nonetheless, Hurston's early published stories suggest that as she searched for a vocation, she was, like Benedict, struggling with both Victorian and modern ideas. Unlike Benedict, however, Hurston far more explicitly breaks with the Victorian past and what she associates with it—namely, the constrictions and limitations of an immanent femininity and black rural life. Her early stories assume the necessity of extricating oneself from both domesticity and provincial black life in order to reach what she calls "the horizon," a transcendent, free world beyond history.[20] What is interesting about these early stories, however, is that while they reject domesticity and rural folk culture in a conventionally modernist fashion, they also seem to recognize that there is a troubling politics to such rejections. These stories insist that to be free, an individual must break from the constricting past, but they also suggest that a clean break may not really be possible. The stage is set in Hurston's preprofessional work, though in a different manner than in Benedict's, for a rethinking of the degraded status of qualities associated with the past (in Hurston's case, provincialism as well as domesticity and subjectivity), a rethinking that anthropology helped her to solidify.

In "John Redding Goes to Sea" (May 1921), John dreams as a child of "riding away to the horizon" on the river near his house.[21] His father, who has been thwarted in the same desire, encourages John, saying "It jes' comes natcheral fuh er man tuh travel. . . . He kain't help wantin' tuh go cause he's a man chile" (*CS*, 4). However, women and domesticity are "weeds" in the river that "tangle up" (2) men. First, John's mother discourages him, seeing his desire for the horizon as the result of "conjuration" (7). She even threatens to curse him if he leaves home. And then, when John impulsively marries, his wife joins in arms with his mother, carrying on "an effective war against him" (7). The curse, or "conjuration," that really tangles him up and finally dooms him, therefore, as it doomed his father, is that of domesticity and its emotional superstitions. Neither John nor his father believe he has been conjured, and to signify John's freedom from such provincialism, he is the only nonwhite character who does not speak in dialect. It is only after he drowns that John can escape the curse of the domestic, provincial, emotive world and travel down the river to the sea. And even then, his father has to prevent John's mother and wife from dragging his corpse back to the shore.

While this story fits into the tradition of male modernist rebellion against a past signified by feminized domesticity, it is also true that John's mother's and wife's fears are ambiguously justified by the story's conclusion. John's voyage to the horizon—and to his death—is precipitated when a white man offers him money to shore up a collapsing bridge. John is not conjured in the manner his mother and wife imagine he is, by a member of the community, but rather by someone and something described as exterior to that community. So if the story is deeply critical of John's wife and mother and how a feminized, provincial black culture "tangles up" the aspirations of its horizon-bound intellectuals, it also suggests that the escape John imagines can come only at great cost—namely, the loss of the self, which is rooted in community. It is a double bind: as John goes to see the horizon, he becomes unrooted and untangled; he goes to sea as a dead man.[22]

In "Drenched in Light" (1924), the dynamics of "John Redding Goes to Sea" are repeated, though with striking modifications and complications. Here modernity and the horizon are not associated with masculinity but with an ambivalently described, antidomestic, white femininity. The young heroine, Isis Watts, dreams of escaping from domesticity and provincial life to an unconstricted world beyond the one in which she lives. At the same time, however, and in a more densely theorized fashion than in "John Redding," that escape involves a troubling financial transaction. "Drenched in Light" came out in 1924, the year before Hurston began to attend Barnard under the sponsorship of Annie Nathan Meyer. The story attests to the mixed feelings of many Harlem Renaissance intellectuals about the freedom that sponsorship enabled as well as the betrayals and constraints it entailed. Like John, Isis wants to escape to the "horizon" (*CS*, 19). Her favorite spot is "the gate post," where she sits, looking "yearningly up the gleaming shell road" (17). But her grandmother perpetually chases her from the perch because she is "too 'oomanish jumpin' up in everybody's face dat pass" (17). Isis's grandmother works to crush Isis's assertive (" 'oomanish") desire for the horizon, restricting her actions in a variety of ways: "Now there are certain things that Grandma Potts felt no one of this female persuasion should do—one was to sit with the knees separated, "settin' brazen" she called it; another was whistling, another playing with boys, neither must a lady cross her legs (19). The narrator's description of gender as a "persuasion" and the random list of actions forbidden to those of the "female persuasion," the fact that Grandma must continually threaten and punish Isis, and even Grandma's "straggling beard" (20) suggest that femininity is a construct—one that constricts the individual.

Isis—the goddess of fecundity—is rescued by a white fairy godmother, who comes from the road and listens to Isis talk about "her trips to the horizon" (23). In the story's denouement, the free, wealthy, but melancholy and desexualized white woman (she is accompanied by "indifferent men" [23]) upsets Grandma's attempt to construct Isis as a member of the "female persuasion." The white woman symbolically purchases Isis from her grandma so as to obtain Isis's "sunshine" (25). Meanwhile, Grandma is transformed in the transaction. Cowed from her usually powerful vociferousness, she humbly lets Isis head down the road to the horizon with the white woman: "Oh, yessum, yessum. . . . Everything's alright, sho' she kin go [with you], yessum," says Grandma (23). Isis is also transformed, seeing this transaction as an acknowledgment of her individuality: "Isis for the first time in her life felt herself appreciated and danced up and down in an ecstasy of joy for a minute" (25). Isis is placed disturbingly in this story between what seems to be the oppressive gender roles deployed by a black mother and the purchasing power of a sexless white woman; however, her position is nonetheless figured as allowing her to achieve an escape to the horizon, an escape she celebrates. If we think about this story as a gloss on the issue of white sponsorship of black artists, it contains the optimistic belief that the individual can simply escape the determination of both the past and the present. At the same time, it uneasily invokes the history of slavery, of blacks sold to whites, of children taken from parents. Sponsorship is, of course, different than slavery, but Hurston nonetheless depicts its disturbing associations with that past.

In these early writings by Benedict and Hurston, then, we see how modernity's theory of rupture exerts an undeniable gravitational pull on these two women intellectuals. But Benedict and Hurston imagine and respond to that pull in somewhat different ways. In these early years, Benedict tries to undermine the notion of rupture by anxiously justifying the ideas that constitute Victorian culture. Hurston, by contrast, criticizes domesticity and provincial culture in no uncertain terms. She imagines a transcendent escape from the messy past, but she does so with an uneasy recognition of what transcendence might really involve. Anthropology, I would argue, enabled Benedict and Hurston to articulate their struggles with Victorian and modern ideas more clearly and to synthesize their analysis of those struggles into their work and specifically into their ideas about objectivity and subjectivity. Anthropology provided them with a professional authority with which to criticize American society and the limitations it placed on women and ethnic or racial others. At the same time, as their preprofessional work shows, they were wary of how modernist forms of authority reproduced the limitations of the larger society. They therefore activated their complex loyalties to the degraded past so as to undermine the assumptions of modernity. In short, they aligned their anthropological work to forms of social criticism from the past that called modernist discourse into question. *Patterns of Culture* and *Seraph on the Suwanee* demonstrate this dynamic for us.

Benedict first achieved national fame with *Patterns of Culture*. The book is equally a manifesto for culture and personality studies within anthropology and an occasion for Benedict to define and describe anthropology for a popular audience.[23] To Benedict, the shift in anthropology from historical reconstruction to psychological studies of culture enables an examination of the discipline itself, for such a shift forces the anthropologist and "his"[24] audience to understand the subjective basis of what they know about themselves and other cultures; they can, therefore, criticize the culture that creates their subjectivity. In other words, the anthropologist works to provide his audience with the tools that would denaturalize their assumptions, and thereby promote self-critique, at the same time that he establishes the basis for a critique of his own authority.

Benedict's polemic appears early on in the book:

> The diversity of cultures can be endlessly documented.... Traits having no intrinsic relation one with the other, and historically independent, merge and become inextricable, providing the occasion for behaviour that has no counterpart in regions that do not make these identifications... The diversity of custom in the world is not, however, a matter which we can only helplessly chronicle.... The significance of cultural behaviour is not exhausted when we have clearly understood that it is local and man-made and hugely variable. It tends also to be integrated. A culture, like an individual, is a more or less consistent pattern of thought and action. Within each culture there come into being characteristic purposes not necessarily shared by other types of society.[25]

Benedict points out the importance of historical reconstruction in anthropology while asserting that its endless tracing out of "diversity" presents an analytical dead end. She has subsequently been heavily criticized both for giving up historical analysis and for being an absolute cultural relativist, but in *Patterns of Culture* she consistently argues that historical reconstruction presents the dead end of absolute cultural relativism itself in which we "helplessly chronicle" cultural histories and differences to no purpose.[26] In contrast to historical reconstruction, she argues, integration allows us to examine a culture in the way we examine an individual so that we see its "consistent" and "characteristic" behaviors, its subjective values, or "emotional and intellectual mainsprings" (*PC*, 46).[27] While such an examination promotes cultural relativism, she insists, it does not lead to absolute relativity: "The recognition of cultural relativity carries with it its own values, which need not be those of the absolutist philosophies" (277). Her argument suggests that we need to represent a culture as a whole—albeit in a provisional fashion—so that we can engage in a value driven, if nonabsolutist, examination of it.

Benedict's metaphor of a culture being integrated like an individual, however, involves two important assumptions. First, she assumes that culture is grounded in subjectivity or emotion. She personifies cultures, arguing that they gain their personalities through their "selection" of the characteristics that suit them best from "the great arc of potential human purposes and motivations" (237). What defines a culture is not so much its individual features but the subjective choices it makes and the form that integrates it: "Without selection no culture could even achieve intelligibility, and the intentions it selects and makes its own are a much more important matter than the particular detail of technology or the marriage formality that it also selects in similar fashion" (237). As Elvin Hatch says, "Like Boas, Benedict was tacitly proposing that reason is subordinate and in a sense epiphenomenal to emotion, for reason is thoroughly distorted by emotional bias."[28] This is a crucial assumption to keep in mind concerning Benedict's claims about the anthropologist's objectivity. Second and more problematically, Benedict assumes that given the subjective ground of cultures (and individuals), they must therefore be integrated: wholes with "consistent" behaviors. This is central to Benedict's thinking, so we need to explore it in more depth.

What authorizes Benedict to make this second, disturbingly holistic assumption about culture? What authorizes her in *Patterns of Culture* to label the Pueblo Indian culture as Apollonian, the Plains as Dionysian, the Dobu as paranoid, and the Kwakiutl as megalomaniac? The anthropologist's authority to describe and denominate other cultures is an issue that obsesses Benedict not only here but in almost all of her texts. Repeatedly, she begins her books with throat-clearing definitions of the anthropologist.[29] *Patterns of Culture*, for example, opens with what seems to be a standard account of the anthropologist as an objective analyst of culture: "To the anthropologist, our customs and those of a New Guinea tribe are two possible social schemes for dealing with a common problem, and in so far as he remains an anthropologist he is bound to avoid any weighting of one in favour of the other. He is interested in human behaviour, not as it is shaped by one tradition, our own, but as it has been shaped by any tradition whatsoever" (*PC*, 1). This description poses the anthropologist as objective, insisting as it does that the anthropologist is unbiased and will not favor his own customs over others. Just a few pages later, however, Benedict argues that the problem of "custom" renders the anthropologist's authority more complicated than she has originally suggested. The perspective of all Westerners has been shaped by what Benedict calls the "historical accident" of Western imperialism, which "has given to our culture a massive universality that we have long ceased to account for historically, and which we read off rather as necessary and inevitable" (6). The assumption of "massive universality" (6), she goes on to explain, afflicts particularly the professional social scientist; in fact, imperialism's effect upon social scientists, she argues, is "a difficulty harder to surmount" (9) than that upon lay people. "Custom," she writes, "did not challenge the attention of social theorists because it was the very stuff of their own thinking: it was the lens without which they could not see at all" (9). This analysis of the social scientist's thinking and perspective as inextricable from the "historical accident" of Western imperialism cannot help but serve to limit the authority Benedict has claimed in describing Pueblo, Plains, Dobu, and Kwakiutl culture.

This is not to say, however, that Benedict simply gives up the possibility of achieving objectivity. On the contrary, she continues to assert the anthropologist's objectivity, but her definition is layered. For example, toward the end of *Patterns of Culture*, she makes the standard Boasian claim that the inductive method leads to objective, scientific truth: "The fieldworker must be faithfully objective. He must chronicle all the relevant behaviour, taking care not to select according to any challenging hypothesis the facts that will fit a thesis" (229).[30] However, she instantly complicates even that muted claim to objectivity: "In theoretical discussions of culture, also, generalizations about the integration of culture will be empty in proportion as they are dogmatic and universalized" (*PC*, 229). To Benedict, objectivity can be achieved only through a rigorously inductive approach, but even so, only flexible and partial truths will be discovered. "It would be absurd," she writes in an apparently critical reference to how her own book could be read, "to cut every culture down to the Procrustean bed of some catchword characterization" (228). The anthropologist's objective knowledge, in brief, is absolutely contingent, his claims circumscribed in similar ways to subjective forms of knowledge. As Richard Handler says, *Patterns of Culture* comes to imply "the impossibility of objective descriptions of individual cultures—or, more precisely of descriptions constructed by an observer occupying neutral ground."[31]

Despite this circumscribed notion of scientific objectivity, however, in the last chapter of the book, "The Individual and the Pattern of Culture," Benedict proposes what anthropological "objectivity" can authoritatively do. Benedict opens the last chapter with the salvo that "One of the most misleading misconceptions" resulting from "nineteenth-century dualism" is the idea that "society and [the] individual are . . . antagonists" (*PC*, 251). Here she refers at least in part to domestic ideology, in which the public sphere of the corrupt market is seen as ruthlessly opposed to the private sphere of emotions.[32] "The problem of the individual," she writes, "is not clarified by stressing the antagonism between culture and the individual, but by stressing their mutual reinforcement" (*PC*, 253). This does not mean, however, that all individuals "find [their society] equally congenial" (255). An integrated culture produces both what is seen as normal and what is seen as abnormal, though it always subordinates the abnormal to the normal (254–70). Such integration leads to "very high prices . . . in terms of human suffering and frustration" (272). The "alienation" of "our psychopaths," she says dryly, "can often be more intelligently handled than by insisting that they adopt the modes that are alien to them" (272). The very dissonance between the "our" and the "they" in this passage emphasizes her point that integration creates a self and an other.

This critique of integration, in which the psychopath is in fact a product of our culture, leads directly into her satirical critique of American society. Throughout the text, she has implicitly (and sometimes explicitly) compared Pueblo, Plains, Dobu, and Kwakiutl cultural integration to that in the United States.[33] In the last chapters of her book, Benedict uses mainstream U.S. culture as exemplary of the worst possible kind of integration. In the U.S., whose representative pattern is, she writes, "Middletown," "Eccentricity is more feared than parasitism. Every sacrifice of time and tranquillity is made in order that no one in the family may have any taint of nonconformity attached to him" (*PC,* 273). Such integration exacts a "staggering" "psychopathic toll" (273); the absolutism of integration in the U.S. produces a psychopathology seen as the norm. As Benedict criticizes U.S. cultural integration, she simultaneously retheorizes anthropological knowledge. While anthropology cannot necessarily provide us with a reliable understanding of others (in part because of our own historically shaped subjective proclivities), she makes clear in these last chapters that it can provide us with the tools to begin to understand our own culture's integration and how it shapes us.

A crucial metaphor sums up her critique of integration and anthropological authority as well as her idea about their uses: "There is . . . one difficult exercise to which we may accustom ourselves as we become increasingly culture-conscious. We may train ourselves to pass judgment upon the dominant traits of our own civilization. It is difficult enough for anyone brought up under their power to recognize them. It is still more difficult to discount, upon necessity, our predilection for them. They are as familiar as an old loved homestead. Any world in which they do not appear seems to us cheerless and untenable" (249). Benedict's use of the domestic metaphor of the old homestead enables her to combine the professional social scientist's critique of cultural integration with a feminist's critique of Victorian domesticity. At the same time, however, the "old homestead," denominates the powerful locus of our emotions as well as the primacy of subjectivity itself, of the way we are attached emotionally to the customs and conventions of our culture. But most crucially, the metaphor, while insisting on the historical power of integration and on the primacy of emotion, imagines an escape from a culture's integration (described as the domestic) through a provisional containment of it within certain borders that then can become an object of critique. Escape from the old homestead would involve continual critique of that homestead, a ceaseless denaturalizing of subjective preferences that would disrupt the self's cultural integration. What anthropology enables is the critique of the domestic self, the individual's historically and culturally based subjectivity, through anthropology's objective (in other words, provisional) knowledge of the world outside.[34]

But if the objective (provisional) knowledge, provided by the anthropologist, enables us to criticize the powerful old homestead, this is a somewhat paradoxical analysis. While objectivity enables us to analyze our own cultural biases, its final aim is to help us "pass judgment" upon those biases. In other words, its task is analysis, but more particularly critique and reform. Richard Handler notes the continuity here between Benedict's ideas and those of Victorian domestic discourse. He says that Benedict saw anthropology as working to "enlighten a broad public facing, during Depression and world war, the task of constructing a more rational and humane social order" and thus that "despite her earlier aspiration to escape women's committees and the associated social services they offered, she never renounced 'service' as an important responsibility. Now, however, woman's duty had been replaced by that of the scientist."[35] Handler's analysis is helpful; however, what is going on in Benedict's work is less a replacement than a tense and conflicted layering of the two in relation to each other so that "woman's duty" calls into question the role of "the scientist" and vice versa.

During World War II and in the years afterward, Benedict asserted even more adamantly than in her prewar writings that the anthropologist's role was to enable a kind of collective form of objective domestic critique. Like Boas, she saw the war as the culmination of Western racism, a racism she describes not only as modern but as the central feature of the modern.[36] In the struggle against modern racism and nationalism, she argues, anthropology must play a central role. She therefore continues to describe domesticity as the central object of anthropological study and at the center of world politics. In the article "Anthropology in Your Life" in the May 1947 *Vassar Alumnae*, for example, she writes:

> Women are particularly fitted to further international and minority understanding by paying attention to *people*. Of course, figures on economic output and on national expenditures and on birthrate—which rate high in discussions of different countries—are of great value, but they are truly important only as one sees how they affect people's habits and values. Women find it easier to see this than most men do, and they are less inclined to label as trivia the details of the daily round of living. . . . It is in the home where every generation first learns the accepted ways of authoritarianism and egalitarianism, and the sanctions that are used for ensuring proper behavior. This is a sphere where women have reason to be good judges; they are sensitive to different ways of handling children. By capitalizing on this understanding women have contributed much to professional anthropology, and it is certainly one of the ways in which they can contribute to the kind of understanding upon which it will be possible to build One World.[37]

Benedict resuscitates here the separation of domesticity and professionalism, women's and men's spheres, objective and subjective forms of knowledge; and she does so in a fashion that can be read as flattering her presumably all-female audience. The sly feminist critique of domesticity that was evident in *Patterns of Culture* has disappeared, replaced apparently by postwar social conservatism. Nonetheless, even here Benedict insists on linking the modernist binaries of the domestic and the professional in ways that force her audience to rethink the relative value and meaning of each. She argues that although the domestic and subjective are labeled as "trivia," they are more important than the numerical facts of "economic output." She furthermore asserts that domesticity creates techniques of study for anthropology—even the central paradigm the discipline relies on—namely, objective domestic critique. Women's domestic analysis of the "details of the daily round of living," Benedict asserts, has "contributed much to professional anthropology." While Benedict's use of domesticity here is less sarcastic and critical than in *Patterns of Culture*, she nonetheless suggests how it can help to dismantle the problematic assumptions at the heart of modern professionalism, a dismantling that makes both domesticity and professionalism look strikingly different.

One of Hurston's most famous statements about the effect of anthropology upon her occurs in *Mules and Men*. She writes:

I was glad when somebody told me, "You may go and collect Negro folklore." In a way it would not be a new experience for me. When I pitched headforemost into the world I landed in the crib of negroism. From the earliest rocking of my cradle, I had known about the capers Brer Rabbit is apt to cut and what the Squinch Owl says from the house top. But it was fitting me like a tight chemise. I couldn't see it for wearing it. It was only when I was off in college, away from my native surroundings, that I could see myself like somebody else and stand off and look at my garment. Then I had to have the spy-glass of anthropology to look through at that.[38]

This dense and deceptively casual analysis of Hurston's relation to anthropology has been interpreted in a number of ways. As Graciela Hernandez has pointed out, the "spy-glass" metaphor can be read as a critique of the violence anthropology inflicts on its subjects through objectification.[39] Along with the critique of anthropology's objective stance, however, there is an analysis of what that stance provides Hurston. First, it denaturalizes the relation between biology and culture. While she is born "in the crib of negroism," negroism is a "garment" that can be taken on and off, a kind of clothing that one does not see because one is "wearing" it, not because one is innately it. Equally important for my argument, however, the specific garment she is wearing is a "tight chemise," suggesting in a similar fashion to "John Redding Goes to Sea" and "Drenched in Light" that to Hurston the racialized femininity assigned to her constricts movement. The "spy-glass of anthropology" reveals the culture's construct of race and gender and enables Hurston to stand apart from and examine the "tight chemise" they create and specifically to examine the chemise she herself wears. In other words, the constrictions of culture, figured as raced and gendered constrictions, deserve scrutiny and self-scrutiny, though the violent, objectivist "spy-glass of anthropology" may be an imperfect means to do so.

Anthropology helped Hurston articulate her complex loyalties to what is figured in much modernist work as the past and the domestic, subjective, and provincial. As a result, like Benedict, culture and personality studies provide important tools for Hurston's work. To begin with, for Hurston, as for Benedict, history is the basis of culture. Finally, however, because she is interested in domestic critique rather than precisely mapping out influence, what she focuses on is cultural integration. In her most explicit statement of cultural theory, *The Florida Negro* (1938), Hurston posits a model of integration much like Benedict's in *Patterns of Culture*:

In folklore, as in everything else that people create, the world is a great, big, old serving platter, and all the local places are like eating-plates. Whatever is on the plate must come out of the platter, but each plate has a flavor of its own because the people take the universal stuff and season it to suit themselves on the plate. And this local flavor is what is known as originality. So when we speak of Florida folklore, we are talking about that Florida flavor that the story—and song-makers have given to the great mass of material that has accumulated in this sort of culture delta. And Florida *is* lush in material because the state attracts such a variety of workers to its industries. (*FMO*, 875)

Florida's "lush" folklore is the result of historical conditions that enabled the intermixing of the cultures of "a variety of workers" in one "local" place. What is significant to Hurston, however, is the way Floridians have flavored their "plate . . . to suit themselves." Active choices based on subjective preferences have led to an integrated culture so that "we [can] speak of Florida folklore" and a "Florida flavor." The importance of subjectivity in this process is underlined by the use of the domestic metaphor of cooking, of seasoning food to suit oneself.

As with Benedict, cultural integration is useful conceptually to Hurston because it enables her to engage in analysis and critique of what she identifies as different kinds of cultural unity. So in *The Florida Negro*, she uses the notion of cultural integration to praise black Floridian culture but also to criticize what she sees as elite national black culture, a critique that she frames through the discourse of anthropology. In the final chapter of *The Florida Negro*, "Art and Such," she begins with a slippery opening salvo, "When the scope of American art is viewed as a whole, the contributions of the Negro are found to be small, if we exclude the anonymous folk creations of music tales and dances" (905). Her point is that we need to include "anonymous folk creations" in our accounts of "American art," but that " 'Race' Men or Women" (906), who have worked to unify black culture, have not allowed such folk art to be recognized as art. She acknowledges that the "tragic pose" (907) and "resent[ful] attitude" (908) of elite national black culture has its roots in history and that it was an important first expression of a silenced people. She insists, however, that this understandable response to historical conditions has become too standardized: "The great Frederick Douglass was the original pattern, no doubt," Hurston writes, using a favorite term of Benedict's, "for these people who went up and down the land making speeches so fixed in type as to become a folk pattern. But Douglass had the combination of a great cause and the propitious moment as a setting for his talents. . . . These others had the wish to be heard and a set of phrases" (906).[40] While the cultural pattern that the "great" Douglass created supported a "great cause," the "original pattern" is now used only in self-serving ways.

Using the idea of elite black culture's integration around dominant patterns, Hurston argues that a central problem with such a pattern is that it enforces clichés and so is ineffectual. The race men and women "want to hear the same thing over and over again even though they already know it by heart, and [it is] certain to be unread by everybody else. It is the same thing as waving the American flag in a poorly constructed play" (*FMO*, 908–9). It is not only that the already memorized critiques of American society promulgated by race leaders bother Hurston but also that they are comparable cultural patterns to the similarly unexamined ones of American nationalism and ethnocentrism. Such clichéd analyses, like those of American nationalism, do no useful work since they remain unread "by everybody" except the race leaders themselves.

Against the richness and appeal of black local Floridian folk culture, Hurston poses black national cultural integration and finds it historically explicable but nevertheless useless.

Hurston's writings, then, involve the subordination of history to integration so that she can engage in objective domestic critique of such integration. In the case of *The Florida Negro,* Hurston seeks to analyze and criticize how black national culture is integrated, even as she praises the way local black Floridian culture is integrated. In Hurston's work, integration becomes an important narrative device that mutes any historical analysis so that she can engage in social analysis—both celebratory and critical. This is evident in her most famous novels and ethnographies.[41] Hurston's subordination of history to integration, of course, has been one of the most controversial features of her work for critics from Richard Wright onward. Since Hurston tended to downplay historical issues in her work, she has been faulted for playing into the generalized stereotypes of white racism, for underplaying the power of that racism, and for essentializing race.

At a risky moment in her career, Hurston seems to have decided to respond to those objections to her work by changing her focus from how black southern culture is integrated to how white southern culture is. *Seraph on the Suwanee* highlights with particular clarity the difficulties critics have had with Hurston's work generally. Those who have praised *Seraph* as a feminist narrative or as a comic novel have willfully shut their eyes to its equally profound misogyny and the deeply problematic nature of its humor. Its seeming reliance on stereotypes about black and white, upper and lower class, men and women has been discreetly ignored, dismissed, or seen as signaling the demise of Hurston's artistry.[42] I would argue, however, that the weaknesses as well as the strengths of the book highlight for us what Hurston saw anthropological discourse as enabling her to do both thematically and formally: to use the idea of cultural integration as a fictional device to denaturalize and objectively criticize for a broad public the formations of race and gender in U.S. culture, even as she acknowledges the centrality of subjectivity to such a project of critique. In *Seraph,* she engages in the paradoxical project of objective domestic critique—but this time focusing on white rather than black southern culture.

At its simplest level, the novel depicts the twenty years of conflict in the marriage of Arvay Henson and Jim Meserve, culminating in their separation and then reconciliation. But the book is also Hurston's most extended analysis and critique of the psychology of white culture and racism. Hurston wanted a broad audience for the novel, and she worked hard to make it appeal to Hollywood.[43] It is therefore a story shaped to fit contemporary narratives about female masochism and the virtues of women subordinating themselves to men.[44] However, both its use of gender melodrama and its insistence that Arvay must, so to speak, pull herself up by her own critique, enable Hurston not only to criticize white America but also to pose that critique as objective, a critique in which the white female self (not the black woman author) discovers its own limitations.[45] Hurston does not need to be explicit about her critique of racist white culture and women's role in that culture, for her white heroine discovers the need for change, not through societal conflict but through the failure of her marriage. Hurston takes enormous risks in the novel as she attempts to appeal to a broad audience. In relying on conventional narratives of the time about gender and race, in relying on her white heroine to discover the problems of racist white culture in her own limited fashion, Hurston's critique could be read as too muted to be of use. Nevertheless, her criticism does succeed, but it does so in uneven and surprising ways.

The novel begins with Hurston's famous technique of multivoiced narration in which the separate voices of the narrator, the townspeople of Sawley, and the central characters interrupt, blend together, and contradict each other. Two voices are most closely linked to each other, however, and are given authority and analytical power: the narrator and Jim Meserve, the latter who has only recently arrived in Sawley. The narrator emphasizes the impoverishment—material, moral, and intellectual—of Sawley, the town into which the heroine, Arvay Henson, is born. The town knows little of its past, little of the world outside, and hence has little understanding of itself. The narrator proposes that the town is integrated by impoverishment, an idea emphasized by the repeated use of the word "few": "[F]ew of these fields [around the town] were intensively cultivated," "Few ever dreamed of venturing any farther east nor west," "Few were concerned with the past," "Few knew and nobody cared."[46] The incest theme that runs throughout the chapters on Sawley—a sterotyped theme in depictions of poor, southern white culture—underlines the mental and moral paucity of life in Sawley.

The narrator emphasizes the town's impoverishment most importantly, however, by describing it as illiterate, unable to "read" or interpret even itself. In the first scenes of the novel, the narrator focuses insistently on vision, on the townspeople's "eyes snapp[ing] in curiosity" (*S*, 18), of their desire to "see for themselves" (7) Jim's courtship of Arvay. But the narrator tells us directly that they are unable to see in any meaningful sense of the term, that they have "no idea who or what Arvay Henson was" (9). And if the town imagines that simply seeing the outside of something is knowledge, then Arvay can similarly see only in the most literal sense. This is evident in Hurston's juxtaposition of the newcomer, Jim Meserve's, vision with that of Arvay's.

Jim is described by Arvay as "first class . . . no common Cracker boy whatsoever" (24). And this is backed up by Jim's ability to read the town and its customs, as the narrator does, anthropologically. Jim notes to himself, for example, that the "usual things" (30) of Sawley's parlors adorn the Hensons' parlor: "the inevitable center table with the big family Bible" and the "ill-assorted pictures" (30) of Civil War and biblical scenes. Just as he sees the "usual things" and customs with the eyes of an outsider, so also, unlike the rest of the town, he immediately sees into Arvay: "Didn't take me long to learn just how you're made, Miss Arvay, and now I know how to handle you," Jim says, telling her also that "you'll get more used to me before long and see into things." "See into what?" (17), Arvay blankly and repeatedly asks from the beginning of the book until her final revelation at the end. There are certainly limitations in Jim's view of Arvay, limitations, as Carby points out, having to do with the "contradictions and conflicts" of gender roles.[47] But as the novel progresses, it is increasingly clear that Arvay must learn to "see into things," as Jim does, if she is to achieve happiness.

So what precisely is wrong with Arvay's perspective, and what is right about Jim's? Hurston's answer lies in her history of lower- and upper-class white culture in the South. Jim's "ancestors had held plantations upon the Alabama River before the War. In that respect, Jim Meserve differed from the rest of the inhabitants of Sawley, who had always been of the poor whites who had scratched out some kind of an existence in the scrub oaks and pines, far removed from the ease of the big estates" (S, 7). In other words, Jim's family background of ease and Arvay's of impoverishment are at the root of their very different ways of seeing, and hence thinking and acting. However, if economic history is at the root of their differences, in Hurston's analysis what matters is the psychological effects of that history. She suggests that scarcity and impoverishment led to a fearfulness and insecurity that integrate poor white southern culture. Repeatedly, she describes Arvay's central emotion as fear, a fear that leads to a scapegoating of racial others. And this scapegoating leads to violence against others as well as against the self.

Two connected examples drive home this analysis of the relation of fear to scapegoating and its violent consequences. First, when Arvay finds out that Jim is a partner with his black "pet,"[48] Joe Kelsey, in a whiskey still, she drives Kelsey and his family from their property. Hurston writes: "Arvay was still too unsure of herself to lay down any ultimatums to her husband, so she took it out on Joe" (S,116). If Arvay hurts the Kelseys, however, she also hurts herself. The Kelsey family was "a part of the pattern of her life," Hurston writes, and their absence "left a vacancy in her days" (118). She also injures her husband and their marriage, "both of them glummed around and snapped at each other" (118) after the Kelsey's departure. The second example is even more dramatic. Jim replaces the Kelseys on their property with a Portugese family, the Corregios, whom Arvay sees as "foreigners, and no foreigners were ever quite white to Arvay" (120). When Arvay and Jim's "queer" son Earl becomes increasingly violent, Arvay blames the foreign "others": "They must have some different scent from regular folks and it maked Earl sick in some way or another. All you got to do is to get rid of 'em and Earl will be all right" (125). Jim disagrees, arguing that Earl's queerness "come through your father's folks" and that Earl's violence has "been there all along" (125). Arvay's refusal to face the "facts" (127) of Earl's violence enables Earl to assault and stab one of the "foreigners," to attempt to slit Arvay's throat, and to shoot at Jim. Both "foreigners" and family suffer.

It is Arvay's destructive fearfulness, a fearfulness that Hurston has rooted in Sawley's historically impoverished culture, that makes Jim leave Arvay: "You love like a coward. Don't take no steps at all" (262). He will return to her only if she "make[s] the first move" (267) toward understanding and meets him on the "high place," where he's been "waiting" (266) for her for a long time. Arvay and Jim can be reconciled in the book's logic only if Arvay can step outside the determination of history, can actively choose to destroy her past and become self-determining. Hurston's description of Arvay's problem and its solution, as in Benedict, are worked out through the metaphor of domesticity, of learning to leave behind the "old homestead."

After Jim leaves Arvay, she is called home to Sawley by the death of her mother. As she packs, Arvay is filled with an unrealistic nostalgia for her hometown:[49] "The corroding poverty of her childhood became a glowing virtue, and a state to be desired. Arvay scorned off learning as a source of evil knowledge and thought fondly of ignorance as the foundation of good-heartedness and honesty. Peace, contentment and virtue hung like a rainbow over turpentine shacks and shanties. There love and free-giving abided. . . . She was going *home!* Home to the good old times and simple, honest things, where greed after money and power had no place (272). These clichés about home, framed sardonically by the narrator, set up the discovery Arvay makes when she returns to Sawley. Earlier descriptions in the novel by Jim and the narrator of Sawley as bumptious and illiterate are supplanted by much more sinister ones of a community integrated by a viciously and violently reactive ignorance. Arvay's mother, Maria, is described as belching and burping her way to an unlamented death, while the rats in the wall can hardly wait to begin eating her. Arvay further discovers at home that her sister, brother-in-law, and their children have not only been living off Maria but also, out of greed, have kept Arvay ignorant of Maria's sickness. In the vicious, cartoonish family arguments that ensue, Arvay's brother-in-law, a defrocked minister, attempts to blackmail Arvay. When blackmail does not succeed, he and his family steal all the possessions in Maria's house, possessions that had been left to Arvay. The rats in the wall are more discreet than the rats in Arvay's family.

This portrayal of poor white southern culture relies on the grotesque stereotypes of "white trash" that, as Annalee Newitz argues, have long soothed white liberals about their own lack of racial bias.[50] And Hurston is clearly appealing to those liberals in her depiction of Sawley. Nonetheless, the grotesque stereotypes also serve another purpose. The switch from the somewhat neutrally toned anthropological analysis of Sawley's culture of impoverishment at the beginning of the novel to the savage satire at the end has the effect of underlining how Arvay is learning to criticize the culture she comes from. As in Benedict, satire works to enforce a thematics of self-critique. For the first time,

Arvay herself begins to see the power of Sawley's culture over her and her family, how Sawley was integrated through impoverishment. Arvay's understanding of her own culture becomes emblematized and contained as an object of critique, as it did in Benedict, in the family's old homestead:

> [T]here stood that house. Now Arvay looked at it with a scrutiny, and darkened . . . it was no house at all. It was an evil, ill-deformed monstropolous accumulation of time and scum. It had soaked in so much of doing-without, of soul-starvation, of brutish vacancy of aim, of absent dreams, envy of trifles, ambitions for littleness, smothered cries and trampled love, that it was a sanctuary of tiny and sanctioned vices. . . . By a lucky chance, she had been carried away from it at a fairly young age, but still, its fumes and vapors had stuck to her sufficiently to scar Jim and bruise her children. . . . No, it was no longer just a building. It had caught a soul of its own now. It caught people and twisted the limbs of their minds. . . . How much had it blinded her from seeing and feeling through the years! (*S*, 306–7)

Arvay decides it is time to clean house, and she does so in an efficient, albeit unconventional, manner: she burns her childhood home to the ground. And burning the house has an immediate and beneficial effect on Arvay: "Looking at the conflagration, exultation swept over her followed by a peaceful calm. It was the first time in her life that she was conscious of feeling that way" (307). Arvay's housecleaning can be read, first of all, as a modernist denial of the determination of history. More importantly however, it can be read as a commentary both on the power of the past and the equal power that a comparative analysis of culture can have. Because she "had been carried away from it at a fairly young age" and so can compare that life with other ways of living, she can see Sawley for what it is. Such a comparative analysis enables, in Hurston's logic, a kind of objective self-critique or domestic critique. It enables Arvay to understand how the past has shaped her manner of "seeing and feeling." She leaves Sawley, never to return again, disabused of her nostalgia for it and presumably free from its power over her.

In Hurston's explanation of the effects of Arvay's revelation, the novel's larger impulse toward collective forms of objective domestic critique and reform becomes more clear. First, and significantly, Arvay begins to treat African Americans more decently. In a story focused on the conflicts between Jim and Arvay, Hurston weaves another one demonstrating that any material wealth Jim has achieved for the family is because of the "underground system in Colored Town" (82) and the friends he makes there. He becomes a rich man because he acts, as he puts it, like a "gentleman" (82) toward blacks. This monetary enrichment is linked inextricably in the novel with cultural enrichment. As Carby points out, Hurston sought to demonstrate in the novel "her ideas of cultural influence and fusion."[51] Jim and Arvay's marriage is celebrated by the songs of the black community, whose beauty cause Arvay at the beginning of the novel to see things momentarily "for the first time from inside" (*S*, 59), though of course it is not until the end of the novel that she can maintain that deeper vision. Later, their son, Kenny, becomes a rich and famous musician because he has learned how to play from Joe Kelsey (250). As Jim says of this cultural relation, which is inextricable from a monetary one, "[W]hite bands up North and in different places like New Orleans are taking over darky music and making more money at it than the darkies used to.... Kenny claims that it is just a matter of time when white artists will take it all over. Getting to it's not considered just darky music and dancing nowadays. It's American and belongs to everybody" (202). That it is the unconcerned businessman Jim who advances this theory of cultural fusion enables us to read it as an objective account of matters, a capitalist's acceptance of the material and immaterial benefits of hybridity. In other words, in Hurston's conservative, rather cynical formulation, having a modicum of gratitude for the wealth and beauty blacks have created in America is, if nothing else, good business.

Arvay's transformation after she has burned down the old homestead is therefore marked by her treating Jeff and Janie Kelsey, the current black caretakers of her house, for the first time like "folks" (314). In an excrutiatingly drawn-out section of the novel, Arvay begins to chat with them, to trust them, even to admire their looks and wonder what they are like as people (312–18). As Jeff, the son of Joe Kelsey, says in surprised reaction to Arvay's transformation, "[E]verybody knows that Mister Jim is quality first-class. Knows how to carry hisself, and then how to treat everybody. Miss Arvay's done come to be just like him" (314).[52] Arvay agrees, telling the Kelseys that she has burned down her home in Sawley and all it stands for and that she does not want to find any residue from Sawley "nowhere around me. If I got any narrowhearted littleness in me [anymore], I hope to God to cut myself and let it run out" (314). Hurston defuses the didactic quality of the narrative here by insisting that Arvay's transformation is the result of quite literally an objective domestic critique.

The novel's didacticism is also deflected through Hurston's use of a standard, postwar, regressive analysis of how women can achieve happiness by realizing that they have "the privilege to serve" and "mother" (351) their husbands. This means that Arvay's "moment of great revelation" (348) at the end of the novel comes when she sees "inside" Jim for the first time, sees that he is "nothing but a little boy to take care of, and he hungered for her hovering... like Kenny when he wore diapers" (351). While Arvay's transformation is charted first in terms of race relations, Hurston packages the racial message in terms of the much more familiar one of woman's acceptance of her maternal power of service.

Finally, however, the ending's race and gender messages are contained within a larger message insisting on the autonomy of the self and its power over history. While Jim lies asleep in her arms, Arvay reviews her life, interpreting the entire narrative we have read, curiously enough, as a story about the autonomy of the self: "All that had happened to her, good or bad, was a part of her own self and had come out of her. Within her own flesh were many mysteries.... What all, Arvay asked of herself, was buried and hidden in human flesh? You toted it around with you all your life time, but you couldn't know. If you just could know, it would be all the religion that anybody needed. And what was in you was bound to come out and stand (349–50). The passage focuses on Arvay's realization of the endless potentiality and productivity of interiority and its freedom from the determination of history ("what was in you was bound to come out and stand").

This solipsisitic, individualistic analysis of the transcendent self, however, means also that the self must become accountable for itself. All of Arvay's conflicts with Jim resulted from Sawley's shaping of her, and the problems that she herself discovers by leaving and then returning to Sawley must be thought through by her. If there are historical reasons for Sawley's integration of itself through impoverishment, Hurston suggests, the hope must be that Sawley's residents will realize this through the opening up of their world via the new highway being built. Through the juxtaposition and mixing of other ways of being with theirs, they will presumably become able to criticize and reform themselves. Social critique relies on objective comparisons. More important and paradoxically, however, social critique depends on objective domestic critique.

In a famous pamphlet, *The Races of Mankind* (1943), Benedict and her coauthor, Gene Weltfish, argue that Hitler has banked on victory in World War II, believing that "he could convince nonwhite races in Asia and Africa that this is a 'white man's war' " and that America is a "no man's land, where peoples of all origins were ready to fall to fighting among themselves."[53] Written for distribution in USO centers and ordered by the army for use in orientation courses, the pamphlet was then notoriously suppressed by the House Military Affairs Commission (and was therefore also widely read) because of its use of statistics showing that northern blacks tested higher on IQ tests than southern whites.[54] Benedict and Weltfish conclude with a crucial and self-reflexively ironic metaphor: "With America's great tradition of democracy, the United States should clean its own house and get ready for a better twenty-first century. Then it could stand unashamed before the Nazis and condemn, without confusion, their doctrines of a Master race."[55] In other words, *The Races of Mankind* argues, as *Patterns of Culture* did, that self-critique or housecleaning of a nation's "great tradition" is always the first order of business, a housecleaning enabled by the objective knowledge of anthropologists. While the pamphlet consistently attacks Nazi racism, domestic racism is the front on which—the pamphlet argues—this war is being fought, "a front no less important . . . than the Production Front and the Inflation Front."[56]

At the end of a letter to Benedict, Hurston comments approvingly on Benedict and Weltfish's pamphlet. Hurston writes, "I read with interest your publication that upset the brass-hats so, and smiled. Facts go down mighty hard with some folks, confirming my conviction that there is nothing so precious that men know as what they *want* to believe."[57] Hurston's analysis of the suppression of *The Races of Mankind* is interesting for a number of reasons. It demonstrates, first of all, how Boasian anthropologists were attentive to each other's work. In this case, the suppression of Benedict's work confirms what Hurston describes as one of her central intellectual convictions: that there are objective "facts" about race but that desires and beliefs (what people "*want* to believe") have a more powerful or real effect upon people than "facts" or knowledge.

The manner in which Hurston frames her attentiveness to Benedict's work, however, demonstrates a compelling tension. As this chapter has argued, the notion that affect has more power than fact is one shared by Benedict and Hurston, among other Boasian-trained anthropologists. Why, then, does Hurston pose this notion as "my conviction" and not as a shared conviction between the two of them or between Boasian-trained anthropologists? The records we have of Benedict and Hurston's relation provide a key to understanding this tension. Both Hurston and Benedict started studying professional anthropology late in life, after struggles with the social roles prescribed them by gender and race. Both studied with Boas when he was switching the emphasis of anthropology from history to the "genius of a people," and both used this conceptual framework, particularly the notion of integration and its cost, not only to subordinate historical analyses of race and gender oppression to psychological ones but also to engage with the question of subjectivity. Their engagement with subjectivity returned them to Victorian domestic reform culture, which they sought to dismiss even as they insisted on its power and resilience. Both insisted, finally, that social analysis must be a kind of domestic critique, a critique that works through a provisional understanding of other cultures but that focuses finally on the self, the only thing one has a right to criticize. Despite the similarities in their ideas and work, however, Benedict's and Hurston's career trajectories were very different.

There is no doubt Benedict faced obstacles in her professional career. Even with Boas's support, she was made only an assistant professor of anthropology at Columbia belatedly in 1931 (associate in 1938), and because she was a woman, she never became chair of the department. Nevertheless, Benedict wielded a fair amount of power at Columbia, and her high status in the profession was acknowledged when she became president of the American Anthropological Association in 1947. After her death, her most famous works remained in print. By contrast, Hurston remained on the margins of the profession, apparently only partly by choice. This meant that she had more freedom than Benedict to pursue other kinds of intellectual work. So, for example, Hurston was a central figure in the Harlem Renaissance, and throughout her life, she alternately wrote and combined fiction and ethnography. At the same time, however, it also meant that she did not have steady institutional support for her work. While Hurston showed exceptional skill at finding patrons to support her research, this support often came at a high price both in terms of the energy she had to expend and in the ways her patrons circumscribed her production. The failure of *Seraph on the Suwanee* in 1948 largely ended Hurston's career.[58] Her writings were out of print and forgotten until the 1970s when Alice Walker and other African American feminists revived her work. For a variety of reasons, including the crucially determining one of institutionalized racism in the academy and in U.S. society more generally, Benedict and her writings could more easily be assimilated into the norms of professional and intellectual discourse than Hurston's could.

The shared limitations both Benedict and Hurston faced as women intellectuals, as well as the different treatment accorded them as a white and black woman, can be gauged in the tension one finds in their letters to each other. As compared to the letters between Boas and Hurston, which while formal and distant in tone are also consistently supportive, the letters between Benedict and Hurston are marked by informality[59] but also by quite rapid alternations between support and covertly competitive anxiety and territoriality. In their early letters, Hurston asks Benedict to edit her work, calls Benedict "Friend," and signs her letters, "Lovingly."[60] Benedict responds by praising and promoting Hurston's work. But even in these early letters, when both were forging their careers, Hurston is consistently asking Benedict to use her influence at Columbia to help Hurston get the money, equipment, or institutional support she needs to continue her research. A low point comes in 1932–33 when Hurston applies for a Guggenheim,[61] and instead of writing a letter of support, Benedict writes confidentially to the Guggenheim that Hurston is not "Guggenheim material." Exercising a gatekeeper's prerogative in the profession, Benedict writes condescendingly that she hopes "some of [Hurston's] patrons will provide the money for this trip and that she'll write up her experiences when she returns in collaboration with some anthropologist."[62] Whether Hurston knew of Benedict's role in her failure to get a Guggenheim that year, it is also true that Hurston's letters generally imply that Benedict is a factotum to Boas. And both before and after Boas's death, Hurston's tone in her letters to Benedict, like that of Benedict's to her, are somewhat condescending. Hurston's statement of support for Benedict's pamphlet, for example, appears at the end of a long letter asking Benedict for research support from Columbia and is subordinated to that request as well as to the already-noted pedagogical presentation to Benedict of Hurston's own "convictions."

Nonetheless, if Hurston's response to Benedict's pamphlet suggests the tensions between two women with similar ideas but experiencing different degrees of exclusion from the professions, it is also true that Hurston's response shows how crucial the relation between anthropology and public debate was to these women. If Boasian anthropologists were attentive to each other's ideas, they were also attentive to the impact their ideas had on the public. Both Benedict and Hurston sought to popularize their work, to create roles for themselves as public intellectuals. They felt, as Benedict says to one colleague, that "people need to be told in words of two syllables what contrasting cultures mean" (*AW*, 321). In the letters that pass between Benedict and Hurston, they consistently support each other's efforts to present their ideas to a broad public. Benedict agrees to help out with the advertising and publicity of Hurston's first two books and congratulates her on the "good reviews" for *Jonah's Gourd Vine*.[63] Similarly, Hurston in a letter to Benedict on *Mules and Men* describes how she is revising it "not for scientists, but for the average reader." She advises Benedict somewhat cynically that she too could "do an Indian book in the same manner," adding that it would "be a big success" and "worth money."[64] This notion of themselves as intellectuals, working to introduce anthropological analyses of different cultures to a large audience for the purpose of social critique (and personal profit), is central to understanding them. It is also central to understanding the ways in which these modernist anthropologists productively retained from Victorian domestic culture a polemical and subjective aim that inheres in and explicitly troubles a simultaneous claim to modern professional objectivity.

Afterword

> *And if . . . you object that to depend upon a profession is only another form of slavery, you will admit from your own experience that to depend upon a profession is a less odious form of slavery than to depend upon a father.*
> —*Virginia Woolf,* Three Guineas

> For the master's tools will never dismantle the master's house. *They may allow us temporarily to beat him at his own game, but they will never enable us to bring about genuine change. And this fact is only threatening to those women who still define the master's house as their only source of support.*
> —Audre Lorde, "The Master's Tools Will Never Dismantle the Master's House"

There are important conflicts in the idea of feminist professionalism in these two famous pronouncements written by a white feminist at the end of the first wave of the women's movement and a black feminist toward the end of the second wave of that movement. The first statement dramatically erases and appropriates the history of unfree black labor in the West to express a seemingly pragmatic preference for the unfreedom of women's professionalism over the unfreedom of women's domesticity. The second highlights the ways in which just such erasures and appropriations of history lead women to reproduce the forms of professionalism and dynamics of power they seek to critique and change. Despite the intense conflict between these two perspectives, however, there is much that also overlaps. The necessity for exiting the "house" (albeit a house defined in different ways) and the profound ambivalence about the professional work that marks this exit is evident in both. In the intense dialogic friction between them as well as in their similarity, these statements provide a useful analogue to *Modern Women, Modern Work*'s thesis.

Virginia Woolf's argument in *Three Guineas*, written on the eve of World War II, is consistently hesitant and self-critical. Why advocate professionalism for women, she asks, given that it is the professional system itself that has caused the war through its hierarchies, its competitiveness, its violence, its exclusiveness, and its greed?[1] What would it matter if women had equal authority to men in economics, law, politics, and culture? Would it change anything, or would the world remain precisely the same? Woolf's skeptical yet hopeful answers are illuminating more than half a century later. In part because Woolf creates a dialogue between her skepticism and hope, and in part because she comes to conclusions that are not always satisfying to us today, *Three Guineas* sheds light on the issue of women's engagement with the modern professions. At the center of Woolf's text is ambivalence—an ambivalence she herself thematizes and that she, in turn, provokes in her reader.

In imagining the difference women's professionalism makes, Woolf rejects any easy modernist narrative of progressive rupture.[2] She describes women of her generation as poised on "the bridge which lies between the old world and the new," between the "private house" (*TG*, 16) and "the world of professional, of public life" (17). It is a bridge, in Woolf's description, not a cliff, for the past and present are undeniably linked in their accession to inequality. There is not a necessary progressive evolution between past and present; instead, the past and present each entail work that she describes as a kind of "slavery." Nonetheless, the bridge represents a new possibility for women, namely a "less odious form of slavery" (16). With their own earned money in hand, or rather the right to have earned money in hand, Woolf writes, "[E]very thought, every sight, every action [looks] different." Admittedly, it is a difference mediated through money—through what Woolf somewhat ironically, somewhat seriously calls "the sacred coin"—but she says in "imagination" at least the difference is important (16).

As Woolf explores what this imaginative difference could mean, she does not deny that in reality it might change nothing. At moments, her skepticism is akin to despair.[3] Nonetheless, in *Three Guineas*, she insists that if professionalism is changed, there is the possibility of a world without war. This change can come about only, however, if women bring ideas and memories from the Old World—memories of the private house and of their exclusion from the professions—into the professions. Women's historic experience of exclusion, and of the traditions that shaped their exclusion, can potentially become the levers by which professionalism itself is reformed (79–84). If women bring the "poverty, chastity, derision and freedom from unreal loyalties" of the past and mix them with "some wealth, some knowledge, and some service to real loyalties" (79), then professionalism could become quite different. Such combinations of old and new, of exclusion and inclusion, will enable women to "enter the professions and yet remain civilized human beings, human beings who discourage war" (79). By forming what Woolf calls an "Outsider's Society" (106), professionalism may be reformed, and social change may possibly occur.

Three Guineas uses its ambivalence about professionalism, in other words, to shape its ideas of a new professionalism and of a more just, less violent society. It insists on highlighting the problems and contradictions of both domesticity and professionalism. It does not idealize exclusion, nor does it retreat into nostalgia or fatalism. Woolf takes full stock of the destructive power of professionalism, but she also recognizes its potential if it is changed. Most important, she imagines how the professions' destructive power can be transformed through a historical memory of women's past. Just as Woolf herself relies on skepticism to shape her hope, so also she imagines the troubling history of professional exclusiveness being transformed by the historic "outsiders" to professionalism who can bring "poverty, chastity, derision and freedom from unreal loyalties" (79) to it. Women and men can thereby become usefully and legitimately professional, an argument that many modernist and contemporary feminists alike have also made.[4]

As numerous feminist critics have pointed out, however, Woolf's own argument enacts some of the problems with professionalism that she herself maps out. *Three Guineas* is narrowly, albeit self-consciously, focused on one class, the "educated man's daughter," rather than on all daughters.[5] Similarly, while Woolf insists that no "human being, whether man or woman, white or black" (66) should be prevented from entering any profession, she nonetheless collapses crucial distinctions between race and gender as well as between unpaid, forced labor and paid or unpaid, alienated labor. The term *slavery* is strikingly inappropriate for describing upper-class Victorian domestic women or upper-class professionals and reveals that for all of Woolf's critical self-consciousness, she is often unable to think through the power differentials between women. The gap between Woolf's ambivalence about women's professionalism and the ambivalence her text creates for us today is instructive. Both to Woolf and *in* Woolf, the disjunction between the ideals of professionalism and its institutional realities are profound.

Audre Lorde's critique of academic professionalism in "The Master's Tools Will Never Dismantle the Master's House" addresses the problems that Woolf analyzes and enforces in *Three Guineas*. The specific issue Lorde's essay takes on is the racism of a feminist academic conference that she had been invited to attend; the larger issue is the historic racism of white feminism. She writes, "It is a particular academic arrogance to assume any discussion of feminist theory without examining our many differences, and without significant input from poor women, Black and Third World women, and lesbians."[6] Broadening the issue beyond the scope of the conference, Lorde continues, "What does it mean when the tools of a racist patriarchy are used to examine the fruits of that same patriarchy?" (*SO*,110–11). Lorde's answer is that "It means that only the most narrow perimeters of change are possible and allowable" (111). As opposed to Woolf's acceptance that the change from domesticity to professionalism may be a minimal one, Lorde nearly a half century later is not satisfied by "narrow" forms of change.

On first reading, Lorde seems to insist on the fundamental necessity for radical modernist rupture with the past. Like Woolf, she addresses the issue of women's professionalism and its relation to the past, but she paints a far different picture. The past has not given a critical edge to women's professionalism. Lorde's famous words—"*the master's tools will never dismantle the master's house*"

(112)—suggest an economic, ideological, political, and linguistic break with history is necessary. In the context of this feminist academic conference, Lorde particularly focuses on the way a shift from claims of universal manhood to those of universal womanhood reproduces the system of oppression and appropriation that feminism theoretically seeks to change. White women professionals, Lorde argues, rely on the same ideological system that subjugates a variety of peoples (white women included). Literally and figuratively, these women still "define the master's house as their only source of support" (112), revealing that they have neither freed themselves from their privileged oppressiveness nor renounced their privileged oppression. To Lorde, domesticity—one of the tools acquired in the master's house—cannot provide the alternative form of historic consciousness that Woolf posits, for it is part of a system of capitalist and racist patriarchy that reproduces precisely that system.

Lorde therefore defines the meaning and importance of outsiders in a very different way than Woolf. She writes: "Those of us who stand outside the circle of this society's definition of acceptable women; those of us who have been forged in the crucibles of difference—those of us who are poor, who are lesbians, who are Black, who are older—know that *survival is not an academic skill.* It is learning how to stand alone, unpopular and sometimes reviled, and how to make common cause with those others identified as outside the structures in order to define and seek a world in which we can all flourish. It is learning how to take our differences and make them strengths" (112). These outsiders stand outside the definition of "acceptable women," outside the circle of the "educated man's daughter." These are outsiders who do not necessarily map onto the domesticity-professionalism binary. Such women exceed that middle-class formulation.

Nonetheless, despite Lorde's embrace of radical modernist rupture, and despite her very different definition of outsiders, Lorde—like Woolf—sees difference as having been created through historical means and so not simply escapable. This is emblematized by the "master's house," an image that relies on the history of slavery to link together—and distinguish—raced, sexed, and classed forms of oppression. Certainly, Lorde wants to think about how reproduction of the same can be disrupted, but absolute rupture from history or complete exteriority to systems of power is arguably not her solution, as some of her critics claim.[7] Lorde's trileveled analysis of how contemporary women's professionalism has reproduced the system it pretends to challenge makes the complexity of her account of history and power clear. She is interested at one level in how white feminists have adopted the universalizing impulse of academic theory that erases historic differences. These white feminists' erasure of difference in their universalizing of gender division results in the entrenchment of difference. At a broader level, Lorde also describes the mechanisms by which "others" have been "*forged in* the crucibles of difference, *identified as* outside the structures" (112, emphasis added). In other words, she is interested in how systems of thought in the past and present construct certain social groups as invisible outsiders within that selfsame system. At yet another level, she wants to examine how those mechanisms also work to keep these others from identifying with each other "to make common cause" (112). Lorde is intensely aware, in other words, that a simple escape from history and systems of power is not the solution.

Like Woolf, except more intensively and critically, then, Lorde's skepticism shapes her hope. Lorde's essay does not finally dismiss women's professionalism or insist on separation from history or structures of power. Rather than arguing for such separation, she attacks it, calling the exclusive separatism of white women's professionalism an "evasion of responsibility" and a "cop-out . . . that keeps Black women's art out of women's exhibitions, Black women's work out of most feminist publications . . . and Black women's texts off your reading lists" (113). Women's professionalism must continuously engage in an unflinching and self-critical examination of its "tools" rather than assuming that historic outsider status creates tools ready to hand. This is not to deny that Lorde is deeply ambivalent about women's differently structured imbrication in the history of systems of power that helped create professionalism. This ambivalence expresses itself through her descriptions of the imaginative, emotional, and political appeal of a black feminist and lesbian separatism to counter white feminist and heterosexual separatism; the persuasive appeals of counterseparatism are never to be gainsaid in Lorde's work. Since white separatism, however, is historically part of a "racist patriarchal thought" whereby white women have not "educated yourselves about Black women and the differences between us" (113), such counterseparatism is not Lorde's ideal solution. Instead, she continues to hold out hope for the possibility of new kinds of education and training about the history of difference that would result in a genuinely transformed kind of professionalism: "In our world, divide and conquer must become define and empower" (112). If Woolf worries about the reproduction of old structures of power as women enter the professions, Lorde insists on finding the tools—historical and critical—to avoid such reproduction.

Reading the ambivalence about the possibilities for feminist professionalism in *Three Guineas* of 1938 and comparing it to the even deeper ambivalence of *Sister Outsider* in 1984 demonstrates why feminist doubt about and conflict over professionalism has been historically, and remains today, an absolute critical necessity. *Modern Women, Modern Work* has highlighted the critical necessity for ambivalence about women's modern professionalism, even as it has insisted on the possibilities that professionalism has provided. It has challenged both Victorian and modern absolutes by showing the ways in which black and white women combined ideas from the "cult of domesticity" with those from the "culture of professionalism" in order to shape the modern professions. In challenging those absolutes, it has shown how the past was used to reform the present as well as how the past (sometimes simultaneously) was used to stabilize the status quo. In the work of modernist women professionals, I have argued, we can see this dynamic enacted with particular clarity. Women's professionalism illustrates the possibilities that the contradictions of modern professionalism created and precluded; it demonstrates the manner in which the domestic "past" could be used to highlight and criticize those contradictions as well as how it could support and create new ones.

I have focused on three central variations of what this dynamic meant for the gendering and racializing of professionalism. There were thinkers like Jewett and Addams who combined ideas about domesticity with ideas about educated expertise to create a new kind of professional social authority. But even as they shaped more expansive forms of expertise, they also walled off expertise, limiting it to women like themselves who were upper class and white. There were other professionals who saw the contradictions of their work quite clearly but nonetheless sought to stabilize a gender- and race-exclusive definition of it. Thinkers like Cather, Tarbell, Norris, and Santayana tried to stabilize the binaries of primitive past-civilized present, domesticity-professionalism in order to guard the borders of expertise from incursions by outsiders as well as to guard expertise from its own contradictions. Their effort at stabilization enabled them to criticize explicitly the untenable logic of domestic transcendence. Because they relied on precisely the logic that they excoriated, however, their critiques of both domesticity and professionalism were contradictory, even incoherent. By contrast, thinkers like Hopkins, Ruffin, Benedict, and Hurston questioned the history and significance of domestic as well as professional ideology, using each ideology to criticize the other. This enabled them to engage in a reevaluation of the bases of exclusive expertise and to change the meaning of professional work, though they faced substantial challenges in sustaining their analyses as well as their work.

While my account of the relation between the domestic and the professional illustrates that professional women often reproduced structural inequality, I have also shown that some women successfully challenged that inequality. Success was uneven, unpredictable, and unsteady, but it did occur. We could nevertheless still ask if these successes were merely local or momentary phenomena. If women and men of different racial and class backgrounds challenged and modified professional exclusivity historically, professionalism nevertheless generally enforces the class divide—the divide between those authorized to speak and those enjoined to listen and obey. Why then, we might ask, is it important for feminists to historicize professional exclusivity and its reform within this larger system of class inequality?

One central answer stands out. While the professions have functioned to reinforce structural inequality, gaining access to them was a crucial goal of both first- and second-wave feminists. Ideally, the professions coincide with feminist notions of work. Ideally, they represent labor that is chosen, that is fulfilling, and that makes the world a better place. Ideally, the professions have provided in the past and could provide in the future, in Vicki Schultz's "utopian" terms, a "life's work . . . work "in which women and men from all walks of life can stand alongside each other as equals, pursuing our chosen projects and forging connected lives." Such work is a "*process*" by which we "*come* to view each other as equal citizens and human beings, each entitled to equal respect and a claim on society's resources because of our shared commitments and contributions."[8] The disjunction between the utopian ideal of such work and the general institutional reality is not a reason to give up the ideal, nor is it a reason to ignore the moments and locations of success. The disjunction, I have shown in this book, has in fact been quite useful in the past as a lever in changing and reforming the reality.

The disjunction could continue to be useful today in this era of multinational, global capitalism. In recent years, the professional-managerial class has seen some of the protections and privileges of their work diminish, though they have not seen them disappear at the rate at which the lower and working classes have. Globalization has so far meant some disruption of middle- and upper-class professions and work communities, but it has meant even more profoundly the disruption of nonprofessional work and its communities. It has meant, most prominently, a continuous assault upon unions, upon the notion of the work community that historically provided protection and forms of solidarity to nonprofessional workers. Professionals need to take heed of this assault, though it has not yet consistently undermined their own protections and privileges. Both upper-class and working-class communities have been (in different degrees) historically exclusive across race, sex, and ethnic lines. Both are experiencing disruptions (though to different degrees). This moment of disruption is also one of possibility, a moment in which we could learn from the failures and successes within and across our work communities—present and past—so that we can create new kinds of work communities together. We need to use the present and past failures and successes to undermine all forms of exclusiveness and to protect everyone in his or her work. We need, in other words, to forge new kinds of work communities by acknowledging and jettisoning those structures that promoted exclusivity or hierarchy.

The ambivalence most feminists thus feel about professionalism should be encouraged. Professionalism's disjunctions need to be highlighted and investigated, even as they continuously shift. Precisely because of these disjunctions and our own ambivalence, we need to think through the significance of women's engagement with professionalism. This engagement registers some of the important struggles and successes as well as the compromises and failures of feminist ideas and ideals about work, and it has much to tell us about how we can shape better and worse models of work for the present and future. The history of women's contribution to modern professionalism can help us reform our work—professional and nonprofessional—within the multinational globalized capitalism of our own era so that we can create more expansive outsiders' societies that would make all forms of work a "life's work."

Notes

Introduction

1. My use of the term *civilization* in this book depends on Gail Bederman's brilliant analysis of it in *Manliness and Civilization* (Chicago: University of Chicago Press, 1995). Bederman shows that the idea of civilization is linked inextricably in late nineteenth- and early twentieth-century American culture to whiteness, masculinity, and sexual specialization through an evolutionary logic, though she also demonstrates how those linkages are undermined and questioned by many thinkers.

2. In Barbara and John Ehrenreich's classic and influential argument, the term *professional-managerial* describes the class of trained experts and managers who became ascendant during the Progressive period in the U.S. They argue that more attention needs to be given to this class. Its belief in democracy and its critique of capitalism enabled the (albeit limited) social reforms of turn-of-the-century Progressivism. They assert that this class could potentially be galvanized again for effective social change in our own era. See Barbara and John Ehrenreich, "The Professional-Managerial Class," *Radical America* 2, no. 2 (March–April 1977): 7–31. *Modern Women, Modern Work* makes a similar argument.

3. One of the most influential nineteenth-century accounts of the relation of the sexual to the modern capitalist division of labor is, of course, that of Karl Marx and Friedrich Engels. At times, they argue that the primitive sexual breakdown of labor is the first incipiently capitalist one. At other times, they describe the sexual division of labor as a "natural" division onto which was grafted the inequities of a larger economic system. See, for example, *The German Ideology* (1845–46) and *The Origin of the Family, Private Property, and the State* (1884). This infamously unresolved problematic reveals a number of tensions in Marx's and Engels's thinking. Most important for my argument is the way in which the sexual division of labor becomes for them the site of a nostalgic and romantic primitivism that is in sharp contrast to the progressive histories they generally narrate and that is imagined through a Victorian separate-spheres ideology. As we shall see in a moment, nostalgia about the "primitive" sexual division of labor is not unique to Marx and Engels but characterizes as well the ideas of those social commentators who are critical of their work, most notably for this chapter, Emile Durkheim. See Friedrich Engels and Karl Marx, *The German Ideology* (New York: International Publishers, 1970); Friedrich Engels, *The Origin of the Family, Private Property, and the State: In the Light of the Researches of Lewis H. Morgan* (New York: International Publishers, 1972).

4. I use *progressive* to refer to contemporary notions of progress linked to ideas about the importance of the occupational division of labor. Such notions overlap with the Progressive social and political movement of the 1890s–1910s but involve repercussions beyond its specific manifestation. The Progressive movement depended on "progressive" ideas about modern expertise in solving the problems of laissez-faire capitalism.

148   Notes to Page 2

Both forms of progressivism can imply our current sense of the word (i.e., critical and linked to transformative thinking and politics); however, the terms can at the same time be absolutely disassociated from our contemporary use of the word and simply be indicative of the gender and race ideas of the time. It will be clear from the context if I am linking progressive ideas to the Progressive movement or to our contemporary sense of what is progressive.

5. Barbara Welter and Burton Bledstein brought these two terms into the debates about domestic and professional culture respectively in *Dimity Convictions* (Athens: Ohio University Press, 1976) and *The Culture of Professionalism* (New York: W. W. Norton, 1976, respectively). Welter's original term was *cult of true womanhood*, but that term morphed into *cult of domesticity*.

6. I use the terms *modernity*, *modern*, and *modernism* somewhat interchangeably despite the multiple debates about each term and their relation to each other. The first tends to be associated with economic, social, and political changes; the second with a period of time; the third with cultural productions. For a useful and succinct analysis of the debates surrounding the three terms, see Rita Felski, *The Gender of Modernity* (Cambridge: Harvard University Press, 1995), 11–16. Following Felski, I link the three through the notion of their rhetorical "enunciation of a process of differentiation, and act of separation from the past" (13). By relying on this shared feature of the three terms, I am able to connect social and economic developments to aesthetic and philosophical ones within a given period of time.

7. See studies by Nina Baym, *Woman's Fiction* (Ithaca: Cornell University Press, 1978); Nancy Cott, *The Bonds of Womanhood* (New Haven: Yale University Press, 1977); Ann Douglas, *The Feminization of American Culture* (New York: Doubleday, 1988); Mary Kelley, *Private Women, Public Stage* (New York: Oxford University Press, 1984); Lora Romero, *Home Fronts: Domesticity and Its Critics in the Antebellum U.S.* (Durham: Duke University Press, 1997); Mary Ryan, *The Empire of the Mother* (New York: Harrington Press, 1985); Shirley Samuels, ed., *The Culture of Sentiment* (Ithaca: Cornell University Press, 1993); Kathryn Kish Sklar, *Catharine Beecher* (New Haven: Yale University Press, 1973); Jane Tompkins, *Sensational Designs* (New York: Oxford University Press, 1985); Welter, *Dimity Convictions*.

8. See Bledstein, *Professionalism;* Nancy Glazener, *Reading for Realism* (Durham: Duke University Press, 1997); Samuel Haber, *The Quest for Authority and Honor in the Professions* (Chicago: University of Chicago Press, 1991); Thomas Haskell, *The Emergence of Professional Social Science: The American Social Science Association and the Nineteenth-Century Crisis of Authority* (Urbana: University of Illinois Press, 1977); Nathan O. Hatch, ed., *The Professions in American History* (Notre Dame: University of Notre Dame Press, 1988); Magali Sarfatti Larson, *The Rise of Professionalism* (Berkeley and Los Angeles: University of California Press, 1977); Dana D. Nelson, *National Manhood* (Durham: Duke University Press, 1998); Peter Novick, *That Noble Dream* (New York: Cambridge University Press, 1993); Thomas Strychacz, *Modernism, Mass Culture, and Professionalism* (New York: Cambridge University Press, 1991); Robert H. Wiebe, *The Search for Order, 1877–1920* (New York: Hill and Wang, 1967); Christopher Wilson, *The Labor of Words: Literary Professionalism in the Progressive Era* (Athens: University of Georgia Press, 1985).

9. Raymond Williams, *The Politics of Modernism*, ed. Tony Pinkey (New York: Verso, 1989), 38. Williams has contributed more generally to the contemporary rethinking of periodization through his notion that culture always contains dominant, residual, and emergent elements in it, a notion to which this book is clearly indebted. See his *Marxism and Literature* (London: Oxford University Press, 1977). Nonetheless, the title to this introduction refers instead to Michel Foucault's *History of Sexuality* both because of his importance in challenging ideas about periodization of Victorian and modern culture,

and also because of his focus on the discourses of disciplines and professions as well as the reverse discourses that develop out of them. See Michel Foucault, *History of Sexuality*, trans. Robert Hurley (New York: Vintage, 1980).

10. See Cathy Davidson, ed., "No More Separate Spheres!" Spec. issue of *American Literature* 70, no. 3 (1998): 133–59; Linda K. Kerber, "Separate Spheres, Female Worlds, Woman's Place: The Rhetoric of Women's History," in *Toward an Intellectual History of Women* (Chapel Hill: University of North Carolina Press, 1997), 159–99.

11. The studies that have most influenced my understanding of the relation of Victorian and modern culture are those by Ann Ardis, *New Women, New Novels* (New Brunswick: Rutgers University Press, 1990); Bederman, *Civilization;* Hazel V. Carby, *Reconstructing Womanhood: The Emergence of the Afro-American Woman Novelist* (New York: Oxford University Press, 1987); Suzanne Clark, *Sentimental Modernism: Women Writers and the Revolution of the Word* (Bloomington: University of Indiana Press, 1991); Desley Deacon, *Elsie Clews Parson: Inventing Modern Life* (Chicago: University of Chicago Press, 1997); Felski, *Modernity;* Alice Gambrell, *Women Intellectuals, Modernism, and Difference: Transatlantic Culture, 1919–45* (New York: Cambridge University Press, 1997); June Howard, *Publishing the Family* (Durham: Duke University Press, 2001); Tamar Katz, *Impressionist Subjects: Gender, Interiority, and Modernist Fiction in England* (Urbana: University of Illinois Press, 2000); Rosalind Rosenberg, *Beyond Separate Spheres: Intellectual Roots of Modern Feminism* (New Haven: Yale University Press, 1982); Margaret Rossiter, *Women Scientists in America: Struggles and Strategies to 1940* (Baltimore: Johns Hopkins University Press, 1982); Helene Silverberg, ed., *Gender and American Social Science: The Formative Years* (Princeton: Princeton University Press, 1998); Laura Wexler, *Tender Violence: Domestic Visions in an Age of U.S. Imperialism* (Chapel Hill: University of North Carolina Press, 2000); C. Wilson, *Labor*.

12. See Bledstein, *Professionalism;* N. Hatch, *The Professions;* Larson, *Rise of Professionalism*, hereafter *RP*. One measure of this is in the formation of national professional associations. In the U.S., Larson points out, eleven of thirteen contemporary professions formed national associations between 1840 and 1887 (5). See also Bledstein, *Professionalism*, 84.

13. Novick, *Noble Dream*, 31.

14. Larson makes this argument most forcefully in *RP*.

15. Larson outlines how the appeal to past traditions is a crucial legitimating strategy of Progressive professionalism (*RP*), while Haber in *Authority and Honor* discusses specifically the important role that the eighteenth-century gentleman had in nineteenth- and twentieth-century professionalism. One could also read professionalism's appeal to the past through T. J. Jackson Lears's notion of the importance of antimodernist arguments to the creation of cultural modernism in *No Place of Grace: Antimodernism and the Transformation of American Culture* (New York: Pantheon, 1981). Bruce Robbins's incisive account of the relation of past and present in contemporary professional discourse has particularly influenced my own. Robbins shows how an embedded rhetoric of past-ness functions in professionalism. He argues that central to professional discourse is the secular jeremiad, in which the past purity of a profession is compared to its current fallen state in order to create new formulations of professionalism. See *Secular Vocations: Intellectuals, Professionalism, Culture* (New York: Verso, 1993), hereafter cited as *SV*. Likewise, crucial to my argument is Bederman's analysis of how the temporal categories of primitive and civilized are used in a variety of ways in the gendered and racialized discourse of "manliness and civilization" that saturated turn-of-the-century American culture, including professionalism.

16. Cott, *Bonds of Womanhood*, 8, hereafter cited as *BW*. See also Shirley Samuels's incisive account of this dynamic in sentimentalism, the representational form of domestic culture (*Sentiment*, 3–4).

17. In other words, some of the earliest analyses of domesticity that describe it as a nineteenth-century phenomenon already begin to point out the ways in which it exceeds those dates, though they do not articulate this conception of it fully or explain its implications for understanding professionalism more generally. On the protomodern, protoprofessional nature of domesticity, see Kelley, *Private Women;* Sklar, *Beecher;* and Ryan, *Empire.*

18. Just as periodizing domesticity has proven controversial, so also has periodizing professionalism. Some describe professionalism primarily as a Victorian social formation (Bledstein, *Professionalism;* Haber, *The Professions;* and Nelson, *National*). Many other historians and theorists see it as a Progressive era or modern one. See Ehrenreich and Ehrenreich, "Professional-Managerial"; Richard Hofstadter, *The Age of Reform* (New York: Vintage, 1955); Larson, *RP;* Daniel T. Rodgers, "In Search of Progressivism," *Reviews in American History* 10, no. 4 (Dec. 1982): 113–32; Wiebe, *Search.*

19. Howard, *Publishing*, 6.

20. Joan Jacobs Brumberg, "Women in the Professions: A Research Agenda for American Historians," *Reviews in American History* 10, no. 2 (1982): 275; Anthony Giddens, Introduction, *Emile Durkheim: Selected Writings* (New York: Cambridge University Press), 39.

21. It is interesting to note that Durkheim was consistently critical of Marxist thought, and in *The Division of Labor* he analyzes the significance of the capitalist division of labor in a profoundly different way than Marx. Nevertheless, as we shall see, Durkheim's generally progressive narrative is disrupted by nostalgia, a nostalgia that like Marx's, gets located in his own history of the sexual division of labor. In this, his argument seems more related to Marx's than it first appears. For more on Durkheim's differences with Marxism, see Steven Lukes, *Emile Durkheim: His Life and Work* (London: Penguin, 1973), 140–48.

22. Emile Durkheim, *The Division of Labor in Society*, trans. George Simpson (London: Collier-Macmillan, 1964), 56 (hereafter cited parenthetically as *DL*).

23. For a helpful discussion of Spencer, see Bederman, *Civilization*, 26–28.

24. For fuller discussions of *The Division*'s relation to the development of sociology, see Giddens, "Introduction," 29–38; Dominick LaCapra, *Emile Durkheim: Sociologist and Philosopher* (Ithaca: Cornell University Press, 1972), 82–83; Steven Lukes, *Durkheim*, chapter 3.

25. See LaCapra's helpful analysis of the way Durkheim distinguishes sociology from other disciplines (*Durkheim*, 124–25).

26. On Durkheim's modernism, see Giddens, *Writings*, 38–43.

27. I borrow this notion of mechanisms that work to articulate the connections between discourses, even as they try to separate or contain them, from Mark Seltzer, *Bodies and Machines* (New York: Routledge, 1992).

28. This is the famous way in which Marlow in *Heart of Darkness* (1899) describes European women's relation to a brutally rationalized imperialism. Joseph Conrad's insistence that domesticity and professionalism are utterly opposed, his equally strong insistence that they are similar, and finally his insistence that domesticity is morally more reprehensible than professionalism is characteristically modern. By being "out of it," Marlow suggests that European women are more deeply implicated in the horrors of imperialism than European men. The domestic sphere of Marlow's Aunt and Kurtz's Intended is imagined as separate from the public world of men and reality, but at the same time, its disembodied logic functions in precisely the same manner as the rationalized logic of the Accountant. Nonetheless, Marlow finally argues that domesticity is far more sinister and, through the links he makes between the Intended and the Queen, more "primitive."

29. Brumberg, "Women in the Professions."

30. Feminist historians have traced this quite carefully in the Progressive period. See especially Regina Kunzel, *Fallen Women, Problem Girls: Unmarried Mothers and the Professionalization of Social Work* (New Haven: Yale University Press, 1993); Robyn Muncy, *Creating a Female Dominion in American Reform, 1890–1935* (New York: Oxford University Press, 1991); Rosenberg, *Beyond Separate Spheres;* Rossiter, *Women Scientists;* Wexler, *Tender Violence.*

31. It went through nine editions between 1898 and 1920 (Bederman, *Civilization*, 122).

32. Charlotte Perkins (Stetson) Gilman, *Women and Economics* (New York: Small, Maynard and Co., 1899), 67 (hereafter cited parenthetically as *WAE*.)

33. Similarly, in her book *The Home* (1903), Gilman both revises and depends upon the ideas formulated in her great aunts Harriet Beecher Stowe and Catharine Beecher's classic nineteenth-century treatise of domesticity, *The American Woman's Home* (1869). In *The Home*, Gilman carefully deconstructs the separation of the private and the public spheres through a kind of muckraking account of the "reality" of the home that contrasts profoundly with classic accounts of domesticity, like that of Stowe and Beecher. Gilman nonetheless concludes in the last sentences of the book that the ideas associated with the home cannot be relinquished but that those ideas need to be brought into the world so as to "make the world our home at last," a proposition also promulgated by her great aunts. Charlotte Perkins Gilman, *The Home* (New York: Charlton, 1910), 347.

34. Cited in Bederman, *Civilization*, 122, 134.

35. Gambrell, *Women Intellectuals*, 2.

36. As Stephanie J. Shaw points out in her study of black women's professionalism at the turn of the century, the class and status of black women professionals change dramatically when they are viewed from within by the black community and from without by the white community. While the white community saw black women professionals as lower-class and low-level professionals, black women and their communities viewed these women as middle- or upper-class and as fully professionalized. Shaw does not make this distinction in order to minimize class and race politics in America but to describe what black women and their communities' perception enabled black women to do—despite the politics in the nation more broadly. See *What a Woman Ought to Be and Do: Black Professional and Women Workers during the Jim Crow Era* (Chicago: University of Chicago Press, 1996).

37. On Ida B. Wells, see Bederman, *Civilization*, chapter 2. For Williams's, Cooper's, Early's, and Brown's talks, see May Wright Sewall, ed., *The World's Congress of Representative Women* (Chicago: Rand, McNally, 1894). See also Mrs. N. F. Mossell, *The Work of the Afro-American Woman* (1894, 1908; New York: Oxford University Press, 1988); and Annie Nathan Meyer, ed., *Women's Work in America* (New York: Henry Holt, 1891). Much later, Meyer sponsored Zora Neale Hurston's education at Barnard, and one cannot help but wonder if Mossell's text had an influence on Meyer's thinking.

38. In this I am following the logic of Robbins and Sandra Harding, who both argue that distinctions can be made about professional discourse and that professions can affect the larger society, just as the larger society affects professions. By contrast, Stanley Fish sees professions as homogeneous and enclosed entities that can change from within but that have little effect on the larger society. See Stanley Fish, *Professional Correctness: Literary Studies and Political Change* (Oxford: Clarendon Press, 1995); and Sandra Harding, *Whose Science? Whose Knowledge? Thinking from Women's Lives* (Ithaca: Cornell University Press, 1991).

39. Foucault, *History of Sexuality*, 100–101.

40. On corporate or incorporated culture, see Alan Trachtenberg, *The Incorporation of America* (New York: Hill and Wang, 1982); on consumer culture, see Richard

Wightman Fox and T. J. Jackson Lears, ed., *The Culture of Consumption* (New York: Pantheon, 1983).

41. Joan Wallach Scott, *Gender and the Politics of History* (New York: Columbia University Press, 1988), 42–43. This point is particularly important concerning women's texts, about which the usual separation of aesthetics from reality is exacerbated by a quite contrary one in which texts are seen (both positively and negatively) as unmediated transcriptions of lived experience that can be read as transparent. For three helpful and different critiques of this latter notion of women's literary texts, see Gambrell, *Women Intellectuals;* Molly Hite, *The Other Side of the Story: Structures and Strategies of Contemporary Feminist Narrative* (Ithaca: Cornell University Press, 1989); and Carla Kaplan, *The Erotics of Talk: Women's Writing and Feminist Paradigms* (New York: Oxford University Press, 1996).

42. As Shaw points out in *What a Woman Ought to Be and Do,* by examining self-perception, membership in a given community, and effectiveness, we can revise our understanding and history of professionalism.

43. Catherine Gallagher and Stephen Greenblatt, *Practicing New Historicism* (Chicago: University of Chicago Press, 2000), 14.

44. Ibid., 51.

45. Ibid., chapter 2.

46. Kaplan, *Talk,* 7, 13–14.

47. Ibid., 15.

48. Kaplan's definition of an "erotics of talk," which depends on Audre Lorde's ideas about dialogue and erotics, focuses on the performative desire for an ideal listener and the social criticism that is enabled when that desire is frustrated. My book, by contrast, does not analyze the performative nature of such talk, though like Kaplan, it explores the utopian hopes that undergird women's dialogues with each other, the power dynamics that profoundly challenge those hopes, and the social criticism that ensues out of that dialectic.

49. I have conceptualized these dialogues in a somewhat similar way to Carol Batker's notion of the "networks of influence" between politically active women journalists in the early twentieth century. Like her, I have therefore focused on how women's "networks of influence" reveal "shared" as well as "jagged and uneasy" use of discourses and tropes. I am, however, less interested than she is in tracing the institutional or personal connections between these women and men and more interested in the weaknesses and strengths of the discourses used. Carol J. Batker, *Reforming Fictions* (New York: Columbia University Press, 2000), 10. I would add that the dialogue between men and women deserves more exploration than it has currently received or than I have engaged in here. For recent work thinking through the history of and problems with the segregation of men and women's texts, see Karen Kilcup, ed., *Soft Canons: Women Writers and Masculine Tradition* (Iowa City: University of Iowa Press, 1999).

50. In recent years, social theorists have increasingly argued that in our own era of multinational and globalized capitalism, professionalism has itself been undermined. While the professions cannot claim the level of prestige or protection they did in the past, I would argue that it is premature, and as I suggest in my afterword, self-defeating to insist their influence and power is at an end. Robbins's analysis in *SV* of contemporary professionalism is helpful here in that he powerfully shows how a rhetoric of decline and fall is typical of professional reinvention (see note 15). More importantly, however, I would follow the logic of many critics of postmodernism in suggesting that while the broad economic, social, and cultural changes we are seeing can be called postmodern, our analyses of these changes are often indebted to the narratives of modernity, which read

historical change as absolute rupture. For these reasons, I refuse to separate prematurely our contemporary professionalism from the professionalism of the modern period.

Chapter 1

1. Sarah Orne Jewett, *Deephaven* (1877; London: Osgood, McIlvaine, and Co., 1893), 3 (hereafter cited parenthetically as *DH*).

2. Jewett repeatedly described her call to vocation in this way. See Sarah Orne Jewett, *Letters*, ed. Annie Fields (Boston: Houghton Mifflin, 1911), 228; and *Sarah Orne Jewett Letters*, ed. Richard Cary (Waterville, Maine: Colby College Press, 1967), 83–84, 164.

3. My questions are clearly indebted to Raymond Williams's groundbreaking analysis of the recurrent yet shifting use of the pastoral in British literature and culture in *The Country and the City* (New York: Oxford University Press, 1973).

4. The phrase *seed-bed* comes from Harriet Beecher Stowe, *Oldtown Folks* (1869; New Brunswick: Rutgers University Press, 1987), 3. For analyses of the relations of city to country in this time and the perceptions about that relation, see Dona Brown, *Inventing New England* (Washington D.C.: Smithsonian, 1995); Hofstadter, *Reform;* Lears, *No Place of Grace;* Gabriel Kolko, *Main Currents in Modern American History* (New York: Pantheon Books, 1984); Jay Martin, *Harvests of Change* (Englewood Cliffs: Prentice-Hall, 1967); Trachtenberg, *Incorporation;* Wiebe, *Search*.

5. The best example of this is Vernon Louis Parrington, *Main Currents in American Thought: The Beginnings of Critical Realism in America, 1860–1920*, vol. 3 (New York: Harcourt, Brace, and Company, 1930). Parrington was clearly influenced by George Santayana's powerfully effective account of the genteel tradition. I discuss the importance of this concept to the gendering of professional literary studies in the U.S. in Chapter 3. A less virulent version of the same argument is evident in Van Wyck Brooks, *New England Indian Summer* (New York: E. P. Dutton, 1940).

6. See, among others, Elizabeth Ammons, "Going in Circles: The Female Geography of Jewett's *Country of the Pointed Firs*," *Studies in the Literary Imagination* 16, no. 2 (1983): 83–92; Josephine Donovan, *Sarah Orne Jewett* (New York: Frederick Ungar, 1980); Judith Fetterley, " 'Not in the Least American': Nineteenth-Century Literary Regionalism as UnAmerican Literature," in *Nineteenth-Century American Women Writers*, ed. Karen Kilcup (Oxford: Blackwell, 1998), 15–32; Marjorie Pryse, " 'Distilling Essences': Regionalism and 'Women's Culture'," *American Literary Realism* 25, no. 2 (winter 1993): 1–15; Margaret Roman, *Sarah Orne Jewett: Reconstructing Gender* (Tuscaloosa: University of Alabama Press, 1992); Sandra Zagarell, "Narratives of Community: The Identification of a Genre," *Signs* 13, no. 3 (1988): 498–527.

7. See Richard Brodhead, *Cultures of Letters* (Chicago: University of Chicago Press, 1993); James M. Cox, "Regionalism: A Diminished Thing," in *The Columbia Literary History of the U.S.*, ed. Emory Elliott (New York: Columbia University Press, 1988): 761–84; Alfred Habegger, *Gender, Fantasy, and Realism in American Literature* (New York: Columbia University Press, 1982). Brodhead's argument has been particularly influential in recent debates about regionalism. For two arguments that take on Brodhead's rather unilinear account of how the literary market shaped regionalism in a more empirical fashion than mine, see Nancy Glazener, *Reading for Realism* (Durham: Duke University Press, 1997); Charles Johanningsmeier, "Sarah Orne Jewett and Mary E. Wilkins (Freeman): Two Shrewd Businesswomen in Search of New Markets," *New England Quarterly* 70, no. 1 (March 1997): 57–82.

8. On form as both historically mutable and real, see especially June Howard, *Form*

and History in American Literary Naturalism (Chapel Hill: University of North Carolina Press, 1985), 7–10.

9. Howard and Zagarell make similar arguments about how to overcome what they describe as an impasse in recent scholarly debates about Jewett between feminists and historicists. They suggest that the impasse in Jewett studies can be resolved by rethinking our insistence on critique or celebration and on unilinear definitions and periodizations. See June Howard, "Unraveling Regions, Unsettling Periods: Sarah Orne Jewett and American Literary History," *American Literature* 68, no. 2 (1996): 365–84; Sandra Zagarell, "Crosscurrents: Registers of Nordicism, Community, and Culture in Jewett's *Pointed Firs*," *Yale Journal of Criticism* 10, no. 2 (fall 1997): 355–70.

10. Lora Romero, *Home Fronts: Domesticity and Its Critics in the Antebellum U.S.* (Durham: Duke University Press, 1997), 5) hereafter cited parenthetically as *HF*). Romero's analysis of how even Foucauldian-inspired historicist readings depend on idealized agency is particularly deft and demonstrates the assumptions that inform powerful historicist work like that of Brodhead (84–87).

11. While focusing on the overlap between feminist and old and new historicist readings of Jewett, I want to insist that there are important differences between them. Nevertheless, I am emphasizing the overlap between these readings in order to rethink the impasse between feminist and historicist methodologies.

12. Romero focuses on the nineteenth-century domestic woman but argues, like most critics, that the "oppositionalist binarism" (*HF*, 87) of hegemony and resistance that figures idealized agency as crucial in aesthetics dates to the Enlightenment. See also Ronald Schleifer, *Modernism and Time* (New York: Cambridge University Press, 2000), x–xii.

13. Henry James, *The Notebooks of Henry James*, ed. F. O. Matthiessen and Kenneth B. Murdock (New York: Oxford University Press, 1947), 129; Thorstein Veblen, *The Theory of the Leisure Class* (1899; reprint, New York: New American Library, 1953), 56. Despite Veblen's sarcasm, he saw the cultivated "new woman" as a progressive development. Her "disinterested motives" (225), while somewhat class-bound, represented a promising survival of "non-invidious interest" (passim) in pecuniary culture.

14. Stephanie Foote, *Regional Fictions: Culture and Identity in Nineteenth-Century American Literature* (Madison: University of Wisconsin Press, 2001).

15. See note 15 in my introductory chapter on the ways the past was useful to progressive professional discourse generally. Don Kirschner adds relevant information to the issue on progressive professional temporality for my argument on Jewett and Addams. He argues that a double-pronged temporality characterizes the work of first generation, urban "new professionals" (11). These social workers sought to solve problems of urbanization largely through a recourse to ideas about democracy and community of their "village" past. Kirschner thereby links progressive reform to regionalism. I add to his argument by pointing to the gendered inflection of these links. Don S. Kirschner, *The Paradox of Professionalism: Reform and the Public Sphere* (New York: Greenwood Press, 1986).

16. Jewett and Addams met socially and seemed to have known each other's work fairly well. Although Jewett's friend and companion for thirty years, Annie Fields, was a reform activist who helped found a settlement house in Boston as well as the Associated Charities of Boston, which she directed from 1879 to 1894, Jewett was politically much more conservative than Addams. On Annie Fields's activism and Jewett's response to it, see Judith Fryer, "What Goes on in the Ladies Room? Sarah Orne Jewett, Annie Fields, and Their Community of Women," *Massachusetts Review* 30, no. 4 (1989): 610–28. While the relations between these women would be interesting to trace in depth, as indicated in the introduction, I am not primarily concerned in tracing direct

influences. Instead, I want to explicate common discursive responses of different professionals across disciplinary lines.

17. For a fascinating reading of Jane Addams and Hull-House that also analyzes how Addams combined ideas about domesticity and culture, see Shannon Jackson, *Lines of Activity: Performance, Historiography, Hull-House Domesticity* (Ann Arbor: University of Michigan Press, 2000). While Jackson and I both analyze the flexibility that this combination enabled, Jackson focuses on the way it could bleed into forms of social control, and I criticize the race and class politics that inhere in its strategies of authorization.

18. Scholarly studies of both Jewett and Addams have shown how each explicitly invoked the racist ideas of the time in their work. While those analyses inform mine, I am focusing on the link between class and race, and their implicit rather than explict racism. On Addams's and the settlement house movement's racism, see especially Elisabeth Lasch-Quinn, *Black Neighbors: Race and the Limits of Reform in the American Settlement House Movement* (Chapel Hill: University of North Carolina Press, 1993). For Jewett, see Elizabeth Ammons, "Material Culture, Empire, and Jewett's *Pointed Firs*," in *New Essays on* The Country of the Pointed Firs, ed. June Howard (New York: Cambridge University Press, 1994): 81–99; Amy Kaplan, "Nation, Region, and Empire," in *The Columbia History of the American Novel*, ed. Emory Elliott (New York: Columbia University Press, 1991), 240–66; Zagarell, "Crosscurrents," and "*Pointed Firs*' Portrayal of Community and the Exclusion of Difference," in *New Essays on* Country of the Pointed Firs: 39–60. Addams's and Jewett's racism worked in different ways. Addams was an important white ally in the black struggle for social justice and helped found the NAACP. She was an antinativist and antiimperialist. Her anxiety about alienating conservative allies, however, led her to compromise on issues like segregation and lynching. Similarly, while she developed a quite nuanced idea of cultural pluralism, it depended on notions of culture as whole and so perforce excluded groups that she saw as irrevocably divorced from their native culture (most prominently, as Lasch-Quinn shows, African Americans). Jewett, by contrast, espoused ideas about Anglo-Saxon superiority and was a nativist and imperialist, though as Zagarell points out in "Crosscurrents," these different racisms map out unevenly in her work.

19. Henry Steele Commager, foreword to *Twenty Years at Hull-House*, by Jane Addams (New York: New American Library, 1938), vii–xviii (hereafter cited parenthetically as *H-H*). I cite Commager's phrase because whatever Cedarville was indeed like during Addams's childhood, she effectively portrays it as a characteristically American country village.

20. Women dominated the settlement house movement in America from its inception. See Allen F. Davis, *Spearheads for Reform* (New York: Oxford University Press, 1967); Kathryn Kish Sklar, *Florence Kelley and the Nation's Work* (New Haven: Yale University Press, 1995); Dorothy Ross, "Gendered Social Knowledge: Domestic Discourse, Jane Addams, and the Possibilities of Social Science," in *Gender and American Social Science*, ed. Helene Silverberg (Princeton: Princeton University Press, 1998): 235–64; Judith Ann Trolander, *Professionalism and Social Change* (New York: Columbia University Press, 1987).

21. Addams compares in the same passage not only the girl's cultivated uselessness in relation to her grandmother and great-grandmother's uncultivated usefulness but also that of the daughter's to the mother's (*H-H*, 64).

22. For a succinct analysis of the increasing radicalism of Hull-House, see Mina Carson, *Settlement Folk: Social Thought and the American Settlement Movement* (Chicago: University of Chicago Press, 1990), chapter 4. Carson makes the point that this radicalism was the logical outcome of Hull-House's notion of itself as a mediator of political disputes, a notion I am arguing was deeply indebted to domestic ideology. See also Jackson, *Lines of Activity* and Sklar, *Florence Kelley*.

23. In *No Place of Grace*, Lears uses *Twenty Years at Hull-House* and Addams's work to discuss the antimodernism of late-nineteenth century "arts and crafts ideology." Lears argues that because Addams and other arts and crafts ideologues sought personal fulfillment through premodern work rather than new ways to improve the degrading and alienated forms that modernized labor was taking, they capitulated to "capitalist cultural hegemony" (80). While Lears's analysis is extremely helpful, one issue that his analysis does not explore is that of leisure: how premodern labor became an object of quest for the bourgeoisie, an object to be kept other to the self as well as to be—as he argues—forcefully integrated into their life. Relatedly, Lears does not discuss the relation between gender, and arts and craft ideology. While Addams's ideas do indeed seem to fit Lears's concept of antimodernism, she links her alienation to her exclusion from the "work of the world," and she wants to return specifically to domesticity.

24. For a longer formulation of Addams's notion of cosmopolitanism, see her *Newer Ideals of Peace* (New York: Macmillan, 1906). Like her conception of cultural pluralism, Addams's notion of cosmopolitanism is nuanced and complex; however, it is also a problematically holistic, idealized, and aestheticized conception.

25. Because one of the main concerns of the settlement house was shaping public opinion, it was important to relay a safe and inoffensive image to the public. Historians have shown what kind of problems settlement house and social workers created for themselves in their attempt to present acceptable images of their work. Both domestic and professional language ended up foreclosing some of the more radical impulses of their social activism. See Kunzel, *Fallen Women*; Trolander, *Social Change*.

26. Jane Addams, *Women and Public Housekeeping* (New York: National American Woman Suffrage Association, 1913), unpaginated.

27. Davis, *Spearheads*, x; Trolander, *Social Change*, chapters 2–3.

28. In later years, Addams acknowledged both the cost of the claim to unprofessionalism and suggested the ways that settlement house workers had been in the past and had since become professional. See my essay, "The Authority of Experience: Jane Addams and Hull-House," in *Women's Experience of Modernity*, ed. Ann Ardis and Leslie Lewis (Baltimore: Johns Hopkins University Press, 2003), 47–62.

29. On the progressives' optimistic belief that the visual or textual exposure of problems would lead to social transformation, see Carson, *Settlement Folk*; Richard Hofstadter, *The Progressive Movement* (New York: Simon and Schuster, 1986), 4–5; and Trolander, *Social Change*.

30. Addams, "Women and Public Housekeeping."

31. Other critics than me have noted how serious Jewett was about her vocation as a writer and how her writing describes and enacts professional ideals. Brodhead in *Cultures* and Elizabeth Ammons in *Conflicting Stories* (New York: Oxford University Press, 1991) describe her as one of the first American women who saw herself as an artist and claimed a kind of ethical duty to her writing. Cecilia Tichi describes Jewett as a "new woman" writer, trying to describe as well as create, work for women. "Women Writers and the New Woman," 589–606.

32. Sarah Orne Jewett, *The Country of the Pointed Firs*, in *The Best Short Stories of Sarah Orne Jewett*, vol. 1, ed. Willa Cather (Boston: Houghton Mifflin, 1925), 173–74, hereafter cited as *CPF*.

33. The use of the term *botanist* at this moment underlines the narrator's belief in her larger worldview. A few pages before she has described Mrs. Todd, in her ideas and expressions, as "nothing if not botanical" (*CPF*, 167). Here she appropriates the role of botanist from Mrs. Todd, in order to describe Mrs. Todd herself.

34. Julie A. Matthaei, *An Economic History of Women in America* (New York: Schocken Books, 1982), 49.

35. For example, Mrs. Todd alone is described as "a huge sibyl" (10, 289), an "oracle" (139), "Medea" (209, 290), "grand and architectural, like a caryatide" (46), "a large figure of Victory" (61), "Antigone alone on the Theban plain" (78), "cousin . . . to the ancient deities" (259), and having wisdom that "belong[s] to any age, like an idyl of Theocritus" (93).

36. That the narrator's cultural knowledge is finally what breaks down barriers between her and the residents of Dunnet Landing is further suggested by her uncanny ability to make all the people of Dunnet Landing, of whatever class or sex, feel comfortable with her and confide in her. While, as noted before, Mrs. Todd guides her in the art of "seein' folks," the narrator surpasses her teacher's skills. Captain Littlepage, Elijah Tilley, and William Todd talk as easily in the narrator as do Mrs. Todd, Mrs. Blackett, and the "Queen's Twin." For similar analyses of the touristic sensibility in regionalist literature generally, see Brodhead, *Cultures;* Kaplan, "Nation, Region, and Empire."

37. Sarah Orne Jewett, "The Old Town of Berwick," *New England Magazine,* n.s., 10 (July 1894): 16.

38. Ibid., 14.

Chapter 2

1. Pauline E. Hopkins, *Contending Forces: A Romance Illustrative of Negro Life North and South* (1900; reprint, New York: Oxford University Press, 1988), 115, emphasis added. Hereafter cited as *CF.*

2. Hazel V. Carby, *Reconstructing Womanhood: The Emergence of the Afro-American Woman Novelist,* 30, hereafter cited parenthetically as *RW.*

3. Paula Giddings, *When and Where I Enter: The Impact of Black Women on Race and Sex in America* (New York: W. Morrow, 1984), 41–54.

4. Stephanie Shaw discusses the ways in which black professional women problematize simple class dichotomies, for they often came from impoverished families and did not earn sums comparable to white professionals. It is also true, she says, that black women's work in the Jim Crow era would not fit classic definitions of professionalism; however, these women's high status within their communities and their subjective perceptions of themselves, Shaw argues convincingly, defines them as professionals *What a Woman Ought to Be and Do: Black Professional and Women Workers during the Jim Crow Era* (Chicago: University of Chicago Press, 1996), 210–13, 1–10. Following Shaw's logic, I describe the women in this chapter as middle- and upper-class professionals despite the problems with such terms.

5. I am borrowing here from Donna Haraway's well-known notion of "situated knowledges" in which she argues that feminists must sustain in their work "*simultaneously* an account of radical historical contingency for all knowledge claims and knowing subjects, a critical practice for recognizing our own 'semiotic technologies' for making meanings, *and* a no-nonsense commitment to faithful accounts of a 'real' world" (579). I am adapting Haraway's notion, however, so I can focus on the problem of contextualizing claims to expertise or authoritative knowledge generally rather than scientific or "objective" knowledge particularly. Donna Haraway, "Situated Knowledges: The Science Question in Feminism and the Privilege of Partial Perspective," *Feminist Studies* 14, no. 3 (fall 1988): 575–99.

6. Benedict Anderson, *Imagined Communities* (New York: Verso, 1993), 195, 197.

7. The racist regionalist stories of Thomas Nelson Page and Thomas Dixon, and the films of D. W. Griffith, among others, authorized the defeated Confederates' view of

history and had a massive impact upon the nation culturally, socially, and politically. See Michael Rogin, " 'The Sword Became a Flashing Vision': D. W. Griffith's *The Birth of a Nation*," *Representations* 9 (1995): 150–95; Joel Williamson, *The Crucible of Race* (New York: Oxford University Press, 1984). For analyses of how unified notions of professional discipline were created through racism in the antebellum and Jim Crow eras respectively, see Dana D. Nelson, *National Manhood: Capitalist Citizenship and the Imagined Fraternity of White Men* (Durham: Duke University Press, 1998; and Peter Novick, *That Noble Dream: The "Objectivity Question" and the American Historical Profession* (New York: Cambridge University Press, 1993).

8. Charles Chesnutt's famous diary entries in the 1880s perhaps provide the best example of black writers' belief that regionalism could be used to contest racism and authorize a new political voice. Richard Brodhead, *Cultures of Letters* (Chicago: University of Chicago Press, 1993, 190–97).

9. Ann Du Cille and Claudia Tate make similar points, arguing that critics neglect postbellum black women's fiction because U.S. literary criticism is often burdened with ahistorical and-or expressivist assumptions about cultural production. Ann Du Cille, *The Coupling Convention* (New York: Oxford University Press, 1993); Claudia Tate, *Domestic Allegories of Political Desire* (New York: Oxford University Press, 1992).

10. Elsewhere, Carby distinguishes between different forms of regionalism and argues that the contemporary critical preference for regionalist fictions of rural blacks romanticizes and aestheticizes the folk roots of African American culture and denies the significance of black urban consciousness and of black history more generally. "The Politics of Fiction, Anthropology, and the Folk: Zora Neale Hurston," in *New Essays on Their Eyes Were Watching God*, ed. Michael Awkward (New York: Cambridge University Press, 1990): 71–93. Carby's critique is instructive, and I discuss it more fully in Chapter 5. I am arguing, however, that regionalism can be rural or urban in form and can be used to revise as much as reify the "aboriginal essence" (Anderson, *Imagined*, 195) of a nation.

11. Dickson D. Bruce Jr., *Black American Writing from the Nadir* (Baton Rouge: Louisiana State University Press, 1989), 190–91; Brodhead, *Cultures*, 206. Wilson Jeremiah Moses similarly criticizes black nationalists at the turn of the century for offering "reform panaceas . . . aimed at achieving assimilationist ends through separatist means" (30). *The Golden Age of Black Nationalism, 1850–1925* (Hamden, Conn.: Archon, 1978). As with the critics of literary regionalism, I would argue that Moses's views of nationalist "reform panaceas" could be more thoroughly contextualized and problematized.

12. Critics have noted in a variety of ways the tension in Hopkins's work between generalizability and specificity. This tension, they show, is linked to the high stakes surrounding representation and representativeness for blacks at the turn of the century. See C. K. Doreski, *Writing America Black: Race Rhetoric in the Public Sphere* (New York: Cambridge University Press, 1998); Jennie A. Kassanoff, " 'Fate Has Linked Us Together': Blood, Gender, and the Politics of Representation in Pauline Hopkins's *Of One Blood*," in *The Unruly Voice*, ed. John Cullen Gruesser (Urbana: University of Illinois Press, 1996), 158–81; Kate McCullough, "Slavery, Sexuality, and Genre: Pauline Hopkins and the Representation of Female Desire," ed. John Cullen Gruesser, 21–49. This tension is evident also in black women's professionalism more generally at this time, which historians describe as having an ethic of "socially responsible individualism" (Shaw, *What A Woman Ought to Be and Do*, 2; see also Wanda A. Hendricks, *Gender, Race, and Politics in the Midwest: Black Club Women in Illinois* (Bloomington: Indiana University Press, 1998), 26–39.

13. Hopkins was not only involved in and wrote about the women's club movement

but also read chapters of *Contending Forces* aloud to members of the Woman's Era Club of Boston, under the leadership of Josephine St. Pierre Ruffin (Carby, *RW,* 120).

14. For different discussions of the complex relation of the club movement to feminism, see Karen J. Blair, *The Clubwoman as Feminist* (New York: Holmes and Meier, 1980); Ann Ruggles Gere, *Intimate Practices: Literacy and Cultural Work in U.S. Women's Clubs, 1880–1920* (Urbana: University of Illinois Press, 1997); Giddings, *The Impact of Black Women on Race and Sex in America*; Hendricks, *Gender, Race, and Politics*; Dorothy Salem, *To Better Our World: Black Women in Organized Reform, 1890–1920* (Brooklyn: Carlson, 1990); Anne Firor Scott, *Natural Allies: Women's Associations in American History* (Urbana: University of Illinois Press, 1991).

15. Giddings, *The Impact of Black Women*, 108–16.

16. Josephine St. Pierre Ruffin, "Publishers' Announcement," *Woman's Era* 1, no. 1 (March 24, 1894): 8.

17. I am indebted to Anderson's theory of the relation between newspapers and nationalism in the eighteenth century in *Imagined* for my analysis.

18. Fannie Barrier Williams, "The Club Movement among Colored Women of America," in *A New Negro for a New Century*, ed. Booker T. Washington, Fannie Barrier Williams, and N. B. Wood (1900; reprint, New York: Arno, 1969), 390.

19. Josephine St. Pierre Ruffin, "Editorial Greeting," *Woman's Era* 1, no. 1 (March 24, 1894): 8.

20. Ruffin, ed., *Woman's Era:* 1, no. 1: p 7; see also in Ruffin, ed., *Woman's Era* 1, no. 2 (May 1894): 3–4; 1, no. 3 (June 1894): 5, 9; 1, no. 4 (July 1894): 6; 1, no. 8 (November 1894); 2, no. 3 (June 1895); 2, no. 4 (July 1895); 2–3, 12.

21. As time went on, for example, visual material was also included to highlight the text and focus the reader's attention on it.

22. "News from the Clubs," *Woman's Era* 1, no. 1 (March 24, 1894): 4.

23. Josephine St. Pierre Ruffin, "Let us Confer Together," *Woman's Era* 2, no. 3 (June 1895): 8.

24. Ibid.

25. Ibid. Ruffin studiously avoids describing the attack or its author in the pages of *Woman's Era*, as do most of the club women, refusing to provide him with any publicity. The significance of the letter, however, was that while written by an "obscure editor in a Missouri town" ("The Club Movement," 396–97), as Fannie Barrier Williams puts it, the letter was sent to Florence Belgarnie, who was an important English ally in the fight against lynching in the United States.

26. Ibid. Ruffin might well have been describing Boston as the best place to create counterrepresentations because of its importance to the development of publishing in the nineteenth century and specifically to abolitionist publications. Alice Ames Winter, of the white General Federation of Women's Clubs, similarly advised club women that "publicity . . . is so great an element in club success that it weighs almost one-half of the total measure of club activities." *The Business of Being a Club Woman* (New York: Century, 1925), 164. If public representation was crucial for middle-class, white women—negotiating their political activism for the first time through a generally hostile male press—it was even more so for black women, as they themselves recognized. Frances Harper's novel *Iola Leroy* (1892), for example, repeatedly argues that it is representation that creates public opinion and politics, and it is representation that can change public opinion and politics. *Iola Leroy* (New York: Oxford University Press, 1988), 114–16, 262–63, 282.

27. Josephine St. Pierre Ruffin, "Address of Josephine Pierre St. Ruffin, President of the Conference," *Woman's Era* 2, no. 6 (August 1895): 15.

28. Ibid.

29. Ibid., 14.
30. Ibid., 15.
31. Ibid., 14, emphasis added.
32. Because of her story "Aunt Lindy" (1891), Matthews has herself been described as "among the first of the black . . . regionalist writers." Bruce, *Black American Writing*, 55.
33. Victoria Earle Matthews, "The Value of Race Literature," *Massachusetts Review* 27, no. 2 (Summer 1986): 176; hereafter cited parenthetically as *RL*.
34. I interpret "counter-irritants" as meaning representations that counter the racist texts of the mainstream. It is possible that Matthews means that literature is only a superficial cure to the larger disease of racism, though this seems unlikely, given the high valuation she ascribes to literature throughout the rest of the essay.
35. Salem, *To Better Our World*, 7–10. Ruffin was at the center of the most infamous action taken to exclude black women from involvement in the white General Federation of Women's Clubs. See Blair, *Clubwoman as Feminist*, 108–9. The General Federation of Women's Clubs's official history describes this incident as a battle between northern and southern clubs, and concludes gratefully that the whole matter was "tactfully" put "in abeyance." *History of the General Federation of Women's Clubs* (New York: General Federation of Women's Clubs, 1912), 129–31.
36. Salem, *To Better Our World*, 17–19.
37. Pauline E. Hopkins, "Famous Women of the Negro Race: Educators," in *Colored American Magazine* 5, no. 3 (July 1902): 206–13; "Famous Women of the Negro Race: Club Life among Colored Women," in *Colored American Magazine* 5, no. 4 (August 1902): 273–77; "Echoes from the Annual Convention of Colored Northeastern Federation of Colored Women's Clubs" 6, no. 10 (October 1903): 709–13.
38. Hopkins, "Club Life among Colored Women, 275; "Echoes from the Annual Convention," 712.
39. Hopkins, "Club Life Among Colored Women," 277; "Echoes from the Annual Convention," 713.
40. Ibid.; ibid.
41. See Du Cille, *Coupling Convention;* Tate, *Domestic Allegories;* Richard Yarborough, introduction to *Contending Forces*, by Pauline E. Hopkins.
42. See also Carby, *RW*, 128–30.
43. Later in the text, Hopkins states that "Races are like families" (*CF*, 198), which would seem to contradict the notion of one "human family." But she goes on to state that races change, depending on the circumstances and environment in which they find themselves. So, though she at first seems to be relying on ideas about nation as race prevalent in the nineteenth century, she finally argues that races are constructed by a given context. On the close relations between nineteenth-century ideas about race and nation, see Reginald Horsman, *Race and Manifest Destiny* (Cambridge: Harvard University Press, 1981).
44. This is clearly meant to be an analysis of the present as well as the past. Because Hopkins sees the past as central to understanding the present and because her aim is to reconstruct (as Carby says) the past in order to change the present, she presents this dynamic as historical.
45. Hopkins leaves Mrs. Montfort's lineage unexplained. On the one hand, Hopkins suggests her beauty is the result of a black relative. On the other hand, Mrs. Montfort's good looks create the suspicion of her black blood amongst a people who have no information on her and who want to kill her husband, rape her, and steal their property. Carby convincingly argues that the ambiguity about her lineage helps enforce the notion that this whipping symbolizes the rape of African American women (*RW*, 132).
46. Claudia Tate makes a similar point, arguing that in *Contending Forces* the home

and domesticity represent allegorically the political aspirations of the black community, particularly those of African American women. *Domestic Allegories*, 160–66.

47. Langley's bizarre death in the Klondike, surrounded by gold and his dead companions, does not simply provide a moral on greed and individualism (Carby, *RW*, 139); rather, I would argue, it is also an American's revision of Frankenstein, a commentary on what *Contending Forces* sees as the monstrous American myth of the self-made man.

48. For discussions of the complexity of the uplift ideology of black women professionals and club members, see Hendricks, *Gender, Race, and Politics;* Shaw, *What a Woman Ought to Be and Do*.

49. That is, Hopkins criticizes the Republican Party's betrayal of African Americans in the post-Reconstruction period.

50. For a very different reading of this meeting, see Tate, *Domestic Allegories*, 165.

51. Elizabeth Blackmar and Roy Rosenzweig, *The Park and the People* (New York: Holt, 1992).

52. Critics have read Sappho's name in a variety of ways—as referring to the novel's homoerotic subtext as well as to its analysis of black women's artistry. I want to add to these readings that the naming of the character furthermore demonstrates the kinds of intertextual relations between literary and political texts and ideas during this time. Harper's novel *Iola Leroy*, for example, uses Ida Wells's pen name for its main heroine, while Sappho, as already noted, appears in Victoria Earle Matthews's talk at the first meeting of the NACW.

53. Cited in Yarborough, introduction to *Contending Forces*, xliii.

54. Carby, *RW*; Frances Smith Foster, *Written By Herself* (Bloomington: University of Indiana Press, 1993); Tate, *Domestic Allegories*.

55. Williams, "The Club Movement," 384, 383–84, 382, 416, respectively.

Chapter 3

1. My argument builds here on the accounts of historians and critics of the resistance women experienced from the turn of the century to World War II in the professions in the British and American contexts. Penina Migdal Glazer and Miriam Slater, *Unequal Colleagues: The Entrance of Women into the Professions, 1890–1940* (New Brunswick: Rutgers University Press, 1987); Regina Kunzel, *Fallen Women: Problem Girls: Unmarried Mothers and the Professionalization of Social Work* (New Haven: Yale University Press, 1993); Rosaline Rosenberg, *Beyond Separate Spheres: Intellectual Roots of Modern Feminism* (New Haven: Yale University Press, 1982); Margaret Rossiter, *Women Scientists in America: Struggles and Strategies to 1940* (Baltimore: Johns Hopkins University Press, 1982). My account of race and gender ideology of turn-of-the-century literary professionalization depends on recent work on both the profession and its central forms—realism and naturalism. See Michael Davitt Bell, *The Problem of American Realism* (Chicago: University of Chicago Press, 1993); Nancy Bentley, *The Ethnography of Manners* (New York: Cambridge University Press, 1995); Daniel H. Borus, *Writing Realism: Howells, James, and Norris in the Mass Market* (Chapel Hill: University of North Carolina Press, 1989); Donna M. Campbell, *Resisting Regionalism* (Athens: Ohio University Press, 1997); Susan Coultrap-McQuin, *Doing Literary Business* (Chapel Hill: University of North Carolina Press, 1990); Philip Fisher, *Hard Facts* (New York: Oxford University Press, 1985); Nina E. Fortin and Gaye Tuchman, *Edging Women Out: Victorian Novelists, Publishers, and Social Change* (New Haven: Yale University Press, 1989); Nancy Glazener, *Reading for Realism* (Durham: Duke University Press, 1997); Gerald Graff, *Professing Literature: An Institutional History* (Chicago: University of Chicago Press, 1989); June Howard, *Form and History in Ameri-*

can Literary Naturalism (Chapel Hill: University of North Carolina Press, 1985); Amy Kaplan, *The Social Construction of American Realism* (Chicago: University of Chicago Press, 1988); Paul Lauter, "Shaping the American Literary Canon: A Case Study from the Twenties," in *Canons and Contexts* (New York: Oxford University Press, 1991), 22–47; Donald Pizer, *The Theory and Practice of American Literary Naturalism* (Carbondale: Southern Illinois University Press, 1993); Mark Seltzer, *Bodies and Machines* (New York: Routledge, 1992); Elaine Showalter, *Sexual Anarchy: Gender and Culture at the Fin de Siecle* (New York: Viking, 1990); Kenneth Warren, *Black and White Strangers: Race and American Literary Realism* (Chicago: University of Chicago Press, 1993); Christopher Wilson, *The Labor of Words: Literary Professionalism in the Progressive Era* (Athens: University of Georgia Press, 1985).

2. This is a permutation of the same logic Huyssen describes in his famous essay, "Mass Culture as Woman: Modernism's Other," in *After the Great Divide* (Bloomington: University of Indiana Press, 1986).

3. Bell, *Problem;* Borus, *Writing;* Campbell, *Resisting;* Alfred Habegger, *Gender, Fantasy, and Realism in American Literature* (New York: Columbia University Press, 1982); C. Wilson, *Labor.*

4. Boyesen was a professor at Columbia as well as a fiction writer and magazine writer. Similarly, despite his claims to the contrary, Norris was an academically trained writer, studying literature, first, at the University of California, Berkeley (1890–94) and then, later, at Harvard (1894–95). His novel *Vandover and the Brute* is dedicated to a professor at Harvard, Lewis Gates, whose literary criticism helped shape Norris's views. See Frank Norris, *The Literary Criticism of Frank Norris*, ed. Donald Pizer (Austin: University Texas Press, 1964), xvii, hereafter cited parenthetically as *LC*. Norris's literary studies were preceded by his studies in painting from 1887–88 in Paris at the Academie Julian. The professionalism of the academicians who taught Norris, William Dillingham argues convincingly, had a major impact on Norris's work. *Frank Norris: Instinct and Art* (Lincoln: University of Nebraska Press, 1969), 14–24.

5. For lists of the many U.S. writers and critics from the early to late twentieth century who were influenced by Santayana, see Robert Dawidoff, *The Genteel Tradition and the Sacred Rage* (Chapel Hill: University of North Carolina Press, 1992), 151; Douglas L. Wilson, ed., *The Genteel Tradition: Nine Essays by George Santayana* (Cambridge: Harvard University Press, 1967), 16–25.

6. I am not the first to link Norris and Santayana. William Dillingham shows how Norris has long been seen by many critics and writers as following Santayana's thinking by breaking with the genteel tradition. Dillingham argues, as I do, that Norris is in fact closely linked to the genteel tradition; however, Dillingham sees that as a personal proclivity rather than as inhering in Norris's professionalism. "Frank Norris and the Genteel Tradition," in *Critical Essays on Frank Norris*, ed. Don Graham (Boston: Hall, 1980): 194–204.

7. Norris often used the terms *romanticism* and *naturalism* indistinguishably in order to define them against realism, as is the case here. For his use of these three terms, see Pizer's analysis in Norris, *LC*, 69–70.

8. This essay appeared in the *Boston Evening Transcript* in late 1901, as did Norris's essay "Why Women Should Write the Best Novels: And Why They Don't," which I discuss below. Norris was also solicited to write serious-minded essays about the novelist's profession in the same time for the reformist journal *World's Work* ("The True Reward of the Novelist," "The Need of a Literary Conscience" [1901]). Joseph R. McElrath Jr., *Frank Norris Revisited* (New York: Twayne, 1992), 104–5.

9. This is Showalter's helpful term for the highly popular, masculinist, imperial ro-

mances of turn-of-the-century England (*Anarchy*, chapter 5). Norris admired Kipling's romances and is clearly influenced by their gender politics (Pizer, *LC*, 20–23).

10. For different variations of this basic narrative, see John C. Conder, *Naturalism in American Fiction: The Classic Phase* (Lexington: University of Kentucky Press, 1984); Habegger, *Gender;* Lee Clark Mitchell, *Determined Fictions: American Literacy Naturalism* (New York: Columbia University Press, 1991); Charles Walcutt, *American Literary Naturalism: A Divided Stream* (Minneapolis: University of Minnesota Press, 1956). Habegger does include sentimentalism in his version of the basic narrative, but the trajectory remains the same: realism is the "crucial middle m[a]n" (65) between sentimentalism and naturalism, enabling the birth of the serious "masculine" (65) form of naturalism.

11. Sentimental elements have been identified in individual naturalist texts; however, critics generally do not focus on the relationship between the two forms. Fisher is an exception in that he directly and systematically links sentimentalism to naturalism. Fisher's emphasis, however, is the opposite of mine. He argues that sentimentalism is a precursor to naturalism, that it has "an awareness" (*Hard Facts*, 126) of " 'forces'—climate, inheritance, and economic system" (125) that is "unmatched in American literature until Naturalism fifty years later" (126). By contrast, I argue that sentimentalism is crucial to naturalism's oppositional self-definition, though I would agree with Fisher that there are more similarities between the two forms than we expect. Howard also provides a suggestive but brief account of the relation between sentimental and naturalist texts (*Form*). While Campbell in *Resisting* focuses on the relation between women realist regionalists and male naturalists, her argument supports mine.

12. Seltzer, *Bodies and Machines*, 27, hereafter cited parenthetically as *BAM*.

13. Graff, *Professing*, 38, 62.

14. I am indebted here particularly to Borus, *Writing*, and C. Wilson, *Labor*, for their analyses of the paradoxes of professionalism for realist and naturalist writers. My account differs from theirs in seeing gender as absolutely crucial to the attempt to resolve these paradoxes.

15. H. H. Boyesen, "The American Novelist and His Public," in *Literary and Social Silhouettes* (New York: Harper, 1894), 41–42, hereafter cited parenthetically as *AN*.

16. Lora Romero, *Home Fronts: Domesticity and Its Critics in the Antebellum U.S.* (Durham: Duke University Press, 1997), 12–13, hereafter cited parenthetically as *HF*.

17. This instability, minus the vituperativeness of Boyesen's essay, is also evident in William Dean Howells's essay "The Man of Letters as a Man of Business," first published in 1893. Howells argues that finally the writer must please women, who constitute his public (21) and that such a public is fickle (13–18). Howells does see this female public, much like Boyesen, as threatening to feminize the author (5–6, 30–31), though he also argues that a serious author who sells well may escape such feminization (30–31). "The Man of Letters as a Man of Business," in *Literature and Life* (1893, reprint, 1902; New York: Harper and Brothers, 1911).

18. Norris's anxiety about the training women received is evidenced by the fact that this is an almost word-for-word repetition of the same idea in "Novelists to Order—While You Wait" (1903) (*LC*, 15).

19. Eve Sedgwick, *Epistemology of the Closet* (Berkeley and Los Angeles: University of California Press, 1990), 145, 148.

20. Critics who have traced the way in which abstract issues become personalized and domesticated in the sentimental novel include Armstrong; Douglas, *Feminization;* Ryan; and Tompkins. Similarly, critics who have traced the workings of force in the naturalist novel include Fisher; Howard, *Form;* Michaels, *Gold Standard;* Mitchell; Pizer *Theory;* Seltzer; and Walcutt.

21. Frank Norris, *The Octopus* (1901; reprint, New York: Penguin, 1986), 467, hereafter cited parenthetically as *TO*.

22. I am indebted to Seltzer's reading of this scene in *BAM*, though I am focusing on the mother as a figure of a personalized sentimentalism, while he focuses on the mother as part of a gendered scientific account of reproduction.

23. S. Behrman's death is also intensely sentimental in the way it enacts "revenge" upon an individual. Norris tries to explain this away by locating the sentimentality in Behrman, not in the narrative. Because Behrman becomes himself "sentiment[al]" (*TO*, 639) about the wheat he has obtained rather than acting as an unwitting agent of abstract force, he can be killed off. Before Behrman became sentimental about the wheat, he was, as Presley points out, impervious to death.

24. See for example, Stephen Crane's *Maggie: A Girl of the Streets;* Jack London's *Martin Eden* and *John Barleycorn;* and Norris's *Vandover and the Brute*.

25. Presley's beliefs are posed in contrast not only to the dainty society ladies of San Francisco but more pointedly to those of Annie Derrick, the genteel wife of one of the ranchers. The contrast between Presley and Annie Derrick is a particularly important one because Annie, like Presley, Annixter, and Vanamee, is college educated. Norris makes clear here, as in his literary criticism, that a college education is crucial in forming men's most profound intellectual and emotional ties and that coeds can never be included in such a fraternity. Annie's education, however, renders her unfit for camraderie with him, for it has provided her not with naturalist but with sentimental aesthetics: "Her taste was of the delicacy of point lace.... She read ... the little toy magazines, full of the flaccid banalities of the 'Minor Poets'" (*TO*, 61). Therefore, in the logic of the narrative, Presley wisely ignores her tentative gestures toward friendship (61).

26. See Amy Kaplan and Laura Wexler respectively on how domestic discourse informed imperialist logic and how imperialist logic informed domestic discourse. Kaplan, "Manifest Domesticity," in "No More Separate Spheres!", ed. Cathy Davidson, spec. issue of American Literature 70, no. 3 (1988): 581–606; Wexler, *Tender Violence: Domestic Visions in an Age of U.S. Imperialism* (Chapel Hill: University of North Carolina Press, 2000).

27. John Ballowe, introduction to *George Santayana's America*, by George Santayana (Urbana: University of Illinois Press, 1967), 4–5.

28. In this poem, Santayana criticized Harvard intellectuals, like William James, for their pacifism during the Spanish-American War, describing such critique as a feminized and vitiated refusal of reality and also as a nativist refusal of racial or cultural intermixing. Admittedly, Young Sammy's seduction and rape of Cuba, Puerto Rico, and the Philippines reveal him to be somewhat crude, but the poem defends his actions as those expected of a virile youth. In addition, the poem blames Uncle Sam for the bad training he gave Young Sammy. Uncle Sam has created a democracy that is "a chance majority" (D. Wilson, *Genteel Tradition*, 31), which fosters both "mediocrity" and "competition" (32). Young Sammy, however crude he may be, represents the hope for a more virile and stronger democracy.

29. D. Wilson, *Genteel Tradition*, 39–40, hereafter cited as *GT*.

30. D. Wilson points out that the masculine-feminine divide is not just metaphoric but also literal to Santayana. This is evident in Santayana's description of American schooling as run exclusively by "chiefly unmarried women, sensitive, faithful, and feeble," who wrap "all things intellectual ... in a feminine veil" (*GT*, 13).

31. Santayana's implicit reference to the "transparent eyeball" of Emerson's essay "Nature" (1830) is rendered explicit a few pages later. Santayana writes approvingly of Emerson's concept of the "speculative eye before which all passes, which bridges the distances and compares the combatants" (*GT*, 50). Santayana uses this eye to make the

point that Emerson's thinking transcends his time: "On the side of his genius Emerson broke away from all conditions of age or country and represented nothing except intelligence itself" (*GT,* 50). He also uses Emerson's notion later in the essay, as we shall see, to argue that man transcends even transcendent nature.

32. Through an analysis of the ideas of William James, Santayana seems, at first, to propose a solution to the cultural expert's tragic dilemma. James's "pragmatist philosophy" represents the "true America, and . . . in a measure the whole ultra-modern, radical world" (*GT,* 54). Like "normal practical masculine American" thought (*GT,* 55), Santayana writes, and also like "biology and Darwinism" (*GT,* 56), pragmatism shows the dynamic relation between theory and practice, individual and environment (*GT,* 57). It thereby balances its separation and involvement in American society. But the more Santayana talks about James, the more it becomes clear that he sees James's work as only giving "a rude shock to the genteel tradition"(*GT,* 59) and not fundamentally upsetting it. In fact, he repeatedly says, not only may James be wrong, but also James may simply be creating a new genteel tradition (*GT,* 60–61). Santayana recognizes, in other words, that despite pragmatism's brave words about "life" and its "normal" masculinity (*GT,* 55), it is after all expert discourse, separated from "life" despite, or perhaps we could say because of, its claim to the authority of experience as well as theory.

33. Dawidoff, *Sacred Rage,* 145, 157.

34. Interestingly, this vein of criticism has been rejuvenated by Douglas's feminist version of it. Both her books build on Santayana's and Beer's analyses of the gendering of American consumer culture in order to criticize the vicarious and mendacious ways women have had to fight to gain a voice in American society and culture. The latter book is particularly useful for showing how the "Titaness" functioned powerfully in the modernists' cultural imaginary, even if at times there is a slippage in Douglas's logic (as there is in Santayana's and Beer's) about whether this titaness was a real social force or a purely imaginary one.

35. I think particularly here of new historicist and pragmatist critics like Richard Brodhead, Walter Benn Michaels, and Stanley Fish.

36. Peter Carafiol, *The American Ideal* (New York: Oxford University Press, 1991), 34.

37. For similar critiques of new historicism and pragmatic criticism, see Romero, *HF;* Brook Thomas, *The New Historicism and Other Old-Fashioned Topics* (Princeton: Princeton University Press, 1991).

38. Willa Sibert Cather, *The World and the Parish: Willa Cather's Articles and Reviews,* vol. 2, ed. William M. Curtin (Lincoln: University of Nebraska Press, 1970), 747, hereafter parenthetically as *WP.*

Chapter 4

1. See particularly Deborah Carlin's elegant account of how Cather's work and its politics have been read through the lens of biography. Carlin focuses on how this has resulted in Cather's later works being neglected. *Cather, Canon, and the Politics of Reading* (Amherst: University of Massachusetts Press, 1992), chapter 1. Joan Acocella also discusses how Cather's work and its politics have been read reductively through the lens of biography. Acocella's argument is, however, somewhat peculiar since she roots this critical tendency in 1930s left-leaning, misogynist literary criticism while nonetheless arguing that it is "women [critics]" (2) (i.e., feminist and queer critics) who are to blame for reductionist analyses of Cather. *Willa Cather and the Politics of Criticism* (Lincoln: University of Nebraska Press, 2000).

2. Marilee Lindemann, *Willa Cather: Queering America* (New York: Columbia Univer-

sity Press, 1999), chapters 3–4; Guy Reynolds, *Willa Cather in Context: Progress, Race, Empire* (New York: St. Martin's, 1996).

3. See Eve Sedgwick for an analysis of this double bind in which the "open secret" of the closet results in exposures, protections, and both, none of which necessarily lead to a queer-friendly politics. *Epistemology of the Closet* (Berkeley and Los Angeles: University of California Press, 1990).

4. Hermione Lee, *Willa Cather: Double Lives* (New York: Pantheon, 1989); Lindemann, *Queering*.

5. Alice Gambrell, *Women Intellectuals, Modernism, and Difference: Transatlantic Culture, 1919–45*; (New York: Cambridge University Press, 1997; Carla Kaplan, *The Erotics of Talk: Women's Writing and Feminist Paradigms* (New York: Oxford University Press, 1996).

6. Guy Reynolds in *Context* notes how Cather's notion of professionalism links her with Progressivism, but he focuses primarily on how her pluralism proves her association with Progressivism (13–24).

7. I am adapting Tarbell's phrase, which is meant to signify contempt for independent oil producers who sold out to Standard Oil. *All in a Day's Work* (New York: Macmillan, 1939), 83. Later in the autobiography, she engages in a long critique on the standardization of American life, which she links to nationalization, consumerism, and the growth of a mass culture (394–96). As we shall see, however, this phrase resonates for the professional journalist of this period as well. Cather also used the notion of standardization critically, a term that she also linked explicitly to nationalism and mass culture, specifically the "indiscriminate Americanization of immigrants. *Willa Cather in Person*, ed. L. Brent Bohlke (Lincoln: University of Nebraska Press, 1986), 145–49, 146.

8. Jean Chalaby argues that "objective" balance in the Anglo-American context created the illusion of an apolitical consensus, or generalized public opinion, which was used to legitimate and authorize professional journalism over and against the political parties. *The Invention of Journalism* (New York: St. Martin's, 1998), 133–37. This certainly is the case in Tarbell's work. It also resonates with Cather's claim to literature as an escape from politics. The apolitical notion of public opinion that informs both their works, however, authorizes itself finally through their personal integrity.

9. An early statement on the advent of journalistic professionalism, Edwin L. Shuman's *Practical Journalism* (1903), demonstrates the logical contradictions that journalists faced as they professionalized as well as how they were manifest in a confused gendering. On the one hand, Shuman argues that because the "modern newspaper is a business enterprise" based on "sound financial principles" (16), it does not express "private" (17), "partizan" (77–78), or "personal" (86) views. In short, it is no longer political; rather it is professional (x, 30) and simply expresses public opinion (17, 36). But this analysis breaks down in his chapter "Women in Newspaper Work," in which he tries to limit women's participation in journalism and anxiously highlights the way journalists do not simply express public opinion but manipulate it. Shuman argues that the reason women should not become journalists is that they want to reform the world while the purpose of journalism is to make a profit (158). A reporter must tell the story as her newspaper tells her to, even if it is untrue (150). The problem here, Shuman continues, is that women lose their "bloom" and "many feminine characteristics" when they cannot tell "the whole truth" (150–51). Shuman's assertion that a newspaper is no place for the "whole truth" or for "opinion" is consistent with his earlier claim that journalistic professionalism is a commercial proposition. His implication that journalists regularly report only "one set of facts" (150), facts that are dictated to them by the newspaper, however, conflicts with his notion of the purity of commercialism. The book concludes with a reassertion that journalism (as well as advertising) is a high-minded profession because it is a commercial proposition. But femininity in Shuman's book, the emblem

of purity, of the "whole truth," registers his underlying anxiety that commercialism is in fact a problem for journalistic professionalism. *Practical Journalism* (1903; reprint, New York: Appleton, 1920).

10. Haber argues that while professionalism is read as a sign of modernization, it depends on older notions of masculine authority from the eighteenth century. Haber's account of the historical roots of modern professionalism is useful for my project as a whole. He does not, however, discuss in any detail the politics of gender and race that is a crucial part of professionalism's history nor how the past could be referred to by professionals for a variety of ends. *The Quest for Authority and Honor in the Professions* (Chicago: University of Chicago Press, 1991).

11. For example, looking at Ida Wells Barnett's journalism, which worked to undermine the link made at the turn of the century between white masculinity and progress, through its use of facts and muckraking, results in a very different answer to this question. Gail Bederman, *Manliness and Civilization* (Chicago: University of Chicago Press, 1995), chapter 2.

12. This comparison also helps us to think about what is shared between forms of writing and authority that we separate. This separation is characterized by Cather herself as that between the journalist's focus on "the teeming, gleaming stream of the present" and the literary author's selection from that of "the eternal material of art." *Not under Forty* (New York: Knopf, 1936), 40, hereafter cited as *NF.* Cather had contradictory ways of describing journalism and the connection between her career as a journalist and her career as a literary author. At times, she said journalism was formative in training and disciplining her writing; more frequently, however, she described journalism as the antithesis, even the enemy, of literature. While her conflicting views on the subject make a study in themselves, I am interested less in her views on journalism than on how the journalistic conflict with commercialism, one she herself notes in her analyses of journalism, influenced her literary work formally and thematically. For Cather's different view on journalism, see Cather, *The World and the Parish: Willa Cather's Articles and Reviews*, ed. William M. Curtin (Lincoln: University of Nebraska Press, 1970), 1:272, 2:528; Cather, *The Kingdom of Art: Willa Cather's First Principles and Critical Statements*, ed. Bernice Slote (Lincoln: University of Nebraska Press, 1966), 332, 450–52; Cather, *Willa Cather in Person*, ed. L. Brent Bohlke (Lincoln: University of Nebraska Press, 1986), 12, 15, 21, 92.

13. Chalaby, *Invention;* Robert Miraldi, *Muckraking and Objectivity* (New York: Greenwood, 1990); Dan Schiller, *Objectivity and the News* (Philadelphia: University of Pennsylvania Press, 1981); Michael Schudson, *Discovering the News* (New York: Basic Books, 1978); Christopher Wilson, *The Labor of Words: Literary Professionalism in the Progressive Era* (Athens: University of Georgia Press, 1985).

14. Schudson, *Discovering*, 71–87.

15. Ibid., 122.

16. Ibid., 151.

17. Ibid., 7.

18. Or, as Schiller puts it, objectivity becomes a prominent and debated issue in the 1890s because there was a growing sense that the press was distorting and hiding the truth about class conflict in the period (*Objectivity*, 184–89).

19. The term *muckraking* was coined by Theodore Roosevelt in 1906 and was then applied derogatorily to a variety of kinds of Progressive journalism. Privately, Roosevelt worried that Progressive exposés of business and politics were "building up a revolutionary feeling" in the nation (Miraldi, *Muckraking*, 26).

20. Hamilton Holt, *Commercialism and Journalism* (Boston: Houghton Mifflin, 1909), 2, hereafter cited as *CJ.*

21. Importantly, however, as the inaugural advertisement of the series asserts, the essays are professionally balanced. The ad authorizes Irwin by citing his year and a half of study and investigation. Such study leads to a fair and balanced account: "This is not a muckraking series . . . [It] disclose[s] the evil as well as the good side of our press. Everybody knows there is a good side as well as a bad side to American journalism. . . . It would be easy to muckrake American journalism—to take an instance here, a defect there, and by massing detrimental truths present a picture of a press untrue to its ancient tribunate of the people. We have avoided that. We have tried to take the broad view of journalism, the virtues with the defects." "The American Newspaper: A Study of Journalism in Relation to the Public," *Collier's* 46, no. 17 (January 14, 1911: 12. Muckraking, the ad argues, is a kind of journalism that is value driven and distorts the truth through its focus on "defects." Irwin's essays are authoritative because they show us what "everybody knows," i.e., a balanced consensus of the good and bad sides of American journalism.

22. Will Irwin, "The American Newspaper: The Power of the Press," *Collier's* 46, no. 18 (January 21, 1911): 15.

23. Will Irwin, "The American Newspaper: The Unhealthy Alliance," *Collier's* 47, no. 11 (June 3, 1911): 34.

24. Ibid.

25. Ibid., 19

26. Ibid., 31, 34.

27. Will Irwin, "The American Newspaper: The New Era," *Collier's* 47, no. 16 (July 8, 1911), 16.

28. Will Irwin, "The American Newspaper: The Voice of a Generation," 47, no. 19 (July 29, 1911): 23.

29. Ibid., 16.

30. Samuel McClure with Willa Cather, *My Autobiography* (1913; reprint, New York: Frederick Stokes, 1914), 246–47.

31. Frank Luther Mott, *A History of American Magazines, 1885–1905*, vol. 4 (Cambridge: Harvard University Press, 1957), 590–93.

32. When Tarbell's series on Napoleon debuted in November 1894, circulation jumped from 24,500 to 65,000, and by the end of the series there were 100,000 subscribers. Kathleen Brady, *Ida Tarbell: Portrait of a Mcukraker* (New York: Putnam, 1984), 91–92.

33. For Tarbell's Lincoln series, circulation went from 120,000 in August 1895 to 250,000 by December 1895, according to McClure (*Autobiography*, 221). Brady further adds that between November 1895 when McClure's published the daguerrotype of Lincoln and December 1895, circulation went from 175,000 to 250,000 (*Ida Tarbell*, 98). The Napoleon and Lincoln biographies are also instructive because they depend thematically on a focus on the personal qualities of the two men, qualities that made them leaders of their nations. They are both described as hardworking, self-made men whose genius lay in their eye for detail. Napoleon lacked the perfect integrity of Lincoln; nonetheless, like him, Napoleon helped in that crucial task of rebuilding a nation in the aftermath of civil war.

34. McClure, *Autobiography*, 238.

35. Tarbell also played with this metaphor, describing or using her sources to describe Rockefeller as Napoleonic. *The History of Standard Oil*, (1904; reprint, Gloucester: Peter Smith, 1963), 2:12, 63, 232, hereafter cited as *SO*.

36. Tarbell, *SO*, 1:50–51, 68, 99, 100–103, 109, 120–21, 145, 148, 155–56, 230–31; 2:64–66, 132–33; also "John D. Rockefeller: A Character Study," *McClure's*, 25, no. 3 (July 1905): 226–49; 25, no. 4 (August 1905): 386–98.

37. Cited in Brady, *Ida Tarbell*, 148.

38. Schudson in *Discovering* also discusses how the reporter was invented in the 1880s and 1890s and became a kind of character in his own stories and worked to create personally distinctive and popular styles of writing (chapter 2). Unlike me, however, he sees such a character as proving that the "ideal of objectivity" had not yet become normative.

39. Mary E. Tomkins, *Ida M. Tarbell* (New York: Twayne, 1974), 151.

40. Still powerful today, this myth depends for its allure on the individual character of Tarbell, but more generically on her character as a lady. The lady outwits the robber baron, on the one hand, because he assumes her gentility and disengagement from economics and politics. On the other hand, because she is genteel and disengaged from economics, not even the robber baron can intimidate her or sway her convictions. If the gentleman contributes to the figuration of professionalism, the lady can easily do so as well. See Brady in *Ida Tarbell* on both the 1905 Broadway version of the Tarbell myth (169–70) and how Tarbell manipulated her image as a lady to dramatic effect during her public speaking engagements (156). Another way to understand these contradictory ideals of impersonality and personality is to think through the implications of bylines. While newspapers did not use bylines regularly until the 1920s (Schudson, *Discovering*, 145), magazines consistently did so in the post–Civil War years. Bylines make journalists accountable to the public for their facts. The paradox, of course, is that the character of the individual journalist becomes part of the story, part of the way the objectivity of a story is verified.

41. Tarbell, *Day's Work*, 256. Among McClure's various schemes for raising money, he apparently promised potential investors in 1905 that he would halt muckraking temporarily (Miraldi, *Muckraking*, 59, 66). Tarbell focuses, however, on McClure's desire to found a larger corporate conglomeration. Brady provides a useful account of the staff's dissatisfaction with McClure's grandiose plans, as well as with his philandering, and the tensions and daily battles they caused in the office (169–75). Cather would most likely have been aware of these tensions when she was hired, since some of the staff members stayed on after the mass resignation of 1906.

42. Brady, *Ida Tarbell*, 178–84; 208–10; Miraldi, *Muckraking*, 65–66.

43. The apparently tense relation between Cather and Tarbell deserves more analysis than I can give it. For brief and conflicting accounts of their relation, see Brady, *Ida Tarbell*, 134; Edith Lewis, *Willa Cather Living: A Personal Record* (New York: Knopf, 1953), 59; 290–92, 352. Sharon O'Brien, *Willa Cather: The Emerging Voice* (New York: Oxford University Press, 1987).

45. Ida Tarbell, *The Business of Being a Woman* (1912; reprint, New York: Macmillan, 1925), 1, 42, 43, hereafter cited as *BW*.

46. This is not an uncommon reading of the new woman, though of course the significance of it lies in that it is a reading by a new woman herself. On critical accounts of the new woman, see Ann Ardis, *New Women, New Novels* (New Brunswick: Rutgers University Press, 1990).

47. Tarbell's next book, *The Ways of Women* (1914; reprint, New York: Macmillan, 1915), takes this up in greater detail.

48. Her readers would have been familiar with her credentials as a much-celebrated female journalist. And these credentials are used to promote the book. Under its title, she is identified as "Associate Editor of the 'American Magazine,' Author of 'Life of Abraham Lincoln,' 'History of Standard Oil Co.,' 'He Knew Lincoln,' etc."

49. Cited in Brady, *Ida Tarbell*, 152.

50. Samuel McClure, Editorial, *McClure's* 22, no. 1 (November 1903): 111.

51. Richard Digby-Jones, *The Journalist as Reformer: Henry Demarest Lloyd and Wealth against Commonwealth* (Westport, Conn: Greenwood, 1996), 101–25.

52. McClure, editorial, 111.

53. Cited in Brady, *Ida Tarbell*, 148.

54. Cited in Tomkins, *Ida M. Tarbell*, 137. This is an argument repeated in the present. See, for example, how Brady reads Tarbell's analysis of Rockefeller (*Ida Tarbell*, 155–56)

55. Similarly, a review of the Gary biography was titled "The Taming of Ida M. Tarbell" (Tomkins, 136–37). Her work is read as representing her personal integrity or her succumbing to pressure rather than a case of larger institutional pressures for professional writers in corporate capitalism.

56. Other scholars have put this dynamic in a different way. Acocella in *Politics of Criticism* castigates critics for relying extensively on Cather's biography but then relies extensively on Cather's biography to show how Cather transcends her biography. Lee in *Double Lives* discusses the way Cather both denies and insists on personal and impersonal readings of her novels, as does Carlin in *Politics of Reading;* Rosowski sees Cather as a romantic who rejects scientism and materialism and seeks to validate imaginative thought and the mind. Susan Rosowski, *The Voyage Perilous* (University of Nebraska Press, 1986).

57. For her other critical comments on women writers' subjectivity and hence failure, see Cather, *WP,* 1:276–77, 362–63; Cather, *Kingdom,* 347–48, 406, 409. Edith Lewis, Cather's companion for many years, also discusses Cather's distaste for personalism in writing and her notion of her voice as an author as a masculine and impersonal one. Lewis, *Willa Cather Living* 32–33, 84.

58. See also Cather, *Kingdom,* 406.

59. This passage comes from a positive review of the actor E. S. Willard. Here she links objectivity with the refusal to sell out. She writes, "Acting has become one of the most intensely subjective of the arts," with actors commissioning plays that suit their personality (*WP,* 1:485). "Personality," writes Cather, "is the menace of the drama today" (488). Cather's critique of celebrity, the selling of self, as in "Ardessa," emphasizes its reliance on the interchangeable terms *subjectivity* and *personality.* Actors who indulge in their subjectivity and personality "finally paralyze ... the purely creative impulse" and are "shut ... from the stars" (486). Cather admires Willard "because he is the antithesis of all this," because he "keeps his personality so entirely out of his work." She states that "Behind each part you recognize the same piercing mentality, but his physical and emotional personality he leaves behind him" (486). His acting is "dispassionate" and "lacks warmth" (487), and in this he is like James (486). In this review Cather associates the personal with flattering narcissism for the artist and with flattering emotionalism for the audience. Subjectivity, in other words, produces commercialized art that sells personality, that sells individual subjectivity. (See also *WP,* 1:94, 259, 271; 2:748). Especially see her interview with the "Bookman" in 1921, after the successes of *My Antonia* and *Youth and the Bright Medusa* in which she says that she is "trying to cut out all analysis, observation, description ... to make things and people tell their own story simply by juxtaposition, without any persuasion or explanation on my part" (*In Person,* 4). She uses an example of juxtaposing an orange and a vase, saying "I want the reader to see the orange and the vase—beyond that, I am out of it ... I'd like the writing to be lost in the object" (24). Cather also links her "detached" (44) aesthetic in another interview in 1921 to a desire to avoid writing "Saturday Evening Post sort of stuff" (44). Only a year later, in "The Novel Demeuble," however, even objects can no longer be the unproblematic signs of impersonality that they were when she juxtaposed an orange and a green vase, since objects by themselves are implicated in market capitalism.

60. See respectively Carlin, *Politicis of Reading;* Lee, *Double Lives;* and for the latter two terms, Rosowski, *Voyage.*

61. Willa Sibert Cather, "On *The Professor's House,*" in *Willa Cather: Stories, Poems, and Other Writings,* ed. Sharon O'Brien (New York: Library of America, 1992), 974.

62. Willa Sibert Cather, *The Professor's House* (New York: Knopf, 1925), 35–36. Hereafter cited as *PH.*

63. I am indebted to Rosowski's similar reading of the "open window" and its effect on the structure of the novel (*Voyage,* chapter 9), though we come to quite different conclusions about it.

64. Some critics have argued that St. Peter is Cather, and the biographical similarities suggest that Cather encouraged such a reading to a degree (Lee, *Double Lives,* 224–25). Lewis even claims that precisely because it is the "most personal" of Cather's novels, it engages in "more symbolic expression" (137). At the same time, however, even as Cather seems to encourage a personal reading of the novel, she insistently poses the narrative as dispassionate about everyone and everything, including St. Peter. The biographical similarities between Cather and St. Peter only make the narrative's "balanced" view of St. Peter more striking.

65. Kathleen accuses her father and the scientist Crane of betraying Tom and his invention through their selfish interest in their own work. While Kathleen's accusation is undermined by the fact that it begins when she is literally "green with envy" because of Rosamond and Marsellus's wealth, her "greenish tinge" disappears, and her eyes, which are red from crying, "expanded and cleared" (*PH,* 80–81). Her argument is given further plausibility by her own unfaltering loyalty to Tom and his memory (127). In addition, St. Peter himself often describes his work as a way of evading personal obligations or duties (19–20, 157), while his passivity is carefully elaborated throughout the narrative. The narrator has already suggested that his passivity has led him to betray Kathleen, just as she accuses him of doing with Tom (60–61, 127).

66. His relation with the puritanical scientist Crane demonstrates how hopeless the fight is and how badly he has been beaten. Their friendship had been based on their shared resistance to the trend of commercialization, but Crane is envious of the money that Marsellus and Rosamond have gained from Tom's death (*PH,* 143–46). While St. Peter and Crane failed often in the past to win this battle (139), now they can no longer even do battle together. Tom's pure research transformed into money corrupts even the seemingly incorruptible Crane. Witnessing Crane's sudden desire for monetary compensation, St. Peter finds (as he does continually in the novel) "everything around him . . . insupportable." In a line that sums up the book's central paradox, St. Peter thinks, "If Outland were here tonight, he might say with Mark Antony, 'My fortunes have corrupted honest men' " (146). Out of the potentially open window that is Tom Outland, out of the ideal of disinterested thinking and work has come the compromised emotional and work relations of every person in the novel.

67. Walter Benn Michaels argues that Cather uses the notion of the "vanishing Indian" to model a nativist form of true, unadulterated, American racial integrity. *Our America: Nativism, Modernism, Pluralism* (Durham: Duke University Press, 1995). While Michaels makes a helpful point, it is also true that Cather does not describe the vanishing Indian as uncompromised. Rather she uses that notion to a more universalist end, namely as a critique of the compromised nature of all desiring relations, a thematics that I am arguing arises for her out of the conflicted and complementary relations between professionalism and consumer culture.

68. She rarely provides an analysis of her feelings. In addition, she had to be convinced by friends to put in details about her family at all (Brady, *Ida Tarbell,* 249–50).

69. Tarbell, *Day's Work*, 280, hereafter cited as *DW*.
70. See, for example, *DW*, 1, 79, 81–82, 141, 254, 299–300, 359, 388, 398.
71. See *DW*, 78, 148, 254, 300.
72. See especially her cagey account of her work with Judge Gary, which emphasizes her need for money after McClure backs out of financing an update of *The History of Standard Oil* (363–71). Brady argues that Tarbell had long disliked Gary and probably wrote the book because she had to support her entire family and take on her brother's debts after his mental breakdown (215–33).
73. Cather, *Kingdom*, 406. Cather's description of *Sapphira* to Viola Roseboro as being about "the terrible in domesticated form" (qtd. in Lee, *Double Lives*, 357) poses it as the antithesis of Stowe's domestic idealizations (though, of course, Stowe in her way focuses also on the "terrible in domesticated form").
74. Willa Sibert Cather, *Sapphira and the Slave Girl* (New York: Vintage, 1968), 237, hereafter cited as *SG*.
75. Carlin provides a thorough examination of the way Cather enforces and validates a racist account of slavery (*Politics of Reading*, chapter 6). Her conclusion that Cather sought to show the good as well as the bad side of slavery (170–71) supports my analysis that the novel seeks to provide a journalistically "balanced" and "objective" account of slavery.

Chapter 5

1. Zora Neale Hurston, *Folklore, Memoirs, and Other Writings*, ed. Cheryl Wall (New York: Library of America, 1995), 910, hereafter cited as *FMO*.
2. Presumably, this is a reference to the popular dialect fiction about blacks by blacks and whites alike—from Charles Chesnutt and Paul Laurence Dunbar to Joel Chandler Harris and Thomas Nelson Page. The connection between regionalism and subjectivity and the criticism of that link implied in Hurston's analysis is one on which many critics still insist. George Hutchinson argues that because of Hurston's anthropological training, her writing "would attempt far more 'realistic,' quasi-ethnographic approaches to folk experience and expression than . . . [her] regionalist precursors." *The Harlem Renaissance in Black and White* (Cambridge: Harvard University Press, 1995), 68. Cheryl Wall also sees Hurston's fiction transcending the limitations of local color fiction because of her scientific training. *Women of the Harlem Renaissance* (Bloomington: University of Indiana Press, 1995), 148–51. Hurston, in contrast to her critics, however, highlights the problem in such assumptions about objectivity.
3. For this dynamic, see Franz Boas's preface to Hurston's *Mules and Men* (1935; reprint, New York: Perennial, 1990), xiii–xiv; contemporaneous reviews of Hurston's work collected in K. A. Appiah and Henry Louis Gates Jr., eds., *Zora Neale Hurston* (New York: Amistad, 1993), 3–36; and Ruth Benedict's advance review in a letter to J. B. Lippincott, 4 October 1935, Ruth Benedict Papers, Vassar College Library.
4. Hurston was not only a novelist but also must be seen as a professional anthropologist. While she never completed her Ph.D. or held an academic position, she did postbaccalaureate work in the 1920s and 1930s supervised by or in dialogue with Franz Boas (and was encouraged by him to complete a Ph.D.); she received a variety of prestigious fellowships for advanced studies in anthropology, including a Rosenwald in 1935 and two Guggenheims in 1936 and 1937; and she published in anthropological journals and was a member of a number of professional organizations, which she lists with apparent pride in her autobiography, *Dust Tracks on a Road* (1942).
5. Hazel V. Carby, "The Politics of Fiction, Anthropology, and the Folk: Zora Neale

Hurston," in *New Essays on* Their Eyes Were Watching God, ed. Michael Awkard (New York: Cambridge University Press, 1990). 77, 79, 89.

6. Graciela Hernandez, "Multiple Subjectivities and Strategic Positionality: Zora Neale Hurston's Experimental Ethnographies," in *Women Writing Culture*, ed. Ruth Behar and Deborah Gordon (Berkeley and Los Angeles: University of California Press, 1995), 156, 160–61. Hernandez's argument about Hurston's relation to anthropology is more typical than Carby's. Repeatedly, critics have sought to demonstrate that while Hurston was trained by modernist anthropologists, her work resisted and undermined anthropological claims to authority. See D. A. Boxwell, " 'Sis Cat' as Ethnographer: Self-Presentation and Self-Inscription in Zora Neale Hurston's *Mules and Men*," *African-American Review* 26 (1992): 605–17; Ronald Bush, "Ethnographic Subjectivity and Zora Neale Hurston's *Tell My Horse.*" *Zora Neale Hurston Forum* 5, no. 2 (1991): 11–17; Deborah Gordon, "The Politics of Ethnographic Authority: Race and Writing in the Ethnography of Margaret Mead and Zora Neale Hurston in *Modernist Anthropology*, ed. Marc Manganaro (Princeton: Princeton University Press, 1990), 146–62. Francoise Lionnet, "Autoethnography: The An-Archic Style of *Dust Tracks on a Road*," in *The Bounds of Race*, ed. Dominick LaCapra (Ithaca: Cornell University Press, 1991), 164–95; Gwendolyn Mikell, "When Horses Talk: Reflections on Zora Neale Hurston's Haitian Anthropology," *Phylon* 48, no. 3 (September 1982): 218–30.

7. As Gerald Graff argues in his study of the professionalization of American literature, disciplines are never unified; to ignore the conflicts and dissenting voices perpetually at work in them is to fantasize, whether nostalgically or critically, about a wholeness that never existed. Nonetheless, it is also true, as I have shown, that certain versions of a discipline can dominate while others are *or retrospectively become* marginalized. At times, the current homogenization of modernist anthropology seems to be linked to the definitional constrictions of periodization, i.e., of positing rupture between modern and postmodern anthropology. For example, one of the most outspoken critics of the claims to objectivity and transparency of modernist anthropology, James Clifford, acknowledges that the current postmodern focus on "text making" and on blurring the "boundary separating art and science" is not a "new attraction" and that many modernist anthropologists, including Malinowski, Mead, Sapir, and Benedict, self-consciously engaged with the literary and the subjective. But though he thus acknowledges that his distinction between modern and postmodern anthropology is somewhat arbitrary or polemical, he insists oddly enough that "until recently literary influences have been held at a distance from the 'rigorous' core of the discipline" (3–4), a somewhat dubious claim, given the prominence of the figures he names. James Clifford and George E. Marcus, eds., *Writing Culture* (Berkeley and Los Angeles: University of California Press, 1986), 2, 3.

8. George Stocking, *The Ethnographer's Magic* (Madison: University Wisconsin Press, 1992), 329–41.

9. George Stocking, ed., *A Franz Boas Reader: The Shaping of American Anthropology, 1883–1911* (Chicago: Midway Reprint, 1989), 18.

10. By displacing the Boas–Hurston connection with that of Benedict–Hurston, I am not implying that the second relationship has priority over the first or that because they were women anthropologists, they were equally alienated from the profession, had necessarily the same ideas, or were bonded in sympathetic sisterhood. As we shall see, their relationship was both supportive and fraught with tension. Nonetheless, Stocking has written that Boas acted the part of "Victorian patriarch" with his students and that while he helped his "daughters," he also assumed that they would never "enjoy all the prerogatives of professionalism." *Selected Papers from the American Anthropologist, 1921–45* (Washington, D.C.: American Anthropological Association, 1976), 7–8. Benedict's and

Hurston's struggles over vocation, their contemporaneity, and the somewhat similar position they were in professionally makes comparing them valuable. For different readings than mine of Hurston and Benedict's relation, see Mark Helbling, *The Harlem Renaissance: The One and the Many* (Westport, Conn.: Greenwood, 1999); Mikell, "When Horses Talk."

11. Susan Hegeman, *Patterns for America* (Princeton: Princeton University Press, 1999), 46.

12. Stocking, *Selected Papers*, 1–2. The conflict between cultural anthropology and the "Waspish 'hard'-science establishment," Stocking shows, coalesced, first, in Boas's expulsion from the American Anthropological Association (AAA) in 1919 for his pacifism in World War I. (Boas had founded the AAA in 1902.) Second, it coalesced in Benedict's midterm resignation as president of AAA in 1947. In this case, AAA was reorganizing itself, and Benedict and Margaret Mead wanted it to be as embracive and federative as possible. They were defeated, as Boas had been, by those who wanted to define anthropology, in a conservative postwar context, as a hard science rather than as "a congeries of subdisciplines, some which still had humanistic orientations" (Stocking, *Selected Papers*, 42). Benedict's resignation speech is extraordinarily nonconciliatory. She insists on a complex geneaology for anthropology and its equal dependence on the sciences and humanities (460–61). She argues "that today the scientific and humanist traditions are not opposites nor mutually exclusive. They are supplementary, and modern anthropology handicaps itself in method and insight by neglecting the work of the great humanists" (462–63). She concludes with the resounding insistence on claiming both objectivity and subjectivity (470). Ruth Benedict, *An Anthropologist at Work: The Writings of Ruth Benedict*, ed. Margaret Mead (Boston: Houghton Mifflin, 1959), hereafter cited as *AW*.

13. The themes that contemporary anthropologists have shown recur in modernist anthropology—the incommensurability of cultures, the heroism of the anthropologist salvaging the tragically disappearing culture of "primitives" and romantic primitivism—do indeed suggest that modernist anthropology often shared the racist assumptions of nineteenth-century "armchair anthropology" that preceded it, assumptions that modernist anthropology claimed it dismantled. For useful critical analyses of modernist anthropology, see Thomas Biolsi, "The Anthropological Construction of 'Indians': Haviland Scudder Mekeel and the Search for the Primitive in Lakota Country," in *Indians and Anthropologists*, ed. Thomas Biolsi and Larry J. Zimmerman (Tucson: University of Arizona Press, 1997), 133–59; Clifford and Marcus, *Writing Culture;* Johannes Fabian, *Time and the Other* (New York: Columbia University Press, 1983); Michael M. J. Fischer and George E. Marcus, *Anthropology as Cultural Critique* (Chicago: University of Chicago Press, 1986).

14. Hegeman, *Patterns*, 64–65.

15. Marc Manganaro has noted the difficulty in periodizing modernism across disciplines, pointing out that some anthropological theorists use the term *modernist* to describe analytical techniques used today rather than in the early twentieth century (6–12). However, like Manganaro, I am using the term *modernist* to describe the "classic" anthropology produced by Boas and his students during the period of anthropology's professionalization, namely from the turn of the century to World War II. "Textual Play, Power, and Cultural Critique: An Orientation," in *Modernist Anthropology: From Fieldwork to Text*, ed. Marc Manganaro (Princeton: Princeton University Press, 1990), 3–47.

16. By their later work, I mean Benedict's postwar writings of the 1940s, described as "National Character" studies. In the case of Hurston, I mean her increasingly reactive writings of the 1950s. See note 58.

17. Margaret Caffrey says that Benedict's journals demonstrate a knowledge of Charlotte Perkins Gilman's *Women and Economics*, though she thinks that Benedict's ideas about parasitism were more strongly influenced by Olive Schreiner's comparable argument in *Women and Labor* (1911). *Ruth Benedict, Stranger in This Land* (Austin: University of Texas Press, 1989), 55, 69–71. Here, however, Benedict is demonstrating that she is both influenced by such ideas and critical of them.

18. Caffrey, for example, argues that Benedict "rejected the validity of Victorian claims upon her as a woman" (*Stranger*, viii–ix).

19. Caffrey points out that Margaret Mead, who edited the journals for publication, emphasized Benedict's domestic inclinations throughout because she wanted to feminize Benedict for a 1950s audience and because of Mead's own "dramatic sentimentalism" (*Stranger*, 400). Likewise, Clifford Geertz has claimed that Mead generally attempted "to incorporate the older woman's persona into her own—making a predecessor look like a successor with a vengeance." *Works and Lives: The Anthropologist as Author* (Stanford: Stanford University Press, 1988), 126. Nonetheless, if Mead highlighted Benedict's struggles with vocation and Victorian gender roles for her own reasons, she did not create those struggles out of whole cloth.

20. The motif of the horizon recurs in a variety of ways throughout Hurston's work and registers her changing ideas about dreams of transcendence and freedom.

21. Zora Neale Hurston, *The Complete Stories*, ed. Henry Louis Gates Jr. and Sieglinde Lemke (New York: Harper Collins, 1995), 2, hereafter cited as *CS*.

22. This story is clearly a revision of W.E.B. Du Bois's "The Coming of John" in *The Souls of Black Folks* (1903). The variations Hurston makes to Du Bois's allegory are striking. On the one hand, she focuses on gender politics within the black community rather than race politics across black and white communities. On the other hand, she is as pessimistic in this story as Du Bois is about race relations. Hurston's reliance on Du Bois here and elsewhere makes her later criticism of him both more unwarranted and more explicable.

23. And *Patterns of Culture* has been popular. Nearly two million copies in two dozen languages have been sold over the years (Geertz, *Works and Lives*, 111). Steve Piker suggests that this makes it "probably the most widely read of all anthropology books." "Classical Culture and Personality," in *Handbook of Psychological Anthropology*, ed. Philip K. Bock (Westport, Conn.: Greenwood, 1994), 17.

24. In Benedict, the anthropologist is always "he." While this can be seen as the standard use of the masculine universal, Benedict's jarring use of it complements the problem of anthropological authority as she poses it in *Patterns of Culture*. I will, therefore, respect her use of it.

25. Ruth Benedict, *Patterns of Culture* (1934; reprint, Boston: Houghton Mifflin, 1989), 45–46, hereafter cited as *PC*.

26. Other scholars who have pointed out that in Benedict's comparativist work, the subordination of history led her toward an emphasis on hermeneutics or the importance of interpretation include Barbara Babcock, " 'Not in the Absolute Singular': Rereading Ruth Benedict, ed. Ruth Behar and Deborah Gordon," in *Women Writing Culture: From Fieldwork to Text*, ed. Marc Manganaro (Princeton: Princeton University Press, 1990) 104–30; and Richard Handler, "Ruth Benedict and the Modernist Sensibility," in *Modernist Anthropology*, 163–80.

27. It is important to note here that throughout this essay I use the term *integration* as culture and personality anthropologists use it to mean the way "A culture, like an individual, is a more or less consistent pattern of thought and action" and has "characteristic purposes" (*PC*, 45–46). I do not use the term in its commonsense meaning as providing equal opportunities and consideration to racial minorities, though certainly

an interesting essay could be written on the tension inhering between the anthropologists' notion of cultural integration and the battles over racial integration that trouble an easy sense of cultural consistency or coherence.

28. Elvin Hatch, *Theories of Man and Culture* (New York: Columbia University Press, 1973), 84.

29. For example, in *The Chrysanthemum and the Sword* (1946), one of Benedict's most troubling books, this stabilizing and its attendant anxiety is evident through an assertively insistent first person who nonetheless depends on the specialized professional techniques of a third-person cultural anthropologist (who is always separated from the "I"). *The Chrysanthemum and the Sword* (Boston: Houghton Mifflin, 1946), 3–9. The oscillation between the first and third person, in this case, seems to call the entire project into question, but as the book goes on, the third-person cultural anthropologist's authority is increasingly stabilized.

30. For analyses of Boas's methodology and the tensions in it, see Stocking, *Reader,* 14–15 and *Selected Papers,* 6–7; E. Hatch, *Theories,* 62–63; Hutchinson, *In Black and White,* 72; and Marshall Hyatt, *Franz Boas: Social Activist* (New York: Greenwood, 1990), 44. Hegeman cites Sapir's comical and critical analysis of Boasian induction: "It is clear that Dr. Boas' unconscious long ago decreed that scientific cathedrals are only for the future, that for the time being spires surmounted by the definitive cross are unseemly, if not indeed sinful, that only cornerstones, unfinished walls, or even an occasional isolated portal are strictly in the service of the Lord" (*Patterns,* 39).

31. Richard Handler, "Ruth Benedict and the Modernist Sensibility," in *Modernist Anthropology: From Fieldwork to Text* (Princeton: Princeton University Press, 1990), 175. Or as Babcock puts it, the book deconstructs the notion of authority, particularly through its "nonabsolutist interpretation" of culture ("Singular," 118). The structure of *Patterns of Culture* enforces Benedict's notion of the contingency of the anthropologist's objectivity and its close relation to subjectivity. The first three chapters promote her thesis about the need for integrative studies of culture, and the next three chapters provide comparative, integrative readings of the Pueblo and Plains Indians, the Dobu, and the Kwakiutl; however, the concluding two chapters of the book strictly limit and revise her "objective" claims about integration in the previous six chapters. In the first of them, "The Nature of Science," Benedict startlingly modifies her thesis about the integration of cultures in a number of ways, particularly by repeating (this time emphatically) that historical reconstruction is absolutely crucial for integrative studies (*PC,* 241–42), by noting the various problems in assuming that a culture is integrated (223, 228–30), by criticizing her own comparative studies as juxtaposing the "incommensurable" (223), and by suggesting that our perception may interfere absolutely with understanding the integration of another culture (228). "The Nature of Science" thus modifies her integrated and comparative readings in the book while also challenging our usual definition of science.

32. Hegeman shows that this is also a critical reference to Sapir's notion of genuine and spurious culture (*Patterns,* 98).

33. In analyzing *The Chrysanthemum and the Sword,* Geertz claims that Benedict carefully structures her comparisons in a satirical form that helps the reader achieve estrangement from U.S. rather than Japanese culture. He argues that the "great originality" of her book is that she emphasizes always that the Japanese are "*really* different" from us. But in the continuous "drumbeat" (*Works and Lives,* 117) of the "Us-Not-us motif" (120), Geertz argues, "Japan comes to look, somehow, less and less erratic and arbitrary while the United States comes to look, somehow, more and more so" (121). "At the close [of *Chrysanthemum*]," writes Geertz, "it is, as it was in *Patterns of Culture,* us that we wonder about. On what, pray tell, do our certainties rest? Not much,

apparently, save that they're ours" (121–22). While I would agree with this analysis in terms of *Patterns of Culture*, in *Chrysanthemum*, Benedict's method fails her, and Japanese, not U.S. culture, looks totally unfamiliar—and strange.

34. This led her in her later work to argue in *Race and Racism* (1942) for what she calls "social engineering," which she describes in terms that suggest it is a collective action led by the anthropologist. Her term highlights how she saw an appeal to science as crucial to what we could call the work of advocacy. And it is precisely that seemingly absolutist appeal to scientific authority that disturbs us today when we contemplate the term *social engineering*.

35. Richard Handler, "Vigorous Male and Aspiring Female," in *Malinowski, Rivers, Benedict and Others*, ed. George Stocking (Madison: University of Wisconsin Press, 1986), 151, 152.

36. For an overview of Boas and Benedict's response to World War II, see Stocking, *Selected Papers*, 34. For Benedict's thesis that the war is the culmination of modern, Western racism, see *Race: Science and Politics* (1940; reprint, New York: Viking, 1947); *Race and Racism* (1942, reprint, London: Routledge, 1959); and *The Races of Mankind*, Public Affairs Pamphlet 85 (New York: Public Affairs Committee, 1943).

37. Ruth Benedict, "Anthropology in Your Life," *Vassar Alumnae*, 32 (May 1947), 11.

38. Hurston, *Mules and Men*, 1.

39. Hernandez, "Multiple Subjectivities," 160.

40. She specifically attacks W.E.B. Du Bois and his call for black didactic, protest art, despite the fact that Du Bois had been quite supportive of many black writers' work that was not didactic, including Hurston's. See Robert Hemenway on Hurston and other modernist Harlem Renaissance authors' ambivalent relation with Du Bois. *Zora Neale Hurston: A Literary Biography* (Urbana: University of Illinois Press, 1977), 37–51.

41. The much-debated tension in *Their Eyes Were Watching God* (1937) between the celebration of rural community and the critique of the way an individual woman fares in it can be understood in terms of Hurston's subordination of history to integrated analyses of culture. Hurston acknowledges the historical reasons for the way in which black Floridian culture constricts Janie's choices—particularly in asides about, among other things, the displaced venom directed toward Janie when she returns to Eatonville (1–2), Janie's grandmother's reason for marrying Janie to Logan Killicks (109), and the impoverished lives of the transient laborers on the muck (125), lives which Hurston otherwise idealizes; however, Hurston makes clear in these asides that if history is crucial in accounting for various conflicts in the story, it is not her central focus. *Their Eyes Were Watching God* (1937; reprint, New York: Perennial, 1990). Similarly, Hurston's book on Jamaica and Haiti, *Tell My Horse* (1938), has been criticized for its nationalistic jingoism, its ethnocentrism, and its exoticizing of cultural difference. And at one level, these accusations stand; however, at another level, Hurston makes clear that she is juxtaposing commonplaces about America's superior civilization and the primitive culture of Jamaica and Haiti in order to denaturalize our assumptions about ourselves. She portrays herself as an American patriot, but her patriotism is often undermined by her informants (83), by the clear, if stagily innocent, parallels she sets up between the "savage" customs of these countries and those of the U.S. (6–7), and most dramatically by sudden frank asides to the reader. An excellent example of the latter occurs near the end of the book, where she discusses a conversation she has with a Haitian friend: "We had gotten to the place where neither of us lied to each other about our respective countries. I freely admitted gangsters, corrupt poitical machines, race prejudice and lynchings. She as frankly deplored bad politics, overemphasized class distinctions, lack of public schools and transportation" (204). If Hurston has focused upon many of the problems in black Jamaica and Haiti, she makes clear here, it is not because there are no such

problems in America. On the contrary, she suggests that she has been lying all along to her reader about America and her patriotism. But if this aside undermines everything she has said about America, the book is still open to the charge that its depiction of Jamaica and Haiti fits racist stereotypes. *Tell My Horse* (1938; reprint, New York: Perennial Library, 1990).

42. Claudia Tate's helpful review of recent criticism on *Seraph* makes a similar point about it as I do. *Psychoanalysis and Black Novels* (New York: Oxford University Press, 1998), 161–63.

43. Hazel Carby, Foreword to *Seraph on the Suwanee*, by Zora Neale Hurston (1948; reprint, New York: Harper Perennial, 1990), x–xii.

44. Tate, *Psychoanalysis*, 156–57.

45. The consistent unlikeableness of the heroine—commented on by Hurston's editor and which Hurston conceded—and the heroine's ambiguous relation to the title underline this point. Arvay certainly does not resemble a conventional seraph, in the sense of an angelic being or of a purifying agent of God. In fact, her only relation to seraphs seems to lie in the definition of that word given by Mrs. Turner in *Their Eyes Were Watching God*. To the mixed-race Mrs. Turner, a seraph is a being with "Caucasian characteristics" (139), and she hopes to attain "her paradise—a heaven of straight-haired, thin-lipped, high-nose boned white seraphs" (139). Through this intertextual joke, Hurston seems to be suggesting that the white seraph here must minister to herself and her "Caucasian" culture by modeling what self-critique would look like.

46. Zora Neale Hurston, *Seraph on the Suwanee* (1948; reprint, New York: Harper Perennial, 1990), 1–2, hereafter cited as *S*.

47. Carby, Foreword, xvi.

48. On this term, see Hurston, "The 'Pet' Negro System," *FMO*.

49. This is a repetition of an earlier trip Arvay takes home. During one of their battles over Earl, Arvay leaves Jim and retreats to Sawley. However, her "ardent championship of her background and her family got a set-back as soon as she stepped off the train," and she sees that Sawley is "poor and shabby and mean" and her family is an "awful gang of Crackers" (*S*, 132–33).

50. Annalee Newitz, "White Savagery and Humiliation, or a New Racial Consciousness in the Media," in *White Trash*, ed. Annalee Newitz and Matt Wray (New York: Routledge, 1997): 131–54.

51. Carby, Foreword, ix.

52. Other lessons follow from that first one of treating blacks decently, including accepting interracial work relations (*S*, 323) and allowing that there are different ways of living and doing things (324).

53. Benedict and Weltfish, *Races*, 2.

54. Caffrey, *Stranger*, 297–98; Judith Schachter Modell, *Ruth Benedict: Patterns of a Life* (Philadelphia: University of Pennsylvania Press, 1983), 253–54.

55. Benedict and Weltfish, *Races*, 31.

56. Ibid., 3.

57. Zora Neale Hurston to Ruth Benedict, 19 June 1945, Ruth Benedict Papers, Vassar College Library.

58. She worked on a number of long manuscripts, but under financially and psychologically debilitating circumstances, and the manuscripts remained unfinished at her death. She also wrote cantankerous short essays on mostly political topics, which seem less carefully thought out and complex than her earlier work. While these essays could be read as a logical endpoint of her belief in "domestic" critique, unlike her early work, history disappears entirely here rather than being a stated but subordinated category. In her infamous repudiation of Brown vs. the Board of Education, for example,

she reads desegregation as really revolving "around the self-respect of my people. How much satisfaction can I get from a court order for somebody to associate with me who does not wish me near them?" (*FMO*, 956). This psychological analysis ignores historical and economic issues in a way that Hurston's earlier writings never did.

59. Helbling also makes this point (*Harlem Renaissance*, 162–63).

60. Zora Neale Hurston to Ruth Benedict, 1934, from Longwood, Fla., Benedict Papers, Vassar College Library.

61. Zora Neale Hurston to Ruth Benedict, 17 April 1932, Benedict Papers, Vassar College Library.

62. Ruth Benedict to Dr. Moe, 15 November 1933, Benedict Papers, Vassar College Library.

63. Ruth Benedict to Zora Neale Hurston, 25 June 1934, Benedict Papers, Vassar College Library.

64. Zora Neale Hurston to Ruth Benedict, undated, Benedict papers, Vassar College Library.

Afterword

1. Virginia Woolf, *Three Guineas* (1938; reprint, New York: Harcourt Brace Jovanovich, 1966), 63–69, hereafter cited as *TG*. Woolf, of course, is not alone in suggesting that occupational specialization and the resulting rationalization and bureaucratization of work is at the heart of the war and its Holocaust. German critical theorists made the same argument during the war and in its aftermath, though outsiders' potential ability to disrupt professionalism was by no means at the center of their analyses.

2. Woolf is usually cited as making the claim to rupture between Victorian past and modern present in "Mr. Bennett and Mrs. Brown" (1923, 1924); here, however, her argument is quite different.

3. The image she uses for her despair is that of a double bind that can be resolved only through suicide. The image is particularly poignant within the context of the war and her own suicide in 1941. She writes: "[W]e, daughters of educated men, are between the devil and the deep sea. Behind us lies the patriarchal system; the private house, with its nullity, its immorality, its hypocrisy, its servility. Before us lies the public world, the professional system, with its possessiveness, its jealousy, its pugnacity, its greed. The one shuts us up like slaves in a harem; the other forces us to circle, like caterpillars head to tail, round and round the mulberry tree, the sacred tree, of property. It is a choice of evils. Each is bad. Had we not better plunge off the bridge into the river; give up the game; declare that the whole of human life is a mistake and so end it?" (*TG*, 74). She decides in *Three Guineas*, however, that there is no reason to give up the game.

4. For a brilliant analysis of the significance of women intellectuals' "insider-outsider" status in professionalism and how women have thematized it to shape their work, see Gambrell, *Women Intellectuals*. Her first chapter and conclusion are particularly useful for their comparison of the ideas of women intellectuals in the 1930s and 1940s about this status and more contemporary debates by thinkers like De Lauretis, hooks, and Spivak.

5. Woolf is quite conscious of her class interests. She provides a useful critique of the problems with upper-class alliances with the working class that involve "adopt[ing] the working-class cause without sacrificing middle-class capital, or sharing working-class experiences" (*TG*, 177). She argues that every class of women needs to work within its class to improve women's status. For that reason her "Outsiders' Society" is limited to

the "educated men's daughters" (106). While Woolf insists on situating every individual within her class context, and the argument is a useful corrective to those that assume women's transcendence of class, she nonetheless too quickly precludes the possibility of cross-class alliances.

6. Audre Lorde, *Sister Outsider* (Trumansburg, N.Y.: Crossing Press, 1984), 110, hereafter cited as *SO*.

7. An interesting example of Lorde's refusal to claim exteriority from systems of power is her discussion with Adrienne Rich about grammar. Rich imagines a separation between writing and grammar, presumably between the freedom of ideas and the restrictions of normative language. Lorde refuses this separation. She describes grammar as not inherently oppressive but as providing both the possibility of freedom and restriction. She describes her experience of teaching grammar thus: "I'd come into my class and say, 'Guess what I found out last night. Tenses are a way of ordering the chaos around time.' I learned that grammar was not arbitrary, that it served a purpose, that it helped to form the ways we thought, that it could be freeing as well as restrictive" (*SO*, 95).

8. Vicki Schultz, "Life's Work," *Columbia Law Review* 100 (2000): 1883, emphasis added.

Bibliography

Acocella, Joan. *Willa Cather and the Politics of Criticism.* Lincoln: University of Nebraska Press, 2000.
Addams, Jane. *Newer Ideals of Peace.* New York: Macmillan, 1906.
———. *Twenty Years at Hull-House.* 1910. Reprint, New York: New American Library, 1938.
———. *Women and Public Housekeeping.* New York: National American Woman Suffrage Association, 1913 (unpaginated).
———. et al. *Hull-House Maps and Papers.* New York: T.Y. Crowell, 1895.
Ammons, Elizabeth. *Conflicting Stories.* New York: Oxford University Press, 1991.
———. "Going in Circles: The Female Geography of Jewett's *Country of the Pointed Firs.*" *Studies in the Literary Imagination* 16, no. 2 (1983): 83–92.
———. "Material Culture, Empire, and Jewett's *Pointed Firs.*" In *New Essays on* The Country of the Pointed Firs, edited by June Howard, 81–99. New York: Cambridge University Press, 1994.
Anderson, Benedict. *Imagined Communities.* New York: Verso, 1993.
Appiah, K. A., and Henry Louis Gates Jr., eds. *Zora Neale Hurston.* New York: Amistad, 1993.
Ardis, Ann. *New Women, New Novels.* New Brunswick: Rutgers University Press, 1990.
Armstrong, Nancy. *Desire and Domestic Fiction.* New York: Oxford University Press, 1987.
Awkward, Michael, ed. *New Essays on* Their Eyes Were Watching God. New York: Cambridge University Press, 1990.
Babcock, Barbara. "'Not in the Absolute Singular': Rereading Ruth Benedict." In *Women Writing Culture,* edited by Ruth Behar and Deborah Gordon, 104–30. Berkeley and Los Angeles: University of California Press, 1995.
Baker, Ray Stannard. *American Chronicle.* New York: Charles Scribner's Sons, 1945.
Ballowe, John. Introduction to *George Santayana's America,* by George Santayana. Urbana: University of Illinois Press, 1967.
Batker, Carol J. *Reforming Fictions: Native, African, and Jewish American Women's Literature and Journalism in the Progressive Era.* New York: Columbia University Press, 2000.
Baym, Nina. *Woman's Fiction.* Ithaca: Cornell University Press, 1978.
Bederman, Gail. *Manliness and Civilization.* Chicago: University of Chicago Press, 1995.
Beer, Thomas. *The Mauve Decade: American Life at the End of the Nineteenth Century.* New York: Knopf, 1926.
Behar, Ruth, and Deborah Gordon, eds. *Women Writing Culture.* Berkeley and Los Angeles: University of California Press, 1995.
Bell, Michael Davitt. *The Problem of American Realism.* Chicago: University of Chicago Press, 1993.
Benedict, Ruth. *An Anthropologist at Work: The Writings of Ruth Benedict.* Ed. Margaret Mead. Boston: Houghton Mifflin, 1959.

182   Bibliography

———. "Anthropology in Your Life." *Vassar Alumnae* 32 (May 1947): 10–11.
———. *The Chrysanthemum and the Sword*. Boston: Houghton Mifflin, 1946.
———. Letter to Dr. Moe. 15 November 1933. Ruth Benedict Papers. Vassar College Library.
———. Letter to J. B. Lippincott. 4 October 1935. Ruth Benedict Papers. Vassar College Library.
———. Letter to Zora Neale Hurston. 25 June 1934. Ruth Benedict Papers. Vassar College Library.
———. *Patterns of Culture*. 1934. Reprint, Boston: Houghton Mifflin, 1989.
———. *Race and Racism*. 1942. Reprint, London: Routledge, 1959.
———. *Race: Science and Politics*. 1940. Reprint, New York: Viking, 1947.
———, and Gene Weltfish. *The Races of Mankind*. Public Affairs Pamphlet 85. New York: Public Affairs Committee, 1943.
Bentley, Nancy. *The Ethnography of Manners*. New York: Cambridge University Press, 1995.
Biolsi Thomas. "The Anthropological Construction of 'Indians': Haviland Scudder Mekeel and the Search for the Primitive in Lakota Country." In *Indians and Anthropologists*, edited by Thomas Biolsi and Larry J. Zimmerman, 133–59. Tucson: University of Arizona Press, 1997.
Blackmar, Elizabeth, and Roy Rosenzweig. *The Park and the People*. New York: Holt, 1992.
Blair, Karen J. *The Clubwoman as Feminist*. New York: Holmes and Meier, 1980.
Bledstein, Burton. *The Culture of Professionalism*. New York: Norton, 1976.
Boas, Franz. Preface to *Mules and Men*, by Zora Neale Hurston. 1935. Reprint, New York: Perennial, 1990.
Borus, Daniel H. *Writing Realism: Howells, James, and Norris in the Mass Market*. Chapel Hill: University of North Carolina Press, 1989.
Boxwell, D. A. " 'Sis Cat' as Ethnographer: Self-Presentation and Self-Inscription in Zora Neale Hurston's *Mules and Men*." *African-American Review* 26 (1992): 605–17.
Boyesen, Hjalmar Hjorth. *Literary and Social Silhouettes*. New York: Harpers, 1894.
Brady, Kathleen. *Ida Tarbell: Portrait of a Muckraker*. New York: Putnam, 1984.
Brodhead, Richard. *Cultures of Letters*. Chicago: University of Chicago Press, 1993.
Brooks, Van Wyck. *New England Indian Summer*. New York: Dutton, 1940.
Brown, Dona. *Inventing New England*. Washington, D.C.: Smithsonian, 1995.
Bruce, Dickson D., Jr. *Black American Writing from the Nadir*. Baton Rouge: Louisiana State University Press, 1989.
Brumberg, Joan Jacobs. "Women in the Professions: A Research Agenda for American Historians." *Reviews in American History* 10, no. 2 (1982): 275–96.
Bush, Ronald. "Ethnographic Subjectivity and Zora Neale Hurston's *Tell My Horse*." *Zora Neale Hurston Forum* 5, no. 2 (1991): 11–17.
Caffrey, Margaret. *Ruth Benedict: Stranger in This Land*. Austin: University of Texas Press, 1989.
Campbell, Donna M. *Resisting Regionalism*. Athens: Ohio University Press, 1997.
Carafiol, Peter. *The American Ideal*. New York: Oxford University Press, 1991.
Carby, Hazel V. Foreword to *Seraph on the Suwanee*, by Zora Neale Hurston. 1948. Reprint, New York: Harper Perennial, 1990.
———. "The Politics of Fiction, Anthropology, and the Folk: Zora Neale Hurston." In *New Essays on* Their Eyes Were Watching God, edited by Michael Awkward, 71–93. New York: Cambridge University Press, 1990.
———. *Reconstructing Womanhood: The Emergence of the Afro-American Woman Novelist*. New York: Oxford University Press, 1987.

Carlin, Deborah. *Cather, Canon, and the Politics of Reading.* Amherst: University of Massachusetts Press, 1992.
Carson, Mina. *Settlement Folk: Social Thought and the American Settlement Movement.* Chicago: University of Chicago Press, 1990.
Cather, Willa. *The Kingdom of Art: Willa Cather's First Principles and Critical Statements.* Ed. Bernice Slote. Lincoln: University of Nebraska Press, 1966.
———. *Not Under Forty.* New York: Knopf, 1936.
———. "On *The Professor's House*." In *Willa Cather: Stories, Poems, and Other Writings*, edited by Sharon O'Brien, 974–75. New York: Library of America, 1992.
———. *The Professor's House.* New York: Knopf, 1925.
———. *Sapphira and the Slave Girl.* New York: Vintage, 1968.
———. *Willa Cather in Person.* Ed. L. Brent Bohlke. Lincoln: University of Nebraska Press, 1986.
———. *The World and the Parish: Willa Cather's Articles and Reviews.* Ed. William M. Curtin. 2 vols. Lincoln: University of Nebraska Press, 1970.
———. "Ardessa." *Century* 96, no. 1 (May 1918): 105–16.
Chalaby, Jean. *The Invention of Journalism.* New York: St. Martin's, 1998.
Chapman, Mary, and Glenn Hendler, eds. *Sentimental Men: Masculinity and the Politics of Affect in American Culture.* Berkeley and Los Angeles: University of California Press, 1999.
Clark, Suzanne. *Sentimental Modernism: Women Writers and the Revolution of the Word.* Bloomington: University of Indiana Press, 1991.
Clifford, James, and George E. Marcus, eds., *Writing Culture.* Berkeley and Los Angeles: University of California Press, 1986.
Commager, Henry Steele. Foreword to *Twenty Years at Hull-House,* by Jane Addams. New York: New American Library, 1938.
Conder, John C. *Naturalism in American Fiction: The Classic Phase.* Lexington: University of Kentucky Press, 1984.
Cott, Nancy. *The Bonds of Womanhood.* New Haven: Yale University Press, 1977.
Coultrap-McQuin, Susan. *Doing Literary Business.* Chapel Hill: University of North Carolina Press, 1990.
Cox, James M. "Regionalism: A Diminished Thing." In *Columbia Literary History of the U.S.,* edited by Emory Elliott, 761–84. New York: Columbia University Press, 1988.
Davidson, Cathy, ed. "No More Separate Spheres!" Spec. issue of *American Literature* 70, no. 3 (1998): 133–59.
Davis, Allen F. *Spearheads for Reform.* New York: Oxford University Press, 1967.
Dawidoff, Robert. *The Genteel Tradition and the Sacred Rage.* Chapel Hill: University of North Carolina Press, 1992.
Deacon, Desley. *Elsie Clews Parson: Inventing Modern Life.* Chicago: University of Chicago Press, 1997.
Digby-Jones, Richard. *The Journalist as Reformer: Henry Demarest Lloyd and Wealth against Commonwealth.* Westport, Conn.: Greenwood, 1996.
Dillingham, William. *Frank Norris: Instinct and Art.* Lincoln: University of Nebraska Press, 1969.
———. "Frank Norris and the Genteel Tradition." In *Critical Essays on Frank Norris,* edited by Don Graham, 194–204. Boston: Hall, 1980.
Donovan, Josephine. *New England Local Color Literature.* New York: Frederick Ungar, 1983.
———. *Sarah Orne Jewett.* New York: Frederick Ungar, 1980.
Doreski, C. K. *Writing America Black: Race Rhetoric in the Public Sphere.* New York: Cambridge University Press, 1998.
Douglas, Ann. *The Feminization of American Culture.* New York: Doubleday, 1988.

———. *Terrible Honesty: Mongrel Manhattan in the 1920s.* New York: Farrar, Straus, and Giroux, 1995.
Du Bois, W.E.B. *The Souls of Black Folks.* Chicago: McClurg, 1903.
Du Cille, Ann. *The Coupling Convention.* New York: Oxford University Press, 1993.
Durkheim, Emile. *The Division of Labor in Society.* Trans. George Simpson. London: Collier-Macmillan, 1964.
Ehrenreich, Barbara and John. "The Professional-Managerial Class." *Radical America* 2, no. 2 (March–April 1977): 7–31.
Elliott, Emory, ed. *Columbia Literary History of the United States.* New York: Columbia University Press, 1988.
———. *The Columbia History of the American Novel.* New York: Columbia University Press, 1991.
Engels, Friedrich Engels, and Karl Marx. *The German Ideology.* New York: International Publishers, 1970.
Engels, Friedrich. *The Origin of the Family, Private Property, and the State: In the Light of the Researches of Lewis H. Morgan.* New York: International Publishers, 1972.
Fabian, Johannes. *Time and the Other.* New York: Columbia University Press, 1983.
Felski, Rita. *The Gender of Modernity.* Cambridge: Harvard University Press, 1995.
Fetterley, Judith. " 'Not in the Least American': Nineteenth-Century Literary Regionalism as UnAmerican Literature." In *Nineteenth-Century American Women Writers,* edited by Karen Kilcup, 15–32. Oxford: Blackwell, 1998.
Fischer Michael M. J., and George E. Marcus. *Anthropology as Cultural Critique.* Chicago: University of Chicago Press, 1986.
Fish, Stanley. *Professional Correctness: Literary Studies and Political Change.* Oxford: Clarendon, 1995.
Fisher, Philip. *Hard Facts.* New York: Oxford University Press, 1985.
Foote, Stephanie. *Regional Fictions: Culture and Identity in Nineteenth-Century American Literature.* Madison: University of Wisconsin Press, 2001.
Fortin, Nina E., and Gaye Tuchman. *Edging Women Out: Victorian Novelists, Publishers, and Social Change.* New Haven: Yale University Press, 1989.
Foster, Frances Smith. *Written by Herself.* Bloomington: University of Indiana Press, 1993.
Foucault, Michel. *History of Sexuality.* Trans. Robert Hurley. New York: Vintage, 1980.
Fox, Richard Wightman, and T. J. Jackson Lears, eds. *The Culture of Consumption.* New York: Pantheon, 1983.
Fryer, Judith. "What Goes on in the Ladies Room? Sarah Orne Jewett, Annie Fields, and Their Community of Women." *Massachusetts Review* 30, no. 4 (1989): 610–28.
Gallagher, Catherine, and Stephen Greenblatt. *Practicing New Historicism.* Chicago: University of Chicago Press, 2000.
Gambrell, Alice. *Women Intellectuals, Modernism, and Difference: Transatlantic Culture, 1919–45.* New York: Cambridge University Press, 1997.
Geertz, Clifford. *Works and Lives: The Anthropologist as Author.* Stanford: Stanford University Press, 1988.
General Federation of Women's Clubs. *History of the General Federation of Women's Clubs.* New York: General Federation of Women's Clubs, 1912.
Gere, Ann Ruggles. *Intimate Practices: Literacy and Cultural Work in U.S. Women's Clubs, 1880–1920.* Urbana: University of Illinois Press, 1997.
Giddens, Anthony. Introduction to *Emile Durkheim: Selected Writings.* New York: Cambridge University Press, 1972.
Giddings, Paula. *When and Where I Enter: The Impact of Black Women on Race and Sex in America.* New York: Morrow, 1984.

Gilman, Charlotte Perkins. *The Home.* New York: Charlton, 1910.
Gilman, Charlotte Perkins (Stetson). *Women and Economics.* New York: Small, Maynard, and Co., 1899.
Glazener, Nancy. *Reading for Realism.* Durham: Duke University Press, 1997.
Glazer, Penina Migdal, and Miriam Slater. *Unequal Colleagues: The Entrance of Women into the Professions, 1890–1940.* New Brunswick: Rutgers University Press, 1987.
Gordon, Deborah. "The Politics of Ethnographic Authority: Race and Writing in the Ethnography of Margaret Mead and Zora Neale Hurston." In *Modernist Anthropology,* edited by Marc Manganaro (Princeton: Princeton University Press, 1990), 146–62.
Graff, Gerald. *Professing Literature: An Institutional History.* Chicago: University of Chicago Press, 1989.
Gruesser, John Cullen, ed. *The Unruly Voice: Rediscovering Pauline Elizabeth Hopkins.* Urbana: University of Illinois Press, 1996.
Habegger, Alfred. *Gender, Fantasy, and Realism in American Literature.* New York: Columbia University Press, 1982.
Haber, Samuel. *The Quest for Authority and Honor in the Professions.* Chicago: University of Chicago Press, 1991.
Handler, Richard. "Ruth Benedict and the Modernist Sensibility." In *Modernist Anthropology: From Fieldwork to Text,* edited by Marc Manganaro (Princeton: Princeton University Press, 1990), 163–80.
———. "Vigorous Male and Aspiring Female: Poetry, Personality, and Culture in Edward Sapir and Ruth Benedict." In *Malinowski, Rivers, Benedict, and Others* edited by George Stocking, 127–55.
Haraway, Donna. "Situated Knowledges: The Science Question in Feminism and the Privilege of Partial Perspective." *Feminist Studies* 14, no. 3 (fall 1988): 575–99.
Harding, Sandra. *Whose Science? Whose Knowledge? Thinking from Women's Lives.* Ithaca: Cornell University Press, 1991.
Harper, Frances. *Iola Leroy.* New York: Oxford University Press, 1988.
Harrell, David. *From Mesa Verde to The Professor's House.* Albuquerque: University of New Mexico Press, 1992.
Haskell, Thomas. *The Emergence of Professional Social Science: The American Social Science Association and the Nineteenth-Century Crisis of Authority.* Urbana: University of Illinois Press, 1977.
Hatch, Elvin. *Theories of Man and Culture.* New York: Columbia University Press, 1973.
Hatch, Nathan O., ed. *The Professions in American History.* Notre Dame: University of Notre Dame Press, 1988.
Hegeman, Susan. *Patterns for America.* Princeton: Princeton University Press, 1999.
Helbling, Mark. *The Harlem Renaissance: The One and the Many.* Westport: Greenwood, 1999.
Hemenway, Robert. *Zora Neale Hurston: A Literary Biography.* Urbana: University of Illinois Press, 1977.
Hendricks, Wanda A. *Gender, Race, and Politics in the Midwest: Black Club Women in Illinois.* Bloomington: Indiana University Press, 1998.
Hernandez, Graciela. "Multiple Subjectivities and Strategic Positionality: Zora Neale Hurston's Experimental Ethnographies." In *Women Writing Culture,* edited by Ruth Behar and Deborah Gordon, 148–65.
Hite, Molly. *The Other Side of the Story: Structures and Strategies of Contemporary Feminist Narrative.* Ithaca: Cornell University Press, 1989.
Hofstadter, Richard. *The Age of Reform.* New York: Vintage, 1955.
———. *The Progressive Movement.* New York: Simon and Schuster, 1986.
Holt, Hamilton. *Commercialism and Journalism.* Boston: Houghton Mifflin, 1909.

Hopkins, Pauline E. *Contending Forces: A Romance Illustrative of Negro Life North and South.* 1900. New York: Oxford University Press, 1988.
———. "Echoes from the Annual Convention of Northeastern Federation of Colored Women's Clubs." *Colored American* 6, no. 10 (October 1903): 709–13.
———. "Famous Women of the Negro Race: Club Life among Colored Women." *Colored American* 5, no. 4 (August 1902): 273–77.
———. "Famous Women of the Negro Race: Educators." *Colored American Magazine* 5, no. 3 (July 1902): 206–13.
Horsman, Reginald. *Race and Manifest Destiny.* Cambridge: Harvard University Press, 1981.
Howard, June. *Form and History in American Literary Naturalism.* Chapel Hill: University of North Carolina Press, 1985.
———. *Publishing the Family.* Durham: Duke University Press, 2001.
———. "Unraveling Regions, Unsettling Periods: Sarah Orne Jewett and American Literary History." *American Literature* 68, no. 2 (1996): 365–84.
———. ed. *New Essays on* The Country of the Pointed Firs. New York: Cambridge University Press, 1994.
Howells, William Dean. 1893, 1902. "The Man of Letters as a Man of Business." *Literature and Life.* New York: Harper and Brothers, 1911. 1–34.
Hurston, Zora Neale. *The Complete Stories.* Ed. Henry Louis Gates Jr. and Sieglinde Lemke. New York: Harper Collins, 1995.
———. *Dust Tracks on a Road.* 1942. Reprint, New York: Perennial, 1991.
———. *Folklore, Memoirs, and Other Writings.* Ed. Cheryl Wall. New York: Library of America, 1995.
———. Letter to Ruth Benedict. 17 April 1932. Ruth Benedict Papers. Vassar College Library.
———. Letter to Ruth Benedict. 1934, from Longwood, Fla. Benedict Papers. Vassar College Library.
———. Letter to Ruth Benedict. 19 June 1945. Benedict Papers. Vassar College Library.
———. Letter to Ruth Benedict. Undated. Benedict Papers. Vassar College Library.
———. *Mules and Men.* 1935. Reprint, New York: Perennial, 1990.
———. *Tell My Horse.* 1938. Reprint, New York: Perennial Library, 1990.
———. *Their Eyes Were Watching God.* 1937. Reprint, New York: Perennial, 1990.
Hutchinson, George. *The Harlem Renaissance in Black and White.* Cambridge: Harvard University Press, 1995.
Huyssen, Andreas. *After the Great Divide.* Bloomington: University of Indiana Press, 1986.
Hyatt, Marshall. *Franz Boas Social Activist.* New York: Greenwood, 1990.
Irwin, Will. "The American Newspaper: A Study of Journalism in Relation to the Public." *Collier's* 46, no. 17 (January 14, 1911): 12.
———. "The American Newspaper: The New Era." *Collier's* 47, no. 16 (July 8, 1911): 15–25.
———. "The American Newspaper: The Power of the Press." *Collier's* 46, no. 18 (January 21, 1911); 15–18.
———. "The American Newspaper: The Unhealthy Alliance." *Collier's* 47, no. 11 (June 3, 1911): 17–34.
———. "The American Newspaper: The Voice of a Generation." *Collier's* 47, no. 19 (July 29, 1911): 15–25.
Jackson, Shannon. *Lines of Activity: Performance, Historiography, Hull-House Domesticity.* Ann Arbor: University of Michigan Press, 2000.

James, Henry. *The Notebooks of Henry James*. Ed. F. O. Matthiessen and Kenneth B. Murdock. New York: Oxford University Press, 1947.
Jewett, Sarah Orne. *The Country of the Pointed Firs*. In *The Best Short Stories of Sarah Orne Jewett*. Vol. 1. Ed. Willa Cather. Boston: Houghton Mifflin, 1925.
———. *Deephaven*. 1877. London: Osgood, McIllvaine, and Co., 1893.
———. *Letters*. Ed. Annie Fields. Boston: Houghton Mifflin, 1911.
———. "The Old Town of Berwick." *New England Magazine*. n.s. 10 (July 1894).
———. *Sarah Orne Jewett Letters*. Ed. Richard Cary. Waterville, Maine: Colby College Press, 1967.
Johanningsmeier, Charles. "Sarah Orne Jewett and Mary E. Wilkins (Freeman): Two Shrewd Businesswomen in Search of New Markets." *New England Quarterly* 70, no. 1 (March 1997): 57–82.
Kaplan, Amy. "Manifest Domesticity." in "No More Separate Spheres!", edited by Cathy Davidson, 581–606. Spec. issue of *American Literature* 70, no. 3 (1998).
———. "Nation, Region, and Empire." In *American Novel, History of the Columbia*, edited by Emory Elliott, 240–66. New York: Columbia University Press, 1991.
———. *The Social Construction of American Realism*. Chicago: University of Chicago Press, 1988.
Kaplan, Carla. *The Erotics of Talk: Women's Writing and Feminist Paradigms*. New York: Oxford University Press, 1996.
Kassanoff, Jennie A. "'Fate Has Linked Us Together': Blood, Gender, and the Politics of Representation in Pauline Hopkins's *Of One Blood*." In *The Unruly Voice*, edited by John Cullen Gruesser, 158–81. Urbana: University of Illinois Press, 1996.
Katz, Tamar. *Impressionist Subjects: Gender, Interiority, and Modernist Fiction in England*. Urbana: University of Illinois Press, 2000.
Kelley, Mary. *Private Women, Public Stage*. New York: Oxford University Press, 1984.
Kerber, Linda K. "Separate Spheres, Female Worlds, Woman's Place: The Rhetoric of Women's History." In *Toward an Intellectual History of Women*. Chapel Hill: University of North Carolina Press, 1997. 159–99.
Kilcup, Karen, ed. *Soft Canons: Women Writers and Masculine Tradition*. Iowa City: University of Iowa Press, 1999.
Kirschner, Don S. *The Paradox of Professionalism: Reform and the Public Sphere*. New York: Greenwood, 1986.
Kolko, Gabriel. *Main Currents in Modern American History*. New York: Pantheon, 1984.
Kunzel, Regina. *Fallen Women, Problem Girls: Unmarried Mothers and the Professionalization of Social Work*. New Haven: Yale University Press, 1993.
LaCapra, Dominick. *Emile Durkheim: Sociologist and Philosopher*. Ithaca: Cornell University Press, 1972.
Larson, Magali Sarfatti. *The Rise of Professionalism: A Sociological Analysis*. Berkeley and Los Angeles: University of California Press, 1977.
Lasch-Quinn, Elisabeth. *Black Neighbors: Race and the Limits of Reform in the American Settlement House Movement*. Chapel Hill: University of North Carolina Press, 1993.
Lauter, Paul. "Shaping the American Literary Canon: A Case Study from the Twenties." In *Canons and Contexts*. New York: Oxford University Press, 1991. 22–47.
Lears, T. J. Jackson. *No Place of Grace: Antimodernism and the Transformation of American Culture*. New York: Pantheon, 1981.
Lee, Hermione. *Willa Cather: Double Lives*. New York: Pantheon, 1989.
Lewis, Edith. *Willa Cather Living: A Personal Record*. New York: Knopf, 1953.
Lindemann, Marilee. *Willa Cather: Queering America*. New York: Columbia University Press, 1999.

Lionnet, Francoise. "Autoethnography: The An-Archic Style of *Dust Tracks on a Road.*" In *The Bounds of Race: Perspectives on Hegemony and Resistance,* edited by Dominick LaCapra, 164–95. Ithaca: Cornell University Press, 1991.

Lippmann, Walter. *Liberty and the News.* 1919. New York: Harcourt, Brace, and Howe, 1920.

Lloyd, Henry Demarest. *Wealth against Commonwealth.* 1894. Reprint, New York: Harper and Brothers, 1902.

Lorde, Audre. *Sister Outsider.* Trumansburg, N.Y.: Crossing Press, 1984.

Lukes, Steven. *Emile Durkheim: His Life and Work.* London: Penguin, 1973.

Lyon, Richard Colton. Introduction to *Santayana on America,* by George Santayana. New York: Harcourt, Brace, 1968.

Manganaro, Marc. "Textual Play, Power, and Cultural Critique: An Orientation." In *Modernist Anthropology: From Fieldwork to Text,* ed. Marc Manganaro (Princeton: Princeton University Press, 1990).

———. *Modernist Anthropology: From Fieldwork to Text.* Princeton: Princeton University Press, 1990.

Martin, Jay. *Harvests of Change.* Englewood Cliffs, N.J.: Prentice-Hall, 1967.

Matthaei, Julie A. *An Economic History of Women in America.* New York: Schocken, 1982.

Matthews, Victoria Earle. "The Value of Race Literature." 1895. Reprint, *Massachusetts Review* 27, no. 2 (summer 1986): 169–76.

McCullough, Kate. "Slavery, Sexuality, and Genre: Pauline Hopkins and the Representation of Female Desire." In *The Unruly Voice: Rediscovering Pauline Elizabeth Hopkins,* edited by John Cullen Gruesser, 21–49. Urbana: University of Illinois Press, 1996.

McClure, Samuel. Editorial. *McClure's* 22, no. 1 (November 1903): 111.

———, with Willa Cather. *My Autobiography.* 1913. Reprint, New York: Frederick Stokes, 1914.

McElrath, Joseph R., Jr. *Frank Norris Revisited.* New York: Twayne, 1992.

Meyer, Annie Nathan, ed. *Women's Work in America.* New York: Henry Holt, 1891.

Michaels, Walter Benn. *The Gold Standard and the Logic of Naturalism.* Berkeley and Los Angeles: University of California Press, 1987.

———. *Our America: Nativism, Modernism, Pluralism.* Durham: Duke University Press, 1995.

Mikell, Gwendolyn. "When Horses Talk: Reflections on Zora Neale Hurston's Haitian Anthropology." *Phylon* 48, no. 3 (September 1982): 218–30.

Miraldi, Robert. *Muckraking and Objectivity.* New York: Greenwood, 1990.

Mitchell, Lee Clark. *Determined Fictions: American Literary Naturalism.* New York: Columbia University Press, 1991.

Modell, Judith Schachter. *Ruth Benedict: Patterns of a Life.* Philadelphia: University of Pennsylvania Press, 1983.

Moses, Wilson Jeremiah. *The Golden Age of Black Nationalism, 1850–1925.* Hamden, Conn.: Archon, 1978.

Mossell, Mrs. N. F. *The Work of the Afro-American Woman.* 1894, 1908. Reprint, New York: Oxford University Press, 1988.

Mott, Frank Luther. *A History of American Magazines, 1885–1905.* Vol. 4. Cambridge: Harvard University Press, 1957.

Muncy, Robyn. *Creating a Female Dominion in American Reform, 1890–1935.* New York: Oxford University Press, 1991.

Nelson, Dana D. *National Manhood: Capitalist Citizenship and the Imagined Fraternity of White Men.* Durham: Duke University Press, 1998.

Newitz, Annalee. "White Savagery and Humiliation, or a New Racial Consciousness in the Media." In *White Trash: Race and Class in America*, edited by Annalee Newitz and Matt Wray, 131–54. New York: Routledge, 1997.

Norris, Frank. *The Literary Criticism of Frank Norris.* Ed. Donald Pizer. Austin: University of Texas Press, 1964.

———. *The Octopus.* 1901. Reprint, New York: Penguin, 1986.

Novick, Peter. *That Noble Dream: The 'Objectivity Question' and the American Historical Profession.* New York: Cambridge University Press, 1993.

O'Brien, Sharon. *Willa Cather: The Emerging Voice.* New York: Oxford University Press, 1987.

Parrington, Vernon Louis. *Main Currents in American Thought: The Beginnings of Critical Realism in America, 1860–1920.* Vol. 3. New York: Harcourt, Brace, and Company, 1930.

Piker, Steve. "Classical Culture and Personality." In *Handbook of Psychological Anthropology,* edited by Philip K. Bock. Westport: Greenwood, 1994.

Pizer, Donald. *The Theory and Practice of American Literary Naturalism.* Carbondale: Southern Illinois University Press, 1993.

Pryse, Marjorie. " 'Distilling Essences': Regionalism and 'Women's Culture'." *American Literary Realism* 25, no. 2 (winter 1993): 1–15.

Reynolds, Guy. *Willa Cather in Context: Progress, Race, Empire.* New York: St. Martin's, 1996.

Robbins, Bruce. *Secular Vocations: Intellectuals, Professionalism, Culture.* New York: Verso, 1993.

Rodgers, Daniel T. "In Search of Progressivism." *Reviews in American History* 10, no. 4 (December 1982): 113–32.

Rogin, Michael. " 'The Sword Became a Flashing Vision': D. W. Griffith's *The Birth of a Nation.*" *Representations* 9 (1995): 150–95.

Roman, Margaret. *Sarah Orne Jewett: Reconstructing Gender.* Tuscaloosa: University of Alabama Press, 1992.

Romero, Lora. *Home Fronts: Domesticity and Its Critics in the Antebellum U.S.* Durham: Duke University Press, 1997.

Rosenberg, Rosalind. *Beyond Separate Spheres: Intellectual Roots of Modern Feminism.* New Haven: Yale University Press, 1982.

Rosowski, Susan. *The Voyage Perilous.* University of Nebraska Press, 1986.

Ross, Dorothy. "Gendered Social Knowledge: Domestic Discourse, Jane Addams, and the Possibilities of Social Science." In *Gender and American Social Science: The Formative Years,* edited by Helene Silverberg, 235–64. Princeton: Princeton University Press, 1998.

Rosenberg, Rosalind. *Beyond Separate Spheres: Intellectual Roots of Modern Feminism.* New Haven: Yale University Press, 1982.

Rossiter, Margaret. *Women Scientists in America: Struggles and Strategies to 1940.* Baltimore: Johns Hopkins University Press, 1982.

Ruffin, Josephine St. Pierre. "Address of Josephine St. Pierre Ruffin, President of the Conference." *Woman's Era* 2, no. 6 (August 1895): 13–15.

———. "Editorial Greeting." *Woman's Era* 1, no. 1 (March 24, 1894): 8.

———. "Publishers' Announcement." *Woman's Era* 1, no. 1 (March 24, 1894): 8.

———. "News from the Clubs." *Woman's Era* 1, no. 1 (March 24, 1894): 4–5.

Ryan, Mary. *The Empire of the Mother.* New York: Harrington, 1985.

Salem, Dorothy. *To Better Our World: Black Women in Organized Reform, 1890–1920.* Brooklyn: Carlson, 1990.

Samuels, Shirley, ed. *The Culture of Sentiment.* Ithaca: Cornell University Press, 1993.

Santayana, George. "The Genteel Tradition in American Philosophy." In *The Genteel*

Tradition: Nine Essays by George Santayana, edited by Douglas L. Wilson, 36–64. Cambridge: Harvard University Press, 1967.

———. "Young Sammy's First Wild Oats." In *The Genteel Tradition: Nine Essays by George Santayana*, edited by Douglas L. Wilson, 26–35. Cambridge: Harvard University Press, 1967.

Sawaya, Francesca. "The Authority of Experience: Jane Addams and Hull-House." In *Women's Experience of Modernity*, edited by Ann Ardis and Leslie Lewis, 47–62. Baltimore: Johns Hopkins University Press, 2003.

Schiller, Dan. *Objectivity and the News*. Philadelphia: University of Pennsylvania Press, 1981.

Schleifer, Ronald. *Modernism and Time*. New York: Cambridge University Press, 2000.

Schreiner, Olive. *Woman and Labor*. London: T. F. Unwin, 1911.

Schudson, Michael. *Discovering the News*. New York: Basic Books, 1978.

Schultz, Vicki. "Life's Work." *Columbia Law Review* 100 (2000): 1881–964.

Scott, Anne Firor. *Natural Allies: Women's Associations in American History*. Urbana: University of Illinois Press, 1991.

Scott, Joan Wallach. *Gender and the Politics of History*. New York: Columbia University Press, 1988.

Sedgwick, Eve. *Epistemology of the Closet*. Berkeley and Los Angeles: University of California Press, 1990.

Seltzer, Mark. *Bodies and Machines*. New York: Routledge, 1992.

Sewall, May Wright, ed. *The World's Congress of Representative Women*. Chicago: Rand, McNally, 1894.

Shaw, Stephanie J. *What a Woman Ought to Be and to Do: Black Professional and Women Workers during the Jim Crow Era*. Chicago: University of Chicago Press, 1996.

Showalter, Elaine. *Sexual Anarchy: Gender and Culture at the Fin de Siecle*. New York: Viking, 1990.

Shuman, Edwin L. *Practical Journalism*. 1903. New York: Appleton, 1920.

Silverberg, Helene, ed. *Gender and American Social Science: The Formative Years*. Princeton: Princeton University Press, 1998.

Sklar, Kathryn Kish. *Catharine Beecher*. New Haven: Yale University Press, 1973.

———. *Florence Kelley and the Nation's Work*. New Haven: Yale University Press, 1995.

Steffens, Lincoln. *The Autobiography of Lincoln Steffens*. New York: Harcourt, Brace, 1931.

Stocking, George. *The Ethnographer's Magic and Other Essays*. Madison: University of Wisconsin Press, 1992.

———, ed. *A Franz Boas Reader: The Shaping of American Anthropology, 1883–1911*. Chicago: Midway Reprint, 1989.

———, ed. *Malinowski, Rivers, Benedict, and Others*. Madison: University of Wisconsin Press, 1986.

———, ed. *Selected Papers from the American Anthropologist, 1921–45*. Washington, D.C.: American Anthropological Association, 1976.

Stowe, Harriet Beecher. *Oldtown Folks*. 1869. New Brunswick: Rutgers University Press, 1987.

Strychacz, Thomas. *Modernism, Mass Culture, and Professionalism*. New York: Cambridge University Press, 1991.

Tarbell, Ida. *All in a Day's Work*. New York: Macmillan, 1939.

———. *The Business of Being a Woman*. 1912. Reprint, New York: Macmillan, 1925.

———. *The History of Standard Oil*. 2 vols. 1904. Reprint, Gloucester: Peter Smith, 1963.

———. "John D. Rockefeller: A Character Study." *McClure's* 25, no. 3 (July 1905): 226–49; 25, no. 4 (August 1905): 386–98.

———. *The Ways of Women*. 1914. Reprint, New York: Macmillan, 1915.

Tate, Claudia. *Domestic Allegories of Political Desire.* New York: Oxford University Press, 1992.
———. *Psychoanalysis and Black Novels.* New York: Oxford University Press, 1998.
Thomas, Brook. *The New Historicism and Other Old-Fashioned Topics.* Princeton: Princeton University Press, 1991.
Tichi, Cecilia. "Women Writers and the New Woman." In *Columbia Literary History of the United States,* edited by Emory Elliott, 589–606. New York: Cambridge University Press, 1988.
Tomkins, Mary E. *Ida M. Tarbell.* New York: Twayne, 1974.
Tompkins, Jane. *Sensational Designs.* New York: Oxford University Press, 1985.
Trachtenberg, Alan. *The Incorporation of America.* New York: Hill and Wang, 1982.
Trolander, Judith Ann. *Professionalism and Social Change.* New York: Columbia University Press, 1987.
Veblen, Thorstein. *The Theory of the Leisure Class.* 1899. New York: New American Library, 1953.
Walcutt, Charles. *American Literary Naturalism: A Divided Stream.* Minneapolis: University of Minnesota Press, 1956.
Wall, Cheryl. *Women of the Harlem Renaissance.* Bloomington: University of Indiana Press, 1995.
Warren, Kenneth. *Black and White Strangers: Race and American Literary Realism.* Chicago: University of Chicago Press, 1993.
Welter, Barbara. *Dimity Convictions.* Athens: Ohio University Press, 1976.
Wexler, Laura. *Tender Violence: Domestic Visions in an Age of U.S. Imperialism.* Chapel Hill: University of North Carolina Press, 2000.
Wiebe, Robert H. *The Search for Order, 1877–1920.* New York: Hill and Wang, 1967.
Williams, Fannie Barrier. "The Club Movement among Colored Women of America." In *A New Negro for a New Century,* edited by Booker T. Washington, Fannie Barrier Williams, and N. B. Wood. 1900. New York: Arno, 1969. 378–405.
Williams, Raymond. *The Country and the City.* New York: Oxford University Press, 1973.
———. *Marxism and Literature.* London: Oxford University Press, 1977.
———. *The Politics of Modernism.* Ed. Tony Pinkey. New York: Verso, 1989.
Williamson, Joel. *The Crucible of Race.* New York: Oxford University Press, 1984.
Wilson, Christopher. *The Labor of Words: Literary Professionalism in the Progressive Era.* Athens: University of Georgia Press, 1985.
Wilson, Douglas L., ed. *The Genteel Tradition: Nine Essays by George Santayana.* Cambridge: Harvard University Press, 1967.
———. Introduction to *The Genteel Tradition: Nine Essays by George Santayana,* edited by Douglas L. Wilson. Cambridge: Harvard University Press, 1967.
Winter, Alice Ames. *The Business of Being a Club Woman.* New York: Century, 1925.
Woolf, Virginia. *Three Guineas.* 1938. New York: Harcourt Brace Jovanovich, 1966.
Yarborough, Richard. Introduction to *Contending Forces: A Romance Illustrative of Negro Life North and South,* by Pauline E. Hopkins. 1900.
Zagarell, Sandra. "Crosscurrents: Registers of Nordicism, Community, and Culture in Jewett's *Pointed Firs.*" *Yale Journal of Criticism* 10, no. 2 (fall 1997): 355–70.
———. "Narratives of Community: The Identification of a Genre." *Signs* 13, no. 3 New York: Oxford University Press, 1988. (spring 1988): 498–527.
———. "*Pointed Firs'* Portrayal of Community and the Exclusion of Difference." In *New Essays on* The Country of the Pointed Firs, edited by June Howard, 39–60.

Index

Addams, Jane, 37, 56, 144; acquaintance with Sarah Orne Jewett, 154 n.16; and racism, 22, 155 n.18. Works: *Hull-House Maps and Papers*, 27; *Twenty Years at Hull-House*, 16, 21, 22–27; "Women and Public Housekeeping," 26, 27
American, 85, 88, 92, 108
Anderson, Benedict, 37, 46, 159 n.17
antifeminism, 16, 94; and racism, ethnocentrism, 83, 98. *See also* feminism
anti-Semitism. *See* Cather, Willa

Baker, Ray Stannard, 85, 86, 88
Baym, Nina, 78
Bederman, Gail, 11, 147 n.1
Beer, Thomas, 77
Benedict, Ruth, 110, 111, 113, 115–16, 144; relationship with Zora Neale Hurston, 135–38. Works: "Anthropology in Your Life," 126; *The Chrysanthemum and the Sword*, 176 nn. 29, 33; journals, 117–18; *Patterns of Culture*, 17, 116, 121–25; *Race and Racism*, 177 n.34; "The Races of Mankind" (with Gene Weltfish), 135–36
Boas, Franz, 113–15, 122, 126, 136–38
Boyesen, H.H., 58, 73, 77; "The American Novelist and His Public," 61–63; professionalism of, 162 n.4
Brodhead, Richard, 38, 153 n.7
Brooks, Van Wyck, 77

Carby, Hazel, 37, 38, 113, 131, 133, 158 n.10
Cather, Willa, 80–83, 111–12, 144; and anti-Semitism, 89, 101–2, 105; career at *McClure's*, 88; on Frank Norris, 78–79. Works: "Ardessa," 88–92; literary criticism, 98–101, 170 n.57; "The Novel Demeuble," 100–101, 106; *The Professor's House*, 17, 83, 101–7; *Sapphira and the Slave Girl*, 107–9, 172 n.75
civilization. *See* modernity
Collier's. See Irwin, Will
Colored American Magazine. See Hopkins, Pauline
cosmopolitanism: in Jane Addams, 26, 32, 156 n.24; in George Santayana, 76
Cott, Nancy, 4
cultivation: in Jane Addams, 21–23, 25–27, 34; in Emile Durkheim, 7; in Sarah Orne Jewett, 21–22, 28, 30, 31–32, 34; in naturalist sentimentalism, 58; Josephine St. Pierre Ruffin's critique of, 40–41; Fannie Barrier Williams's critique of, 54–55;
culture and personality, 114, 121, 127

disinterestedness, 3, 4, 56, 84–85; in Jane Addams and Sarah Orne Jewett, 25–27, 37; in Willa Cather, 82, 91, 102, 105–7; in Emile Durkheim, 6–8; in George Santayana, 73, 78; in Ida Tarbell, 82, 92, 97–98, 107
domesticity: in Jane Addams, 21–24, 26–27, 34; in Ruth Benedict, 111, 115, 117–19, 125; as both modern and primitive, 1; in H. H. Boyesen, 56–58, 63; in Hazel Carby, 37; contradictions of, 4; cult of, 1–2, 26, 28, 148 n.5; in Emile Durkheim, 5–8; in Charlotte Perkins Gilman, 10–12, 151 n.33; in Pauline Hopkins, 39; in Zora Neale Hurston, 111, 115, 119–20, 132–33; in Sarah Orne Jewett, 21–22, 28–32, 34; in Frank Norris, 56–58, 66, 71, 73, 78; in Josephine St. Pierre Ruffin, 40–41; in George Santayana, 56–58, 73–74, 76, 78; standard periodization and definition of, 2, 150 n.17. *See also* imperialism; primitive; sentimentalism

Index

Douglas, Ann, 77, 165 n.34
Du Bois, W. E. B., 26, 54, 175 n.22, 177 n.40
Durkheim, Emile, 10–11, 150 n.21. Works: *Division of Labor in Society*, 5–9; "Some Notes on Occupational Groups," 7–9

expertise: abstract or transcendent, 16, 34–35, 37, 39, 54, 56; situated, 16, 37, 39, 53–55, 56, 157 n.5

feminism: African American, 43, 44, 137, 141; and ambivalence about professionalism, 10, 13, 139–41, 143–46; and criticism of Jewett, 20, 154 nn. 9, 11; dialogistic method of, 15, 152 n.49; white progressive, 34. *See also* antifeminism
Foucault, Michel, 13, 17, 148 n.9

Gambrell, Alice, 12, 152 n.41, 179 n.4
General Federation of Women's Clubs (GFWC), 44–45, 159 n.26
Gilman, Charlotte Perkins (Stetson): and racism, 11–12. Works: *The Home*, 151 n.33; *Women and Economics*, 10–12, 175 n.17
Graff, Gerald, 60, 173 n.7
Greek culture: in Addams, 25–26; in Jewett, 32, 157 n.35. *See also* cosmopolitanism

Haber, Samuel, 82, 167 n.10
Handler, Richard, 124, 125
Harlem Renaissance, 120, 136
Hegeman, Susan, 114–15
Hernandez, Graciela, 113, 127
Holt, Hamilton, 81–82, 91; *Commercialism and Journalism*, 84–86, 96; *Independent*, 84, 85
Hopkins, Pauline, 56, 144; relation with Woman's Era Club, 45, 154 n.13. Works: *Colored American Magazine*, 45, 54; *Contending Forces*, 16, 36
Howard, June, 4, 154 n.9
Hurston, Zora Neale, 110, 111, 115–16, 144; critique of W. E. B. Du Bois, 175 n.22, 177 n.40; relationship with Ruth Benedict, 135–38. Works: "Art and Such," 128–29; "Drenched in Light," 120–21, 127; *The Florida Negro*, 111–13, 127–29; "John Redding Goes to Sea," 119–20, 127; *Jonah's Gourd Vine*, 138; *Mules and Men*, 126, 138; *Seraph on the Suwanee*, 17, 116, 121, 129–35, 137; *Tell My Horse*, 177–78 n.41; *Their Eyes Were Watching God*, 177 n.41, 178 n.45

imperialism, 66, 72, 73, 123, 150 n. 28, 164 nn. 26, 28
Independent. See Holt, Hamilton
integration (anthropological concept of): in Ruth Benedict, 122–25, 136; defined, 175–76 n.27; in Zora Neale Hurston, 127–33, 135, 136
Irwin, Will, 81–82, 91; "The American Newspaper," 84, 85–86; *Collier's*, 84, 85, 86

James, Henry, 21, 99
Jewett, Sarah Orne, 37, 56, 144; acquaintance with Jane Addams, 154 n.16; and racism, 22, 155 n.18. Works: *The Country of the Pointed Firs*, 16, 21, 27–34; *Deephaven*, 19; "The Old Town of Berwick," 35

Kaplan, Amy, 72, 164 n.26
Kaplan, Carla, 15, 152 n.48

Lippmann, Walter, 83, 84
Lloyd, Henry Demarest, 94, 95
Lorde, Audre, 15, 152 n.48; "The Master's Tools Will Never Dismantle the Master's House," 141–43; Virginia Woolf compared to, 139, 143–44

Matthews, Victoria Earle, 45, 52, 160 n.34, 161 n.52. Works: "Aunt Lindy," 160 n.32; "The Value of Race Literature," 43–45, 53
McClure, Samuel, 85, 86, 94
McClure's, 82, 85, 86–88, 94
Mead, Margaret, 113, 175 n.19
Meyer, Annie Nathan, 12, 120, 151 n.37
modernity: and civilization, 1–2, 147 n.1; defined against premodernity, 1–2, 4, 156 n.23; defined in relation to modern, modernism, 148 n.6; periodization of, 2–5, 174 n.13; standard narrative of, 1–2, 116, 121, 140, 152 n.50, 173 n.7
Mossell, Mrs. N.F., 12, 151 n.37
muckraking, 66, 87, 89, 167 nn. 11, 19

National Association of Colored Women (NACW), 37, 39, 43, 45, 51, 53–55
naturalism, 14, 59; and literary professionalism, 57, 66, 161–62 n.1; in Frank Norris, 66–71, 162 n. 7; in George Santayana, 73, 75–76
naturalist sentimentalism, 61, 57–58, 77–78
new historicism, 14–15, 20, 77, 165 nn. 35, 37

Norris, Frank, 73, 94, 109, 144; Willa Cather on, 78–79; and the genteel tradition, 162 n.6; professionalism of, 162 n.4. Works: literary criticism, 63; *The Octopus*, 16, 58, 66–73; "A Plea for Romantic Fiction," 58–59, 65; "Why Women Should Write the Best Novels: And Why They Don't," 63–65

Novick, Peter, 81

objectivity, 16, 17; in anthropology, 113–14; balanced, 82–86, 107–9, 166 n.8; —, in Cather, 89, 91, 101–2, 106–7; —, in Tarbell, 93–97; in Ruth Benedict, 111, 122–26; in Zora Neale Hurston, 111–13, 127–19; "ideal of," 81, 83–84; in Frank Norris, 72, 78; in George Santayana, 58, 73, 78

objective domestic critique, 116, 126, 129, 132–34, 135

occupational division of labor, 1–2, 5–8, 10–12, 147 n.3. *See also* professionalism

Parrington, Vernon Louis, 77, 153 n.5

pastoral, 19, 22, 66, 71

primitive: racial others as, 1–2, 9, 16, 37, 115; women as, 1–2, 9. *See also* domesticity

professionalism: in Jane Addams, 15–16, 21–22, 26–27, 34–35, 154 n.15, 156 nn. 25, 28; and ambivalence, 3–4, 71, 164 n.24; appeals to the past of, 3–4, 82, 149 n.15; in Ruth Benedict, 116–17, 121; in H. H. Boyesen, 61–63; in Willa Cather, 98–101, 107–9; contradictions of, 3–4, 56–57, 60–61, 65, 83, 84; and critique, 114–15, 121; culture of, 1–2, 35, 37, 39, 148 n.5; in Pauline Hopkins, 39; in Zora Neale Hurston, 116–17, 121, 172 n.4; and imperialism, 123, 150 n.28; and impersonality, 81–82, 98, 100; in Sarah Orne Jewett, 15–16, 21–22, 28–29, 34–35, 154 n.15, 156 n.31; in Frank Norris, 63–65, 71–73; opposed to amateurism, 60–61, 69–70, 72; paradoxes of, 8–9, 163 n.14; and personal integrity, 80–82, 96–98, 100; in George Santayana, 73–77; standard periodization and definition of, 2, 150 n.18; in Ida Tarbell, 92–97, 107–9; and the university, 60, 71–72, 164 n.25. *See also* modernity; regionalism; sentimentalism

public intellectuals, 17, 116–17, 137–38

realism, 57, 59, 161–62 n.1

Redfield, Robert, 113

regionalism, 14, 16, 172 n.2; and black women intellectuals, 37, 39, 54–55; criticism about, 20; Pauline Hopkins's use of, 45, 48, 50–53; Virginia Earle Matthews's use of, 43–44; and professionalism, 34, 36; and racism, 38, 157–58 n.7; Josephine St. Pierre Ruffin's use of, 40–43

Robbins, Bruce, 13, 149 n.15, 151 n.38, 152 n.50

Romero, Lora, 20, 62, 154 nn. 10, 12

Ruffin, Josephine St. Pierre, 45, 56, 144; conflict with GFWC, 160 n.35; and Woman's Era Club, 39–41. Works: *Woman's Era*, 16, 39–43; "Editorial Greeting," 40–41

Santayana, George, 77, 94, 109, 144, 153 n.5; writers and critics influenced by, 153 n.5, 162 n.5. Works: "The Genteel Tradition in American Philosophy," 16, 20, 58, 73–77; "Young Sammy's First Wild Oats," 73, 164 n.28

Sapir, Edward, 113, 176 nn. 30, 32

Sappho, 44, 52–53; criticism about, in *Contending Forces*, 161 n.52

Schudson, Michael, 81, 108

Scott, Joan, 14

Sedgwick, Eve, 65

Seltzer, Mark, 60, 77–78, 150 n.27; 164 n.22

sentimentalism, 14, 16; Willa Cather's critique of, 108–9; and domesticity, 57, 149 n.16; Pauline Hopkins's critique of, 45–51; and Frank Norris, 58–59, 65, 66–71; and professionalism, 58, 66, 77; and George Santayana, 73–74

sexual division of labor, 1, 5–8, 10–12, 147 n.3. *See also* domesticity

specialization. *See* occupational division of labor; sexual division of labor

Spencer, Herbert, 5

Steffens, Lincoln, 86, 88, 108

Stocking, George, 113

Stowe, Harriet Beecher, 108–9, 151 n.33, 172 n.73

subjectivity, 16, 17; in anthropology, 113–14; in Ruth Benedict, 122–26; as feminine, 82, 93–94, 99, 112, 115; in Zora Neale Hurston, 127–29; in George Santayana, 58, 76

Tarbell, Ida, 81–83, 85, 86, 88, 111–12, 144. Works: *All in a Day's Work*, 107–8; *The Business of Being a Woman*, 92–94, 98; *The History of Standard Oil*, 17, 83, 86, 87, 94–98, 101; *New Ideals of Business*, 107

Veblen, Thorstein, 21, 75

Washington, Booker T., 54
Wells, Ida B., 12, 51, 151 n.37, 167 n.11

Wexler, Laura, 72, 164 n.26
Williams, Fannie Barrier, 12, 40, 54–55
Williams, Raymond, 2, 148 n.9
Woman's Era. *See* Ruffin, Josephine St. Pierre
Woman's Era Club. *See* Ruffin, Josephine St. Pierre
Woolf, Virginia: Audre Lorde compared to, 139, 143–44; "Mr. Bennett and Mrs. Brown," 179 n.2; *Three Guineas*, 139–41

Acknowledgments

In the variety of places this book was written, I have benefited from the generosity of many people. I would like to thank my graduate school teachers Laura Brown, Walter Cohen, Shirley Samuels, and especially Mark Seltzer for their support over the years. For their advice and encouragement, I also want to express my gratitude to Ann Ardis, Peter Carafiol, Dan Cottom, Alice Gambrell, David Mair, Ron Schleifer, and an anonymous reader. The book was influenced deeply by the interdisciplinary feminist conversation at the Bunting Fellowship Program at the Radcliffe Institute. I want to thank particularly my Bunting writing group—Denise Buell, Lisa Herschbach, Augusta Rohrbach, and Cathy Silber—for their engagement with this project and our productive discussions more generally. My editor, Jerry Singerman, deserves special gratitude for his kindness and efficiency.

The National Endowment for the Humanities provided readers' reports and financial backing at an early stage of this project. Sue Danielson, Sherrie Gradin, Nancy Porter, Shelley Reece, and John Smyth at Portland State University helped me find funds and encouraged me to work on the book during summers. The Bunting Fellowship Program and the English department and the College of Arts and Sciences at the University of Oklahoma generously supported the project with leave time and financial aid so that it could be completed.

Parts of this book have appeared in earlier versions in *Nineteenth-Century Literature*, vol. 48, no. 4 (copyright 1994 by the Regents of the University of California and reprinted by permission of the University of California Press); *Breaking Boundaries: New Perspectives on Regional Women's Writing*, edited by Sherrie Inness and Diana Royer (copyright 1997 by the University of Iowa Press and reprinted by its permission); *Sentimental Men: Masculinity and the Politics of Affect in American Culture*, edited by Mary Chapman and Glenn Hendler (copyright 1999 by the Regents of the University of California and reprinted by permission of the University of California Press). I am grateful for the permission to reuse this material.

The University of Oklahoma has provided me with an exceptional community of friends and interlocutors. I want to thank Julia Abramson, Julie and

Adam Cohen, Cindy Greenwood, Sandie Holguin, Melissa Homestead, Catherine John, Cathy Kelly, Rita Keresztesi, Randy Lewis, and Circe Sturm. I also want to express my gratitude to friends at a distance: Stacy Burton, Julie Gozan and Tom Keck, John Heins, Priya Kapoor, Ari and Lesley Kelman, Antonia Lombard, Kavita Panjabi, Saralinda Subbiondo, Jeremy Telman, and Cathy Tufariello helped out in a variety of ways, all of which mattered. Without Tamar Katz's generous assistance and the model of her work, this book would simply never have been completed. An especial and deep thank-you to Jean Gregorek, who listened, encouraged, and suggested. Her thinking and writing have been absolutely formative to mine throughout the years. She is, as everyone agrees, the greatest one.

Finally, I want to thank my family. The Egans, Pikers, Prestandreas, Rosas, Ryans, and Sawayas have each and all been a source of inspiration and happy distraction. For their generosity, unflagging encouragement, and sense of humor, I particularly want to thank my aunts—Loretta Rosa and Therese and Barbara Sawaya—and my grandmother Rose Sawaya. I also want to express my gratitude to my great uncles Orazio and Salvatore Prestandrea for their kindness in Boston and the pleasure of their company. There are no words sufficient to thank my parents, Ann Rosa and Fares Sawaya, and my sister, Marie Sawaya. They have supported this book in manifold ways, and they have been always and at once the best of everything—comrades, teachers, friends, family, and comic relief. Likewise, there are no words sufficient to thank Josh Piker. He has discussed and read everything here and improved both its conception and its expression. More important, he has been the best, funniest, and wisest company in the world.